EATING THE EMPIRE

EATING THE EMPIRE

Food and Society in Eighteenth-century Britain

TROY BICKHAM

REAKTION BOOKS

For Joanna Innes

Published by Reaktion Books Ltd
Unit 32, Waterside
44–48 Wharf Road
London N1 7UX, uk
www.reaktionbooks.co.uk

First published 2020

Printed and bound in Great Britain by
TJ International, Padstow, Cornwall

A catalogue record for this book is available from the British Library

ISBN 978 1 78914 207 5

CONTENTS

F. Astley, frontispiece of [Walter Raleigh], *A New History of England* (London, 1746). In an early version of what would be repeated innumerable times in the following century, Britannia sits enthroned while the indigenous subjects of her territorial and commercial empire reverently bring her their native goods.

INTRODUCTION

In 1767 the Marsh family welcomed home Edward from his first tour as a junior officer aboard the HMS *Gibraltar*. Edward, who had followed in his father's footsteps and joined the Royal Navy, proudly gave a personal tour of the ship to his family, which included his fourteen-year-old brother, John. Reflecting decades later on the memorable experience, John recalled two things. The first was how Edward 'came home in high spirits' – in sharp contrast to a decade later when he returned in a severely depressed state following a period of confinement as a prisoner of war in America. The second was the food. To share his experiences of living on board the ship, Edward prepared some of the food that he and his comrades often made for themselves, 'particularly Chowder (a kind of fish soup)' and 'a kind of Pancake made with flour and salt water' that Edward called a 'pandoudle'. Anxious to embrace the experience, the family tried it all, with even Edward's father attempting to make a pandoudle himself.[1]

John Marsh is remarkable only in that he recorded much of his long life. The son of a naval officer, Marsh avoided naval service by becoming a lawyer and then inheriting a minor estate via a distant relative. Although the estate had dwindled to the point that it could not support a country gentry lifestyle, it enabled Marsh to enjoy life as a minor member of the provincial urban gentry. When in middle age, Marsh gathered his memories into a series of shorthand journal entries that he collectively called a 'History of my private life' – written for his own reminiscing pleasure and so that his unborn progeny might better know him. As was the case with Marsh's visit to his brother's ship, food was instrumental to Marsh's socialization and memory. Marsh packed his childhood accounts with detailed descriptions of holiday foods, school dinners and tea visits. One of his earliest memories was mischievously devouring a cherry pie with his brothers before leaving for school. Unbeknown to the adult guests at his house, the boys had surgically gutted the pie, leaving only the crust. The incident was met with good humour and became a favourite family anecdote for years to come. Virtually all his accounts of Christmas and other major holidays included descriptions of the food. Like most men of his social class, Marsh routinely went to coffeehouses and drank tea daily with his wife, and his memoirs' most notable conversations, whether they were about politics or family affairs, almost invariably took place in such settings. During the early 1770s he tutted privately at neighbours who in sympathy for the protesting American colonists openly defied national days of prayer and fasting by holding dinner parties. Marsh even credited food with helping him to make the important decision of whether to join the Inner Temple or Lincoln's Inn as he embarked upon a legal career. (He chose the former, being deterred by the 'idea of dining off wooden Trenchers which I had heard was the custom at Lincoln's Inn'.)

Marsh's experiences also highlight how much the British Empire affected the lives of those Britons who never ventured beyond their nation's shores. As a young boy, Marsh mourned the departure for India of his favourite cousin, Elizabeth, who dropped him at school one last time, 'where we took an affectionate leave of each other little thinking we were never to meet again'. In search of adventure and a husband, she found both but died just a few years later. During the American Revolution, Marsh's brothers suffered as prisoners of war of the new United States. Edward died in the West Indies, but not before engaging in an affair with a local free black woman and fathering a son, whom Marsh ultimately brought to England and financially supported. Marsh sent his own son, Henry, to war in 1794 as a lieutenant in the artillery. When Henry was deployed to Africa the following year to capture Cape Town, the worry-sick Marsh purchased a small print of the place, and he and his wife kept their son's letters beside it. Another of his sons won a school prize 'for the best English Verses' – a 160-line poem on the recent successful capture of Seringapatam in India – which Marsh sent to Henry in Africa as part of a care package. The various book clubs to which he belonged favoured histories and travel accounts related to the growing empire, and he sometimes purchased sheet music purportedly from America and Asia for his musical group to play. For Marsh, the empire was full of curiosities, but it could not be reduced to the mere exotic. For him, as for many Britons, the empire was a real place full of personal connections woven into the fabric of everyday life.

THIS BOOK IS not a traditional food history in that it does not tell the history of a particular foodstuff or cuisine. Rather, the present undertaking is more akin to what anthropologists and sociologists call 'foodways', which explore the cultural, social and economic practices of the acquisition, production, preparation, distribution and consumption of food in order to better understand society. As B. W. Higman explains in what he dubs 'social nutrition', food provides virtually everyone, irrespective of social class or gender, with at least some choices.[2] Thus food is less the subject of study and more a means for examining something else. In the case of the present study, food is examined to better understand Britons' relationships with the empire and its influence upon their lives.

Although a long list of definitions of terms would be tedious, addressing at least the two key ones from the book's title helps frame the present discussion. 'Food' is employed here in the broadest possible sense of the word to include both prepared dishes and a wide variety of single commodities. Although much of the twenty-first-century Western medical community would classify many of the commodities discussed here (or at least their most appealing elements) as drugs, they are still treated here under the broad category of food. Certainly, plenty of contemporaries recognized the narcotic elements of what would later be identified as caffeine and nicotine, and many of these goods were initially peddled as medicines in the British Isles. Although the health benefits continued to attract attention, the primary overseas commodities discussed here were predominately advertised, sold and consumed as part of a diet and sold by grocers, rather than apothecaries. So as to include the different modes of consuming these commodities – eating, drinking and, in the case of tobacco, snorting and inhaling – the term 'ingestibles' is employed.

'Empire' is an equally ambiguous and more contentious term. Although the concept of empire requires a general definition in order to be studied, because it is partly a product of human thinking, empire has many forms and is not monolithic. An ongoing problem in the histories of the British Empire is to mistake the Victorian and Edwardian empires as linear, if not inevitable, progressions of the eighteenth century. This is the same fallacy as calling the employees of the Virginia Company who built the Jamestown outpost in 1607 the forbears of the United States. In fact, the eighteenth-century empire was an ever-moving umbrella that covered an array of activities so incongruous that attempts to reconcile it into a semi-central authority provoked its fragmentation via the American Revolution.[3] In consequence, empire is used here in the broadest sense to include Britain's overseas territorial, economic and commercial branches. This is akin to Jacob Price's encompassing description of the eighteenth-century empire as 'both lands indisputably under English or (from 1707) British sovereignty and other territories over which the Crown did not claim sovereignty, but in which the market activities of British subjects were regulated by parliamentary statutes and other emanations of power'.[4] Therefore, empire, as used here, includes such disparate places, peoples and things as New England, the African slave trade and the East India Company; and while China was not part of the British Empire, the portion of the tea trade over which the East India Company claimed a British state-backed monopoly was. It is important to note that Britain's imperial presence must not be instinctively equated with dominance or control, as it too often is in later centuries. This is particularly the case with trade. Whereas colonization in the Chesapeake and Caribbean, in which the native peoples and fauna were cleared for commercial agriculture, was the backbone of tobacco and sugar production, other major trading relationships in the empire had a different power dynamic. To varying degrees of success in the eighteenth century, China controlled tea production and largely set the terms of trade; American Indians did the same with the fur trade, as did African rulers with the slave trade. In all of these cases, European trade required at least some local consent.[5]

Many of the topics discussed here – consumerism, social aspiration, enlightenment, political consciousness – were unique neither to the British nor to the period under consideration. The outpouring of biographies of specific goods – such as sugar or cotton – over the past three decades have highlighted that Britain was part of a global web of commerce throughout the eighteenth century. In fact, Britain's economic growth (as in most other countries) in the eighteenth century relied almost entirely on trade, rather than any significant increase in production.[6] As a result, Britain was as much a recipient of global trends and market forces as a purveyor of them.[7] After all, coffeehouse culture, not just coffee drinking, originated in Arabia, and Britain, however much tea its people drank, was always a secondary market for Chinese production.[8]

Contemporaries certainly conflated and conjoined the various elements of the British Empire during the eighteenth century. The Massachusetts colonists who dumped the East India Company's tea into Boston's harbour in 1774 (celebrated as the Boston Tea Party) in protest against parliamentary taxation considered the tea 'British'. Neither the finer points of the tea's Chinese provenance nor its ownership by the shareholders of the East India Company made a difference; by shipping the tea, the Company was complicit. As the freeholders of nearby Marblehead resolved at a town meeting just days before, 'the late Measures of the East-India Company, in sending to the Colonies their *Tea Loaded with a Duty for raising a Revenue from America*, are to all Intents and Purposes so many Attempts in them and all employed by them to tax Americans.' Therefore, the widely reprinted resolutions continued, 'Tea from Great Britain, subject to a Duty, whether shipped by the East-India Company, or imported by Persons here, shall not be landed in this Town while we have the Means of opposing it.'[9] Most commentators described the territorial and trading elements of the empire as two sides of the same coin. For instance, Malachy Postlethwayt, a government publicist and Royal Africa Company servant, described the British Empire in 1745 as 'a magnificent superstructure of American commerce and naval power on an African foundation'.[10] In justifying the production of his widely read and heavily annotated translation of *The Universal Dictionary of Trade and Commerce* a few years later, Postlethwayt reflected the wider tendency to link trade, empire and the power of the state. 'So I have judged it my duty as a Briton', he declared, '[to show] as empire follows trade, that nation which gains the superiority in trade, must gain the like in dominion'.[11]

This book takes as its primary period of focus what is often referred to as the 'long eighteenth century' – bookended by the accessions of William and Mary via the Revolution of 1688 and

Queen Victoria in 1837. Chronologically framing a book that might be most accurately described as cultural history with two major political events may seem odd, but these dates serve as useful markers. In case of William and Mary, their accession meant embarking on what has been dubbed the 'second hundred years war with France' (1689–1815) and the adaptation of the Dutch fiscal-military state of highly organized, centralized taxation to fund the British military. That, in turn, meant greater interest in taxable trade – imports and exports as well as the consuming habits of Britons. Wars with France and its allies, while ostensibly fought due to political and cultural differences, pitted armies and navies against each other for control of the trade resources that funded them, notably the trading colonies in India, tobacco-producing North American colonies and West Indian sugar islands.

Equally important was the expiration of the Licensing Order in 1694, in which Parliament essentially deregulated print and enabled the creation of a modern newspaper and periodical press. The press connected ordinary Britons through common readings, facilitated national political discussions and contoured British culture through endless commentary.[12] In the case of food, print culture meant the mass production of cookery books, visual advertising, travel accounts that described the eating habits of distant peoples, and commentary and stories in newspapers that linked favourite overseas luxuries with the empire and global trade networks that brought them to British homes. Reading and consumption of the goods of imperial rule and trade goods were intrinsically linked. Visual and literary representations of tea tables and coffeehouses are littered with people reading newspapers and magazines, and the men discussing the latest news are almost invariably depicted as smoking. Such collective social practices helped to form what have been described as national cultural consciousnesses and imagined communities, in which gentlewomen drinking tea in Devonshire engaged virtually with male coffeehouse patrons in Bristol by reading and discussing the same news topics.[13] Equally important, these sorts of interactions (imagined or otherwise) encouraged debate and dissent. As local governments in the Middle East and North Africa learned as coffee drinking spread there during the fifteenth and sixteenth centuries, coffeehouse culture questioned political authority.[14] In eighteenth-century Britain, print culture enabled the raucous political and social debates of the

William Tringham, 'The Rum Grumblers of Great Britain; A New Humorous Political Song' (London, 1762). The scene depicts two coffeehouse patrons reading from a selection of newspapers and complaining about the latest developments in the Seven Years War peace negotiations, with one stating 'D—m the War' and the other 'D—m the Peace'.

coffeehouses to permeate society, resulting in a national population that was both acutely aware of British imperial practices and ready to critique them.[15]

Capping the study in 1837 is less about identifying a conclusion of the topics explored here than it is about recognizing a shift in gears. The eighteenth century has long been recognized as witnessing the transition from the early modern to modern periods for much of Europe and its settled colonies. In many ways, the technological advancements of the Victorians, such as railways, printing techniques and the telegraph, consolidated and made more uniform the developments of the eighteenth century. Victoria's accession is also adjacent to the Slavery Abolition Act of 1833, which marked Britain's emancipation of its African slaves, the backbone of production for many of the goods discussed in the book.

The meteoric rise of the British Empire during this eighteenth century was predictable only with the power of hindsight. Starting with a handful of far-flung settler colonies and trading outposts, the English, and after 1707 British, Empire grew during the long eighteenth century into an entity that claimed sovereignty over nearly a fifth of the world's population and dominated large swathes of the rest through trade and intimidation. Born from over a century of global armed conflicts sometimes, although Eurocentrically, referred to as the second hundred years war with France, the British Empire was a product of violence – perpetrated on combatants and civilians alike. However, commerce, which was inextricably linked to much of the warfare that Britons waged, was equally important. Successful commerce, and the ability to manage and tax it, enabled Britain to punch well above its weight in terms of population, technology and natural resources against both European and global competitors.[16]

To assert that such ingestible products of imperial trade as coffee, tea, sugar and tobacco were important to the growth and prosperity of Britain and its empire during the eighteenth century is an understatement. They were the glue that bound the disparate parts of the empire to each other. To some extent the English, later British, Empire had always been gastronomic. A major part of the East India Company's mandate when founded in 1600 was to trade for exotic Asian goods, including lucrative spices. Although initially established as bases for raiding Spanish shipping and acting as havens for pirates, the English West Indian colonies shifted to highly profitable sugar production as piracy was stamped out – sometimes violently and sometimes amicably. Jamestown, established in 1607 as the first successful English colony in North America, barely clung to existence until tobacco saved it.[17] To produce these lucrative products the English retained African slaves – first a trickle from the Portuguese and other European traders and then a flood as the English, and then British, took control of large swathes of the trade. Thus the British penchant for sweet tea and coffee and a pipeful of tobacco had severe global consequences.

While these events were important to seventeenth-century England and its economy, they paled in significance to the imperial commerce that transpired in the century that followed. Sugar imports from the West Indies rose from 8,176 tons per annum in 1665 to 97,000 tons a century later; the value of imported East India Company tea increased from £8,000 at the end of the seventeenth century to £848,000 75 years later; and coffee imports, initially sourced from the southern Arabian port of Mocha, increased sixteenfold by the 1770s as a result of new plantations in the British West Indies. Even tobacco imports, already well established in the seventeenth century, increased nearly fourfold during the eighteenth century. To put some of these figures into context: the value of tea legally imported to Britain in 1794 exceeded England's total annual government spending just a century earlier and was more than twice what the United States federal government spent that year. Moreover, Britain doubly benefited by trading these goods for British products – largely manufactured ones. At the start of the eighteenth century, British exports were worth a mere £4.46 million, with the empire accounting for less than 15 per cent of the market. Less than a century later, the value of exports had increased more than threefold, and imperial markets accounted for more than half of the overall market.[18]

While such figures irrefutably state the importance of the trade in ingestibles to the British economy, they tell us little about how ordinary Britons connected these goods with the places that produced them. In short, when a group of men gathered in a London coffeehouse and smoked tobacco, Yorkshire ladies sipped sugar-infused tea, or a Glasgow family ate a bowl of Indian curry, to what extent were they aware of the origins of what they ate or the mechanisms of empire that made them available in Britain? Central to Britain's global success was the ability to connect the empire to domestic worlds.[19] Doing so bound ordinary Britons to the empire in such ways that they understood it as central to their prosperity and security and were willing to sacrifice their treasure and blood to protect and expand it. Although the relationship was largely exploitative, many Britons also developed a sense of moral responsibility towards the empire's subjects. While primarily examined as a phenomenon of the Victorian Age and the early twentieth century, the genesis of these connections can be found in the eighteenth century. Exploring these relationships and their development is a central theme of the present study.

A lingering, hotly contested question about Britain and its empire is whether or not people cared about it. For the African taken into the Atlantic slave trade to work on a Jamaican sugar plantation or an American Indian displaced to make way for white colonists' tobacco fields, awareness of imperialism was both acute and incontestable. Ignorance was the privilege of the British at home. Given the option, did the British remain largely oblivious to their empire? For some, this is a politically loaded question, as the legacy of the British

Empire continues to be played out in postcolonial nations and their internal and external disputes around the world.[20] Popular enthusiasm for the empire in this context might be interpreted as complicity, and historical complicity comes with present-day repercussions – not simply in the form of national guilt but also national obligations to make amends. The present study takes no position on the present-day political ramifications of past British imperialism, but it is not intimidated by the hard questions that inform the debate. Strong cases against popular interest in the empire, or at least ambivalence towards it, have been made; however, these studies disproportionately focus on the nineteenth and twentieth centuries, particularly the Victorian and Edwardian eras, when the British Empire was at its zenith and most secure.[21] The eighteenth century was a fundamentally different experience for the empire in terms of growth and security to the extent that the British Empire that emerged at the century's end would have been unfathomable to the English a century earlier. The British spent the century at war, usually winning but precariously on the precipice of defeat – facing the loss of colonies and a host of credible invasion scares of Britain itself. Even as late as 1815, American privateers were marauding British territorial waters and coastlines.[22] At the beginning of the eighteenth century, the English simply sought access to Asian and African markets; in subsequent centuries the British aimed to rule them. In consequence, Britons had different relationships to and understandings of their empire at different points in history; and, just as views of the empire were not stationary, the meanings of things and peoples associated with the empire were not static.

Food offers an invaluable opportunity to better understand British society and its relationships with the empire. Food is essential to human existence, and a considerable amount of our time and energy is spent engaging with it – producing, distributing, selling, buying, preparing, consuming and digesting. Almost as common is the practice of assigning meanings, whether individual or communal, to food. In consequence, the subject of food has been rich ground for scholars investigating social meanings and change, particularly in marking recent shifts, such as the privileged status of organic foods, the slow food movement and same-sex figurines on wedding cakes. Such behaviours also abound in the more distant past. In what Stephen Mennell describes as the 'civilizing of appetite' in his study of early modern English eating, in times of scarcity shows of abundance by the elite were sufficient to confirm their status; however, relative food prosperity, such as Britain experienced in the eighteenth century, meant that people sought more complex ways to assert their status. Taste, fashion and connoisseurship developed as means to provide distinctions in quality as signals of status when quantity alone was insufficient.[23]

Eighteenth-century Britons certainly recognized this phenomenon within their own society. Writing for the *London Magazine* in 1755, 'The Connoisseur' declared that 'those, who have more leisure to study what they shall eat and drink, require something more in their food, than what is barely wholesome or necessary; their palates must be gratified with rich sauces and high-seasoned delicacies.'[24] This also applied to specific commodities. The mere possession of many of the goods of imperial trade discussed here was sufficient to demonstrate wealth and taste when they first arrived in the British Isles. The later ubiquity of these goods necessitated ancillary devices – porcelain sugar bowls, jewelled tobacco boxes and leisurely tea visits in the middle of the working day – for consumers to exhibit their status. In this context of an abundance of choice, the rituals surrounding food flourished as a form of communication, if not a language.[25] In the case of tea in eighteenth-century Britain, the selected type, time of day, frequency of consumption, invited company, vessels used, rituals of preparation and decor of the room in which it was served could all act as conscious statements of social status, wealth and civilized refinement. Mixed-gender dinner parties also boomed during this period with an equally complex set of rules that promoted sociability. These changes turned domestic spaces into public arenas where hosts displayed their wealth and status. Methods of carving meat, placement of dishes, dishware and decor all became subjects of conversation and judgement.

Outside the home, increased urbanization and travel combined with sociability to turn eating into something of a pastime for elite and socially aspiring Britons.[26] While inns, taverns and itinerant food stalls had long peppered the urban landscape, the eighteenth century witnessed the developing of an epicurean scene, complete with printed guidebooks and reviews. At the high end were the taverns and eating houses frequented by the elite. In 'such houses', boasted the *London Pocket Pilot* guidebook, 'are to be met all the most delicate luxuries upon earth and where the fortuned voluptuary may indulge his appetite, not only with all the natural dainties of every season, but with delicacies produced by means of preternatural ingenuity'.[27] Beneath such elite establishments were an array of dining options. Traditional taverns, alehouses, chop-houses and inns as well as the thousands of new coffeehouses and tea gardens worked day and night to satisfy the populace's nutritional needs and epicurean desires.[28] A late eighteenth-century crossover from domestic to public was the highly fashionable 'Pic-Nic supper', described in *The Times*: 'As the expression of a Pic-Nic Supper is become so fashionable . . . it may be necessary to explain it for the information of many of our Readers.' In this period's version, subscribers to the event drew lots to determine which dishes they were obliged to provide to the group. Having different providers of the dishes results in friendly competition, explained *The Times*, 'as each strives to excel; and thus a *Pic-Nic* Supper not only gives rise to much pleasant mirth, but generally can boast of the refinement of the art'.[29]

The heightened socialization of food during the eighteenth century became so prevalent that food served as part of the language of national and regional identities. It is no accident that a letter to the *General Evening Post* in 1779 extolling the virtues of living in Britain and concluding 'As an Englishman I feel the highest pleasure in having had ocular proof that the Parisians neither enjoy the freedom, the conveniences, nor the luxuries of our Londoners', is signed 'Jack Roast Beef'.[30] Images of British food abound in satirical prints and public commentaries of the day, portraying the French as oppressed, American Indians as cannibals and Asian civilizations as decadent. Travellers regularly recorded their longing for their native cuisines and relished opportunities to replicate it with fellow nationals. As Janet Schaw, a young woman travelling through the West Indies and North America, gleefully remarked in her diary following a Scottish-themed dinner:

> We had a sheep killed yesterday, and have had a Scotch dinner under the Tropick in the middle of the Atlantick. We eat haggis, sheep-head, barley-broth and blood puddings. As both our Capt. and Mate are Scots, tho' long from home, they swore they had not seen such an excellent dinner since they left their native land.[31]

For the same reasons, food became a tool for cultural critiques. Concerns about the debilitating effects of luxury, the influence of foreign cultures and any number of political scandals were described both publicly and privately using the imagery of food. In a widely reprinted nostalgic lament for simpler times of less division by social rank, *The Times* emblematically framed its chastisement of the elite via a discussion of Christmas food. 'Within the last half century,' *The Times* declared in its 1790 Christmas Day editorial, 'this annual festivity has lost much of its original mirth and hospitality.' Chastising the elite for no longer opening their houses and rivalling for 'who should be the most splendid, the most generous, and the most charitable on the occasion', *The Times* complained that the social ranks had become segregated. 'This has almost in one respect obliterated the fashion of what was called old English hospitality, and convened the public into what may be called distinct societies, where the individuals are personally known to each other.' As a result of

James Gillray, 'Politeness' (London, 1779). The stout Englishman sits in a sensible, sturdy chair as he consumes a large tankard of frothing ale and huge joint of meat hangs on the wall. The daintily attired Frenchmen sits opposite, pinching snuff on his ornate chair while a brace of frogs hangs behind him. The underlying caption reads 'With Porter Roast Beef and Plumb Pudding well cram'd, Tack English declars that Monsr. May be D—d' and 'The Soup Meagre Frenchmen such Language don't suit. so his Grins Indignation & calls him a Brute.'

greater prosperity, *The Times* explained, isolated celebrations had replaced communal festivities: 'A system of refinement in luxury marks the tables of the rich – the middling rank of life are more enlightened and more selective in their company.' Worse still, *The Times* continued, families increasingly outsourced the preparation of the traditional dishes, once made with great personal love. Although 'there are as many plumb puddings boiled, and as many minced pies made', ladies preferred 'now to possess the art of painting the face and whitening the hands' and had 'kicked the drudgery of mixing pies, tarts, and puddings out of doors'. In consequence, the old traditions of Christmas were to be found only 'Among the trading part of the people, [for whom] beef and pudding, and turkey and chine are almost synonymous with the day'. Among them, *The Times* wistfully proclaimed, 'Young and old join in the festivities and a kind of general joy spreads itself around: business is forgot and pleasure takes the chair.' 'John Bull', *The Times* concluded, 'enjoys his holiday.'[32]

Ultimately, an examination of selected food practices enables a better understanding of how Britons considered and engaged with their rapidly expanding empire and changing world during the long eighteenth century. This book is divided into two parts. The first focuses on how Britain's inhabitants encountered the empire via the ingestible articles of imperial rule and trade and how those goods influenced their lives. The first chapter describes how such goods as coffee, tea, sugar and tobacco changed from novelties to ubiquities, entering even the poorest and remotest of households by the end of the eighteenth century and making them paramount to Britain's economy. The second chapter shifts to the consumers, exploring how the dramatic influx of these goods and the widespread desire for them played a central role in the transformation of Britain into a consumer society.[33] By mid-century, the most common shops were those that sold the ingestible commodities of imperial rule and trade. Savvy entrepreneurs' readiness to meet consumers' demands resulted in practices that transformed the retail trade into something someone in Britain today would find familiar. Customer store credit, mail orders, bulk discounts, luxurious shopping experiences and delivery services all came to bear as shopkeepers endeavoured to secure a share of the market. Among the most innovative developments was visual advertising, which Chapter Three examines. Purveyors of the ingestibles of imperial trade throughout Britain turned to cheap, printed visual

James Gillray, 'Monstrous Craws, at a New Coalition Feast' (London, 1777). The print attacks the expenses of the royal family by depicting the queen, Prince of Wales and king sitting around a table greedily feasting on golden tax revenues, served in a bowl labelled 'John Bull's Blood' – John Bull being a reference to the ordinary people of Britain.

images from the 1740s onwards to entice customers to buy their goods. The selected imagery rammed home the goods' imperial origins and connections, repeatedly reminding consumers of the importance of the empire to something as ordinary as a cup of tea or a pipeful of tobacco.

Part Two shifts focus to consider how practices of food preparation and consumption reflected, shaped and expressed Britons' understandings of themselves and their empire. Britain during the eighteenth century was awash with goods, printed accounts and displays of objects from across the rapidly expanding empire of rule and commerce, and Part Two offers important insights into how people interpreted and responded to this flood of things and information. Chapters Four and Five are tightly linked examinations of cookery. Intertwined with the Enlightenment, the growing popularity of science, interest in the arts and greater emphasis on so-called factual information, cookery was a leading subject of both private and national public discussions. As a woman commented in 1814, when remarking on the British who raced to tour Europe following the conclusion of war with France, 'some of the young men seem better able to criticise French cookery than French conversation, or the Venus or Apollo.'[34] Chapter Four investigates the emergence of a national cuisine in Britain, particularly how it reflected and influenced wider considerations of human civilization, national identity, the power of print culture and women's growing public role as cultural arbiters. Through its exploration of domestic changes in cookery, Chapter Four lays the necessary groundwork for the next two chapters. Chapter Five considers how Britons used cookery as a means to similarly evaluate other cultures' level of development and place them in the hierarchy of civilizations. Engagement with foreign cookery from across the empire also took the form of the increasing number of replicated dishes found in British cookery books and public eateries. Almost universally promoted for their authenticity, these dishes were given place names and background stories. In this context, such dishes served as edible artefacts alongside the other objects from imperial rule and trade that flooded Britain.

Chapter Six describes how the preparation and consumption of foods related to the empire reflected and affected popular politics. Goods such as coffee and tea, along with the copious amounts of sugar that Britons poured into these hot beverages, created an environment ripe for politicization. Purchased outside the home and primarily consumed either in public venues such as coffeehouses or semi-public domestic settings, these goods overtly promoted socialization and conversation. These conversations, whether in the public space of a coffeehouse or the semi-private setting of afternoon tea in someone's home, regularly took a political turn. Even the commodities themselves sometimes assumed political meanings as objects of empire. The combination of public politics, consumerism and shared meanings of imperial goods reached its zenith in the creation of the first widespread consumer boycotts. Initiated as protests of imperial practices and implemented largely by women of the middling ranks, boycotts gave political voices to ordinary British men and women as consumers who, collectively, recognized their paramount role in the economy of Britain and the empire. Critically, the boycotts also plainly demonstrate that ordinary consumers recognized specific goods' association with the empire, and that by purchasing these goods, consumers were supporting its practices.

Together, the chapters demonstrate the paramount role that food played during the eighteenth century in binding domestic life with the British Empire. The connection, like the acquisition and consumption of food itself, had multiple layers. Through food, Britons engaged with each other and the rapidly expanding empire as consumers, curious onlookers, a society in self-reflection, assessors and, ultimately, participants. There were, of course, a range of other ways for Britons to engage with the empire, including the growing newspaper and periodical press, museums, live shows and vast quantities of other material goods, such as porcelain, that flooded into Britain. The present study does not ignore this wider context. After all, men and women drank tea as they discussed a visit to the British Museum to see its ethnographic collections, and coffeehouse patrons read newspapers as they smoked Virginian tobacco. Engaging with food, like reading a vivid account of the African slave trade or holding an Iroquois tomahawk at a London auction, was yet another way that the empire gripped British imaginations. However, food was distinct during this period because it, more than any other experience, connected Britons to their empire, consciously or not.

What emerges from this study of food is an image of a nation in transformation. The English Empire was evolving from a far-flung collection of settled colonies and trading stations clinging precariously to coastlines around the world into a British Empire with a centralized, bureaucratic and heavily armed authority; so, too, was British society. The journey to the confident imperialism of the Victorian Age was neither preordained nor rapid. Instead, it was accretive. The imperial cosmology of the middling British woman in 1800 was fundamentally different from that of her ancestor a hundred years earlier. While other studies of British society and the empire tend to focus on wars as watershed moments, the consideration of food muddies this picture. While war often attracted acute attention and disrupted and opened new trade routes, the flow of goods from imperial trade was governed by a vast array of supply and market factors – often well outside British control. As discussed in the proceeding chapters, tea, for example, became ubiquitous and its price rose and fell not because of war, but primarily as a result of such factors as Chinese decisions about opening trade, parliamentary taxation, changing socialization and fashion in Britain, and the decisions and wider fortunes of the East India Company.

Moreover, while newspaper articles, political pamphlets and books were the primary conduits for information about the world, an examination of food offers insights into how the subject infiltrated the routines of Britons' daily lives as well as their levels of awareness. The question of whether or not the consumption of empire-related foods should be equated with imperialism, or even an awareness of empire, is a fair one. Any assertion that all Britons who drank tea during this period were imperialists is as ridiculous as it is unprovable. However, the evidence, as presented in this book, reveals that food both reflected and affected Britons' engagement with the empire. Consideration of the mechanisms of empire and its relationship to Britain's prosperity is evident in something as seemingly benign as a reader's article in 1812 on the origins of coffee for the *Lady's Monthly Museum*, a moderately successful magazine aimed at middling housewives and the lesser gentry. In it, the writer not only narrates the history of coffee but connects it to the political economy of Britain and the empire, noting how its trade benefited the West Indian colonies, the strength of the navy and the British consumer. Asserting that 'the increased consumption of coffee must be regarded as a public good', she even astutely warns about the dangers of the tea trade with China draining Britain's silver – a problem the East India Company would try to address by selling opium, a consequence of which would be the mid-nineteenth-century Opium Wars.[35]

Equally important, food served as a way for Britons to encounter peoples around the world who were connected to the empire. Visual advertisements displayed products' origins with such images as African slaves growing tobacco in Virginia alongside British ships. Recipes in popular cookery books and dishes at a number of eateries gave consumers a taste of India. Printed discussions of domestic and foreign cookery found in both the tomes of the intellectual elite and cookery books written by housekeepers used food to compare, contrast and critique societies. Importantly, such assessments were not nationalistic rants. Far more often, they were reflective pieces that were critical of British society and complimentary of other cultures. Difference was something to be studied, experienced and, in certain contexts, celebrated. Such connections contributed immeasurably to the growing sense of obligation many ordinary Britons felt towards the more vulnerable peoples living under the empire's rule, which is exemplified by the hundreds of thousands of consumers in the British Isles who abstained from West Indian sugar in protest against the African slave trade and slavery at the end of the late eighteenth century. For them and the public they worked tirelessly to persuade, the connection between eating and the empire was undeniably evident.

PART I

ENCOUNTERING, ACQUIRING *AND* PEDDLING

ONE
THE EMPIRE'S BOUNTY

While London is littered with monuments that pay tribute to the military men who forged the British Empire, the real heroes (or, perhaps, villains, depending on one's perspective) were the humble shopkeepers who peddled small luxuries from faraway lands. In a process Adam Smith described as 'breaking and dividing' in his *Wealth of Nations*, these men and women took the vast quantities of teas, coffees, sugars, spices and tobaccos that poured into Britain and repackaged them in ways that made them accessible to even the poorest and remotest of its inhabitants.[1] By the time Smith published these observations in his seminal work in 1776, the issue was no longer whether or not someone could afford such luxuries of imperial rule and trade; rather, the questions were about what quantity and which quality.

The story of the transition of these goods from rare luxuries to commonplace staples is a remarkable one. The rapid growth of trade in these commodities, both in terms of volume and as a proportion of British trade, is staggering. In fact, if all of the coffee England imported as late as 1724 was distributed evenly, there would be only enough for the average inhabitant to have a weak cup every three weeks, and tea was not much more plentiful.[2] Yet edible commodities of imperial rule and trade were so ubiquitous a generation later that hardly a household could be found without one or more of them. The influx of ingestible goods transformed British diets, social practices and consumer behaviours during the eighteenth century to the extent that they would have been almost unrecognizable a century earlier, and the overseas trade in them became so plentiful as to recontour how the British ran their empire. In consequence, the domestic consumption of these goods transformed how ordinary Britons engaged with the economy and bound them to imperial rule and trade.

Lingering medicines

The favoured products of empire that would play critical roles in shaping Britain's economy and culture were hardly new to the nation's shores at the dawn of the eighteenth century. The entrepreneurial desire to expand existing domestic markets for such luxuries was one of the driving forces of English and Scottish overseas expansion throughout the late sixteenth and seventeenth centuries. Nevertheless, access to most of the goods discussed in this book remained limited well into the eighteenth century, and like other cultures when first introduced to exotic goods, the inhabitants of the British Isles treated such commodities as novelties and medicines.[3] When Samuel Pepys commented on tea in his diary in 1667, he remarked that his wife bought it on the advice of their local apothecary – not a grocer – who had touted it to her as a remedy for 'her cold and defluxions'.[4] Such goods' mystique, and with it much of their medicinal status, dissipated as they became more common.

Although treating such goods as cure-alls for an array of physical maladies may appear to the twenty-first-century reader as quackery, the advice was fairly conventional. Published medical advocates were especially sanguine. A 1712 treatise on *The Virtues and Excellency of the American Tobacco Plant*, for example, assigned tobacco a host of health benefits, including increased circulation, improved digestion and dental health. It also claimed that tobacco prevented scurvy and remedied leprosy. Not satisfied with those incredible assertions, the treatise declared that 'Tobacco also is often a Remedy for Deafness' and that it inoculated the user from plague. There was little tobacco could not supposedly cure, the treatise argued, and therefore 'All Persons who love long Life and Health, will daily have Recourse to the *American* Tobacco, as a noble Remedy.' To achieve the best benefits, the treatise recommended using tobacco as early in life as possible, noting that those who started in their youth 'are never afflicted (or at least very rarely) with Gout, Rheumatisms, Scurvy, or Tooth-ach'. Paramount to success, and likely a major reason for the treatise, was selecting the correct tobacco – the genuine American article – rather than competing types. Anything else was 'very unwholesome and pernicious to anyone that use it'. In fact, the treatise warned, 'Instead of preserving, it destroys Health.'[5]

While *The Virtues and Excellency of the American Tobacco Plant* was especially optimistic about tobacco's medical properties, it was hardly unique. Nor were such claims confined to treatises that can be described as little more than false advertisements. In his authoritative *Physical Dictionary* aimed at professional medical practitioners in 1702, Steven Blankaart reflected the wider circulating literature by assigning Asian tea a myriad of beneficial properties, including being a cure for nightmares, giddiness, dropsy, gout, constipation, fatigue and poor eyesight.[6] Similarly, claims for coffee's curative benefits were vastly exaggerated before its widespread consumption. Its enduring quality as a cure for hangovers, however, remained. As the 1708 *Materia Medica* claimed, 'Coffee Liquor is very usefully and effectually drunk after a Surfeit of hard Drinking' – the favoured remedy still popularly touted, despite scientific doubts, today.[7] While tea maintained its association with good digestion and rejuvenating energy throughout the period, wider use led to a consensus by the 1720s regarding some of its negative effects, including how drinking too much caused nervousness and sleeplessness and how tea stained and damaged teeth.[8] By mid-century, when tea had seen off contenders for the nation's hot beverage of choice as measured by volume of consumption, medical assertions had decidedly slumped, and the discussion shifted to the consumption of tea as a danger of a different kind: luxury.

Oddly, of all the major ingestibles of the empire, tobacco seems to have received the most aggressive defence as a medical remedy during the early decades of the eighteenth century. As in *The Virtues and Excellency of the American Tobacco Plant*, early eighteenth-century proponents advocated tobacco in its various forms as a cure for mouth ulcers, cancerous growths and fevers, among other ailments. One practitioner noted tobacco's dual use as both a pesticide for flies and a cure for haemorrhoids. Counterintuitively, a number of sources advocated tobacco as an effective remedy for asthma, skin irritations and failing eyesight – with one declaring that through regular smoking, 'persons may never come to wear spectacles'. Another common recommended use was to rub its oil on the afflicted areas to cure venereal diseases.[9] Although quackery abounds in the array of prescriptions for using tobacco, and much of the advice was rooted in folk medicine, authoritative sources also initially endorsed tobacco as an effective medicine. The Royal College of Physicians' 1702 edition of *Pharmacopoeia Londinensis* described tobacco as useful for inducing purges and cleanses as well as pain relief, chiefly related to the teeth and gout. It, too, praised tobacco oil as an ointment for venereal disease and noted that 'it cures all manner of Tumors, Wounds, Ulcers, old Sores, Breakings out, Itch, Bitings or Stingings of venomous Beasts' as well as 'Scalds, Burns, Piles, and Gouts of all sorts'. Moreover, 'being dropt into the Ears it helps deafness' and 'bathed upon the Region of the Bladder it breaks the Stone'. Even John Locke praised tobacco for its regularizing effects on one's bowels in his 1693 *Some Thoughts Concerning Education*.[10]

During the second and third decades of the eighteenth century, voices of scepticism began to take hold. They noted tobacco's addictive properties and its negative effects on teeth and gums, as well as how it impaired breathing and agitated digestion. In the 1714 satirical poem *Medicaster Exenteratus, or the Quack's Pourtrait*, tobacco makes the list of fraudulent medicines.

> Intolerable Coxcombs! All this while
> Their *Powders* are no more the sifted Tile.
> Their *Tinctures*, Stale & Verguice stain'd with Brick
> With Brasil some, and some with Turmerick.
> Toads, and Tobacco their Emeticks are;
> And their *Catharticks*, Gall, Hogs-dung, and Tar.[11]

Although tobacco continued to appear in home and folk remedies for several decades, and for much longer as an insect pesticide and repellent, by mid-century it had been removed from most medical treatises, and a consensus was reached on its ill effects. The following, from a 1745 jest book, reflected this: 'One [consumer] asking another which Way a Man might use Tobacco to have any Benefit from it: *By setting up a Shop to sell it,* said he, *for certainly there is not Profit to be had from it any other Way.*'[12] Even the 1757 *London Tradesman*, a guide for parents on choosing a son's career, used the opportunity to complain about the ill effects of tobacco when describing the prospects of a tobacconist.[13]

Yet by then tobacco was entrenched into the daily lives of millions of Britons, who smoked, chewed and snorted more tobacco than ever, irrespective of the strictures issued by medical practitioners as well as moral reformers.[14] In fact, Emanuel Mendes da Costa, a fellow of both the Royal Society and Antiquarian Society, credited the dramatic increase in fossil discoveries, which spurred the development of archaeology as a scientific discipline, to the boom in white clay extraction for tobacco pipes.[15]

The economic importance of the empire's ingestibles

Overestimating the importance of the ingestible products of imperial commerce to the British economy during the eighteenth century is difficult. While many of the goods had long histories in Europe, only in the eighteenth century did they become widely and cheaply available in Britain. During this time, they fundamentally altered Britain's imperial and domestic economies.

Cane sugar, for example, had been available in Europe for upwards of two thousand years, its production originating in Southeast Asia some ten thousand years ago, but the quantities were small and expensive. First appearing in Europe in Greek medicines, the plant was later cultivated in the eastern Mediterranean by Arabs, European Crusaders and Turks, but exorbitant prices ensured it remained the preserve of the elite. Tudor monarchs boasted mini-mountains of it to display their wealth, with fashionable banquets featuring a sugar course in which confectioners sculpted the sweet crystals into spectacular shapes and scenes. The rapid growth of the West Indian plantation system and the African slave trade from the late seventeenth century made sugar affordable to virtually all Britons, who eagerly drove up annual per capita consumption by 2,500 per cent to reach 20 pounds per person by 1800.[16]

Other products experienced similarly rapid growth rates. In 1724 customs officers reported 660 tons of coffee entering England; that annual figure increased fivefold fifty years later.[17] Tobacco had a deeper connection to Britain, having been the economic salvation of England's first successful American colony, Jamestown, in the early seventeenth century.[18] By the 1670s, after tobacco planters had cleared vast swathes of land of native people and fauna and embraced African slave labour, colonies sent tobacco to Britain in quantities that could be measured in millions of pounds weight annually.[19] A century later, annual tobacco imports exceeded 7 million pounds.[20]

Much of the sugar Britons consumed during the eighteenth century went into tea, the consumption of which also grew at an exponential rate. Tea almost invariably came from China, as the commercially produced Indian tea that would eventually dominate the British marketplace would not appear in Britain until the Victorian era. During the seventeenth century, tea trickled into England as curious gifts and the continuation of drinking habits acquired by merchants engaged with Asian trades before the East India Company formally entered into the trade in 1660. Even then, the company initially bought the tea not directly from China, but from the Dutch, who began sending it commercially to the Netherlands in 1637. The growth of tea consumption was, at least initially, slow; in fact, trade with China accounted for a mere 4 per cent of the Asian trade through the 1680s.[21] In this context, tea was a luxury for the elite and upper echelons of the middling ranks, who, like Pepys, enjoyed it in individual servings in coffeehouses or purchased it in small quantities for medicinal purposes.

The turn of the century marked a shift in England's tea trade. Anxious to tap into China's considerable wealth, English merchants sought to invest more heavily in trade with China. Meanwhile, silver-hungry China, where the precious metal commanded a value as much as 50 per cent higher than in European markets, eased a number of trading restrictions placed on European traders, culminating in the opening of Canton, the heart to the tea trade, to British traders in 1713.[22] In consequence, China's share of England's Asian trade rose to 14 per cent by 1706, with England having imported more tea in the previous four years than the whole of the seventeenth century.[23] Even so, these were small quantities compared to the trade that soon blossomed. At the mid-century mark, the East India Company, which held a monopoly on all tea legally imported into the British Isles, had increased its tea trade fortyfold, and for every pound imported in 1711, Britain imported 143 pounds a century later, as tea displaced ale as the favoured breakfast beverage and became the preferred hot beverage throughout the day. Tea was so plentiful that on a given day in 1784, London shop shelves alone carried over 146 tons of it, and by 1835 the British were consuming 40 million pounds of tea each year.[24]

The profits of imperial trade during the eighteenth century helped transform modest towns into thriving commercial cities. At the time of Scotland's Union with England in 1707, Glasgow's population did not exceed 13,000 people. Less than a century later, it had increased sixfold on its way to becoming the second most important city in the British Isles. Much of this boom was on the back of the tobacco trade with the North American colonies, which the rapidly growing port came to dominate by mid-century. By 1762 legal tobacco coming into Glasgow, through which the majority of tobacco imported into Britain flowed, accounted for 85 per cent of Scottish imports from North America and a whopping 47 per cent of all of its imports. In terms of volume, this meant a 3,200 per cent increase between the Act of Union and the eve of the American Revolution.[25]

The tax revenues generated by these goods were unprecedented. For example, the annual duty on sugar in the 1760s was roughly equivalent to the cost of maintaining all the ships in the Royal Navy in peacetime.[26] While well behind sugar's value, tobacco and coffee were no slouches. The tax revenues from tobacco exceeded those collected on all printed goods, including the tens of millions of newspapers that flowed into the taverns, inns and coffeehouses in which tobacco was smoked. The customs duty on coffee in 1774 was enough to build five ships of the line – a fleet more powerful than anything the soon-to-be-independent United States would produce for generations.[27]

Critically, the government was not a passive collector of taxes on these goods, and its attempts to regulate and manipulate these trades provoked wars, desolated indigenous populations and transformed British culture. The tea trade is a prime example. As a commentator aptly reflected in the introduction to his 1835 *Brief Notices on the Tea Plant*, 'Whether we regard Tea as the object of a very extensive branch of British trade, or as the source of much social and individual enjoyment, its importance and claims on our attention come home to us all.'[28] Tea's rise was by no means assured when it first appeared commercially in Britain. Coffee, originally imported through the southern Arabian port of Mocha that had dominated the trade since coffee's fifteenth-century origins as a beverage, had a modest head start. While the East India Company imported less than 23 pounds weight of tea in 1666, all acquired from Amsterdam, coffee stalls and houses by that time had been operating for years and numbered a hundred or more. In fact, coffeepots were more common than teapots during the early eighteenth century, as Britons consumed more coffee than tea until the 1720s.[29]

The government played an instrumental role in compelling a shift in English (British after 1707) and colonial habits. Not quite sure how to handle the hot beverage trade, taxmen initially treated coffee like alcohol and taxed it in brewed form at 4*d* per gallon. Fortunately for those consumers in search of freshness in their coffee, the government shifted to a tax on the dry beans in the 1660s, well before tea established itself in England. A series of tax measures – a mixture of increased duties on coffee and decreased duties on tea – over the first half of the eighteenth century ensured that as more Britons sought caffeine, they increasingly opted for tea. This was no accident. The legal tea trade was controlled entirely by the East India Company, which was a private-public concern. The East India Company had enormous influence during this period. Its reliably

'The Chancellors' Hobby, or More Taxes for John Bull' (London, 1819). The satire depicts the Chancellor of the Exchequer running down John Bull (the personification of ordinary Britons) with a myriad of taxes, particularly those on tobacco, coffee and tea. Bull exclaims, 'What the Devil the fellow at are you going to cram all this Down my Throat Zounds you will choak me'. Taxes on such imperial goods as coffee, tea and tobacco were increasingly controversial, as they became staples in British households, and always provoked public outcries. Yet their ubiquity and Britons' inability to produce them domestically made them prime, lucrative targets for taxation. It was a delicate balance the British government could get wrong, such as in the American colonies in the 1770s.

profitable shares were broadly owned by the political and mercantile elite, it had access to the Bank of England for short-term loans (not unlike the arrangement the British government had), it loaned millions of pounds to the government, and its taxed trade accounted for 11 per cent of total government revenue by the early 1770s. Tea was a crucial part of the company's trade, accounting for between 20 and 40 per cent of its total value by mid-century. Thus protecting the tea trade, and with it the East India Company, was widely seen to be in the nation's best interest.[30]

In contrast, Britain had little hope of controlling the European market in other caffeinated hot beverages. As British demand for coffee rose during the eighteenth century, it came from an increasingly diverse group of sources, including European rivals. In fact, within a few decades of the eighteenth century, the trade with Mocha was irrelevant, because Europeans were spreading production across the world. By the 1780s the Island of San Domingo, then divided by the French and Spanish empires, supplied half of the world's coffee.[31] For similar reasons, hot chocolate, which relied almost exclusively on Spanish imports, never had a chance at dominance – although plenty of people enjoyed it, especially when Sir Hans Sloane, the president of the Royal Society whose private collections would form the basis of the British Museum in 1753, began marketing his patented milk chocolate as a digestive aid.[32] By the time British coffee imports had shifted to their own coffee-producing West Indian colonies in the second half of the century, tea had entrenched itself as the beverage of choice, and so over 90 per cent of coffee imported into Britain was re-exported to northern and central Europe. By the 1780s, British tea consumption was more than seventeen times that of coffee – more than the rest of Europe combined. In fact, Britain and its colonies' demand for tea was so great that the bulk of the tea that the Dutch and other European traders imported by that time also made its way to consumers in Britain and its American colonies, albeit via the black market.[33]

Because virtually all tea imported into Europe relied on Canton as its single source, the East India Company had a better chance of controlling it than coffee, or so the company's directors believed. In consequence, during the early eighteenth century, the company's agents in Canton were instructed to buy as much tea as possible in order to corner the European market. The ploy ultimately failed, primarily because the directors did not fully appreciate how small a part of the global tea trade Europe was or the ability of Chinese producers to adapt. The British managed to squeeze European competitors to the point that the Dutch were forced to buy over a million pounds of tea from the East India Company in the 1720s, but by mid-century the Dutch were importing almost as much as the British, and the French, Danish and Swedish were each importing roughly two-thirds as much.[34] The result was a massive glut that in turn made tea cheaper and more accessible to domestic and colonial consumers. Meanwhile, in an effort to cut wastage and enlarge the market for tea, the company shifted away from the more expensive and delicate green teas in favour of cheaper and hardier black, or 'Bohea' (Wuyi), tea, which went from 37.8 per cent by weight of total tea imports in the 1720s to 63.3 per cent three decades later.[35]

These ingestible commodities also served to bind the desperate pieces of the far-flung British Empire together – economically and culturally. The American Chesapeake colonies existed primarily to produce tobacco for the British Empire, both for domestic consumption and the lucrative re-export trade that gave Britain a favourable trading balance with the rest of Europe. By the same token, the West Indian colonies produced sugar and, to a lesser degree, coffee. Colonists focused on the production of these products at the expense of self-sufficiency. A succession of governments from the mid-seventeenth century onwards actively regulated imperial trade to encourage a web of interdependence between the colonies and the home nation and to promote English shipping. In this mercantilist model, Virginia colonists purposely produced vast quantities of tobacco for export and, with the profits, purchased necessities and luxuries from the rest of the empire. Ideally, Britain served as the hub of manufacturing and the nexus through which all imperial goods flowed (and were taxed). Although fraught with challenges and limitations – objections to it played a major role in the outbreak of the American Revolution, among other conflicts – the model was a cornerstone of the British Empire during the eighteenth century and beyond. The evidence is apparent in colonial household inventories, which, rich and poor alike, are awash with goods from across the empire. Even in the late colonial and early post-revolutionary period, Britain's North American colonies continued to depend on Britain for books, tools and scientific and medical instruments as well as more mundane goods such as textiles – much to the agitation of American commentators who perceived this reliance as eroding the new nation's independence.[36]

The cultural implications were significant. British fashions flowed into the colonies via trade. British books, printed music and clothes dominated the social trends of the colonial middling and elite ranks, as demonstrated by the shelves of lending and private libraries and the wardrobes of the likes of George Washington and Thomas Jefferson, whose cargoes of tobacco destined for Britain were invariably accompanied by detailed shopping lists.[37] The consumption of tea is a prime example. Although tea was available in the American colonies in small quantities not long after it appeared in Britain, consumption did not take off until the 1740s, when the East India Company sought to unload its substantial surplus on the colonists. The plan worked. In the 1710s the East India Company re-exported less than 28,000 pounds of tea to the American colonies (mainland and West Indian); in the 1740s, the amount exceeded 1.4 million, or roughly 7 per cent of the tea the East India Company shipped from Asia. The market for the colony of New York alone during the same period grew from 731 to 441,139 pounds. Such growth rates exceeded even England's impressive increase in tea consumption, and, on a per capita basis, meant that British North American colonists drank roughly twice as much tea as their English counterparts by the middle of the century.[38] With tea came the British culture of tea drinking. Described in detail in subsequent chapters, drinking tea became an opportunity to demonstrate personal taste and wealth – in part by abiding by the rituals of tea drinking, but also through displaying various material accompaniments. Accordingly, colonial households, rich and poor alike, experienced a boom from the mid-century onward in ownership of such British-produced goods as silverware and ceramics, and the Americas overtook continental Europe as a market for them.[39]

Disseminating the ingestibles of empire

The massive influx of and demand for the ingestible products of colonial settlement and imperial trade reshaped British consumer culture. As the subsequent chapters explain, the retailing, advertising, purchasing and consumption of these goods combined to play a central role in the advent of the modern consumer. Critical to this development was the underpinning commercial distribution structure that extended across Britain, ensuring that rural labourers living in the later decades of the eighteenth century had access to a wider range of these goods than aristocrats in London had two generations earlier. Such a remarkable development, however, came with consequences.

Although still sparse in the late seventeenth century, the shops that peddled the ingestibles of empire numbered in the tens of thousands two generations later, reshaping urban and rural landscapes alike. Initially, many of the empire's ingestible goods appeared in apothecaries' shops as medicines, such as the one where Pepys's wife was advised to drink tea to ease her ailments. As tea and coffee became less exotic, savvy entrepreneurs sold small quantities in side arrangements to their primary business. For example, as late as the 1790s, Walthal Fenton, a prosperous clothier and draper in the Staffordshire market town of Newcastle-under-Lyme, purchased substantial quantities of various teas and coffees from London grocers Brewsters & Gillman for his own and several other local shops. A single order for 1791, for example, included thirteen types of tea and three of coffee.[40]

The growth of the market for the empire's ingestibles, combined with the costs associated with establishing oneself in the trade, propelled the rise of dedicated shops. Loosely labelled as 'grocers', such shops were not restricted to guilds and livery companies, such as London's Worshipful Company of Grocers, whose origins date to the fourteenth century. By 1765 there were some 32,234 licensed tea dealers in England and many more unlicensed ones – accounting for roughly a quarter of all shops in England. By 1800 the number of licensed shops had risen to over 62,000, increasing their share to roughly a third of all shops.[41] While some shops in the metropolitan marketplace focused exclusively on one product, most sold the full range of the imperial staples of coffee, tea, sugar and tobacco, alongside an impressive array of spices, dried fruits and other sundries. In smaller markets, and even some towns, grocers acted as something of a general store, offering all sorts of goods from Spanish lemons to Chinese silks. One such store was Ann Gomm's Cotswold village shop in Shipton-under-Wychwood. Although a small operation with recorded sales typically in pennies and occasionally shillings, Gomm nevertheless had an impressive assortment of goods. Her sales records from the 1790s include a wide range of imported coffees, tobaccos, teas, spices, sugars, textiles and ribbons, alongside such familiar domestic supplies as dried fruits, ink, candles, soaps, butter and bacon.[42]

Few prospered more than William Fortnum. The former footman of Queen Anne went into business with Hugh Mason in 1705 to found Fortnum & Mason, the iconic luxury grocery that for over three centuries has supplied the rich and powerful along with anyone else with the means and desire to purchase its famously high-quality goods.[43] From humble beginnings as a small shop in St James's Market, the partners and their successors forged a considerable business empire that served royalty and other elite customers throughout the empire – perhaps most famously Queen Victoria, who sent beef tea to the Crimea for the use of Florence Nightingale.[44] By the early nineteenth century, the shop occupied two adjoining properties in Piccadilly along with a considerable warehouse nearby whose combined contents exceeded the value of £4,000 – roughly the cost of an Arkwright-type one-thousand-spindle mill, the most advanced and expensive piece of industrial machinery of the age.[45]

The domestic trading networks that distributed these goods from port to shop were remarkably extensive, interwoven and overlapping. Formal monopolies and tight-knit interest groups dominated the legal overseas trade of many of the goods, such as the East India Company's government-backed monopoly of the tea trade. In consequence, these goods legally entered Britain in just a handful of port cities. Bristol, Liverpool and Glasgow lassoed much of the Atlantic trade. London, where the East India Company was headquartered, harvested most of the Asian trade. At these cities' auctions the

Fortnum & Mason trade card, *c.* 1775.

'wholesalemen', as Daniel Defoe described them in his 1726 account of the booming networks of English trade, purchased and funnelled the goods to shops and other, lesser, dealers, and on 'into every corner of the kingdom, however remote'.[46]

Although Defoe took a fairly dim view of wholesalers and merchants in general, warning that 'the very boys in the wholesalemen's warehouses, and in merchant's warehouses, will play upon [the ignorant buyer], [and] sell him one thing for another', wholesalers played a critical role in evaluating the quality and value of goods and took great pains to develop their craft.[47] In the case of tea, wholesalers assessed the teas at the East India Company's twice-annual auctions. Initially, the primary distinctions for tea in Britain were Bohea, the common and cheaper black sort, and green tea, but as the century progressed the wide range of teas that reached Britain were categorized into an increasing number of types and grades, which ranged enormously in price. By the late eighteenth century, the company and wholesale buyers had adopted grading systems, enabling some standardization in the market.[48] Nevertheless, much still depended on wholesalers' abilities to evaluate the teas on offer and ensure that both quality and value were disseminated through the chains they supplied. In this context, the first national branding emerged. Among the most famous wholesalers were the Twinings, whose name continues to adorn teas today. First apprenticed to a weaver, Thomas Twining, the founder of the business, shifted to groceries as a young man and then established Tom's Coffee-House in London at the age of 31. He expanded operations with the help of his family, focusing on the wholesale business.[49] By the time of his death in 1741, the Twining name was becoming one of the first nationally recognized brands, thanks to the firm's rapid expansion and successful marketing, which included the novel idea of distributing thousands of advertising trade cards to its wholesale customers. The cards, used as package labels and receipt stationery, featured the Twinings label and space for the local shop to provide its name and address as a reminder of where a satisfied customer might return.

At the level of the individual shop, the market was especially competitive. The inherent portability of these commodities – lightweight, already in a preserved state and durable – meant that individual shopkeepers could ship them to geographically broad customer bases. As the eighteenth century wore on, sellers mushroomed in the tens

Advertisement for John Deck, *c.* 1804. This was one of several trade-card templates associated with Twinings. A blank space, in this case inside the box, provides room for the cards to be altered so as to include the individual shop's name and location.

of thousands across the national landscape, and this meant choices for consumers and fierce national and regional competition among sellers.[50] Even villages could become commercial battlegrounds. In consequence, peddlers of the empire's ingestibles became some of the most entrepreneurial people in Britain, being among the first to establish themselves in new towns, enjoying a diverse customer base and drawing goods from a range of competing suppliers.

Competition was in larger part the result of grocers' utilization of the vast networks of suppliers and customers that extended well beyond their immediate geographic areas. George Milne in Perth, Scotland, who operated a modest-sized business with less than £300-worth of inventory, was typical in that he dealt with a range of wholesalers in multiple port cities.[51] Despite being a small Glasgow-based grocer with a mere £109-worth of stock, James Hunter competed across a huge area, sending goods across Scotland to customers in such places as Strathkinness, Kilbride, Wadestown, Lanark, Mull, Strathaven, Stirling, Darvel and Kilmarnock – all of which had a multitude of geographically closer sellers.[52] Abraham Dent, who operated in the small, landlocked northern market town of Kirkby Stephen in Westmorland (now Cumbria), and whose surviving records span over two decades, provides one of the most complete snapshots of the provincial retail trade. The exact size of Dent and his son's operation is difficult to measure because cash receipts have not survived. However, annual credit-based sales of roughly £500, combined with purchases from suppliers of nearly £700, suggest they operated a good-sized business. They sold a wide variety of goods in their shop but primarily groceries, particularly tea and sugar. Between 1756 and 1777 he bought goods from nearly two hundred suppliers, although most of his goods came from fewer than a dozen, with orders ranging in value from less than £1 to over £100. The suppliers were both regional and national, and Dent regularly switched in order to procure the best prices. His customer base was regional, rather than restricted to his immediate town, with some customers even being much further afield – likely a combination of loyal patrons who had moved, smaller retailers he supplied and retailers with whom he exchanged goods.[53]

Ambitious London retailers also fought for a share of provincial markets, targeting small shops and prosperous middling and gentry households. Alexander Hog, a substantial London grocer who operated from Nicholas Lane, maintained a considerable business with customers throughout Britain with a particularly strong concentration on the east coast of Scotland, where he could boast customers from Inverness to Edinburgh. The billing amounts, such as the one for William Bayne of Cupar for £20 10*s* 9*d*, indicate that the customers were likely a mixture of substantial gentry households and small shops.[54]

By mid-century London grocers advertised with increasing regularity in newspapers outside London. Among the most prolific was the Original Tea-Warehouse. In its advertisements, which appeared in London and provincial newspapers alike from the 1770s, the Original Tea-Warehouse employed an impressive range of tactics to lure customers, including bulk discounts and rush shipping. Its pitch was to fashion itself as a no-frills retailer, providing wholesale prices to the general public. The Original Tea-Warehouse was open to all and ready to 'serve the Nobility, Gentry, Families, Shopkeepers, Coffee-Houses, Tea-Gardens, &c. in Town or Country'. It promised that by eliminating the local-grocer middlemen, simplifying transactions by requiring payment before or on delivery, and exchanging the softer shop experience for a no-frills warehouse, it could offer 'from 10 to 20 per cent lower than the usual Prices' on an assortment of coffees and teas without compromising on quality. This stripped-down approach, akin to the modern megastores that have prospered in similar niches, appealed to bargain-savvy consumers, and the Tea-Warehouse thrived, growing physically into larger premises and spawning imitators.

Such competition put considerable pressure on local sellers, who responded with more advertisements and competitive pricing. For example, in response to the flood of the Original Tea-Warehouse's advertisements in the *Derby Mercury* in the 1780s, J. Bradley, a leading local dealer, advertised with increasing frequency, reminding customers of his shop's variety and competitive prices. Bradley's prices read like a response to the Warehouse's rates, as does his reminder of the variety of other goods his shop offers, unavailable from the

Packing from the Original Tea-Warehouse, which prospered with its wholesale model, changing hands, moving into newer and larger premises, and enlarging its national customer base. By 1830, the time of this advertisement, the business had three prime London locations: Ludgate Hill, Oxford Street and Charing Cross.

Advertisement for J. Bradley from the *Derby Mercury*, 31 January 1782.

Tobacco, Tea, Sugar, &c.
J. BRADLEY,
Of ASHBORNE, Derbyshire,

THINKS proper to acquaint his Friends and the Public, that he is now carrying on the Tobacco Manufactory in all its Branches, and has lately purchaſed a large Aſſortment of Tobacco, Teas, Sugar, Flax, Hops, &c. which he will ſell at the following Prices, until ſome material Alteration happens.

Leaf Tobacco Stalks, 14d. to 16d. per lb.
Leaf Tobacco, 2s. 2d. 2s. 4d. to 2s. 8d. ditto.
Twiſt Tobacco, 2s. 8d.—Fine, 2s. 10d. to 3s.
Saffron Cut, ditto, 20d.—Fine, 2s. to 2s. 4d.
Ditto, very fine, 2s. 6d. 2s. 8d. to 3s.
Good dry Shag ditto, 2s. 4d.—Fine, 2s. 8d. to 2s. 10d.
Snuff, 2s. to 2s. 4d.—Fine, 2s. 8d. 3s. to 3s. 4d.
Fine and full flavour'd Hyſon Tea, 10s. 6d. to 16s.
Fine Souchong and Pekoe, 8s. 9s. to 10s.
Fine Congo, 5s. 6d. 6s. 6d. to 7s.
Good Green, 6s. 8d. 7s.—Fine Singlo, 8s.
Good Bohea, 4s. 6d. 4s. 8d. to 4s. 10d
Coffee, 5s. 5s. 8d.—Beſt, 6s. 4d.
Cocoa, 6d. 12d. 2s.—Beſt, 2s. 4d.
Good Lump Sugar, 11d.—Fine, 12d. 14d. to 16d.
Sugar, 6½d. to 7½d.—Fine 8d. 9d. to 10d.
Ditto, 60s. 70s. 80s. to 90s per Cwt.
Raiſins, 4d. 5d. to 6d.—Currants, 6d. per lb.
Hops, 4d. 5d. to 6d.—Fine 7d. to 8d.
Candles, 6s. 4d. per Dozen.—Soap, 52s. to 60s. per Cwt.
Flax of all Sorts, from 4d. to 12d. per lb.
Hemp of all Sorts, from 3d. to 12d.

With a great Variety of Spices, Drugs, Oils, Paints, Bruſhes, Writing-Paper, Blues, Nails, and ſo forth, ſold Wholeſale and Retail, on the very loweſt Terms the fluctuating Markets will admit of.

J. BRADLEY returns his moſt ſincere Thanks to his Friends and Cuſtomers for the great Encauragement he has hitherto experienced; and he will exert his beſt Endeavours to merit a Continuance of their Favors; and the greateſt Care and Attention will be obſerved in the Execution of their Commands.

Original Tea-Warehouse, ranging from seven types of tobacco to nails. Most noticeably, Bradley's advertisements concluded with a promise of personalized local service – a thinly veiled jab at the impersonal nature of his London competitor. Whereas the Warehouse concludes with a demand that all goods must be paid for on delivery, Bradley 'returns his most sincere Thanks to his Friends and Customers' and promises that 'the greatest Care and Attention will be observed in the Execution of their Commands.'

Illegal markets

Operating alongside, and often within, the vast legal trade in these imperial goods was an enormous black market. Surviving records of the Old Bailey, London's central criminal court, which reach back to 1674, include the theft and illicit resale of the edible products of imperial trade in even its earliest proceedings. Coffee, tobacco, tea, sugar and an array of spices and their associated wares were targets of opportunistic and calculated thefts alike. When a 'fellow of good Name, but poor Condition, and worse Quality' was convicted of highway robbery in April 1667, details of the crime revealed that his victim had no money but offered 'a pound of Tobacco' instead, 'and the pitiful Padder to verifie the Proverb, and play at small

Games rather than be idle, accepted'.[55] The primary source for the illegal trade in the empire's ingestibles was smuggling. The British government's series of decisions to inflate the retail prices of these desired goods, whether by directly taxing them or enforcing monopolies, fuelled the black-market trade in them. A number of other European nations participated in the overseas production and trade in these goods, which meant there were alternative suppliers, and their portability and ubiquity made them virtually impossible to trace once on British shores. A challenge of customs and excise taxes in any nation is finding the delicate balance between taxing as much as possible and pushing ordinary citizens to the black market, thus not merely hurting government revenues but also undermining the government's authority by effectively normalizing illegal behaviour.[56] In this regard, the British government failed miserably.

Although black markets existed for the full range of the ingestible products of imperial rule and trade, tea emerged as the most illegally traded commodity in eighteenth-century Britain. Black-market tobacco was common in the seventeenth century and illicit trade continued into the eighteenth century; however, England's dominance over American production combined with its declining cost and increasing availability served to lessen its prominence. Far more common tobacco-related crimes, or at least ones worth reporting and prosecuting, were thefts of the associated, and more expensive, wares of tobacco use, particularly metal carrying boxes. Often silver and finely crafted, these pocket-sized items were favoured targets of pickpockets and housebreakers. Smoking tobacco seems to have been more a ruse of criminals, meant to disarm potential victims, than the object of theft. For example, a man stole a silver tankard from a 'Victualling-house' in 1679 by ordering a drink and, when the barmaid arrived with it, 'pulling a paper of Tobacco out of his Pocket; he bid her fetch Pipes, and as soon as she was gone, poured out the Tankard and got out the Window' with it. Similarly, two men were convicted the following year of 'Felloniously bearing away eighteen Yards of Broad cloth' out of a London shop with the ploy of pretending to leisurely smoke a pipe of tobacco. While one of them 'held the maid in a Discourse' the other 'carried off the Purchase'.[57]

Legal tea struggled from the start. When the East India Company first began importing tea from China, a host of alternative suppliers from across Europe were already in place. As noted earlier, even the

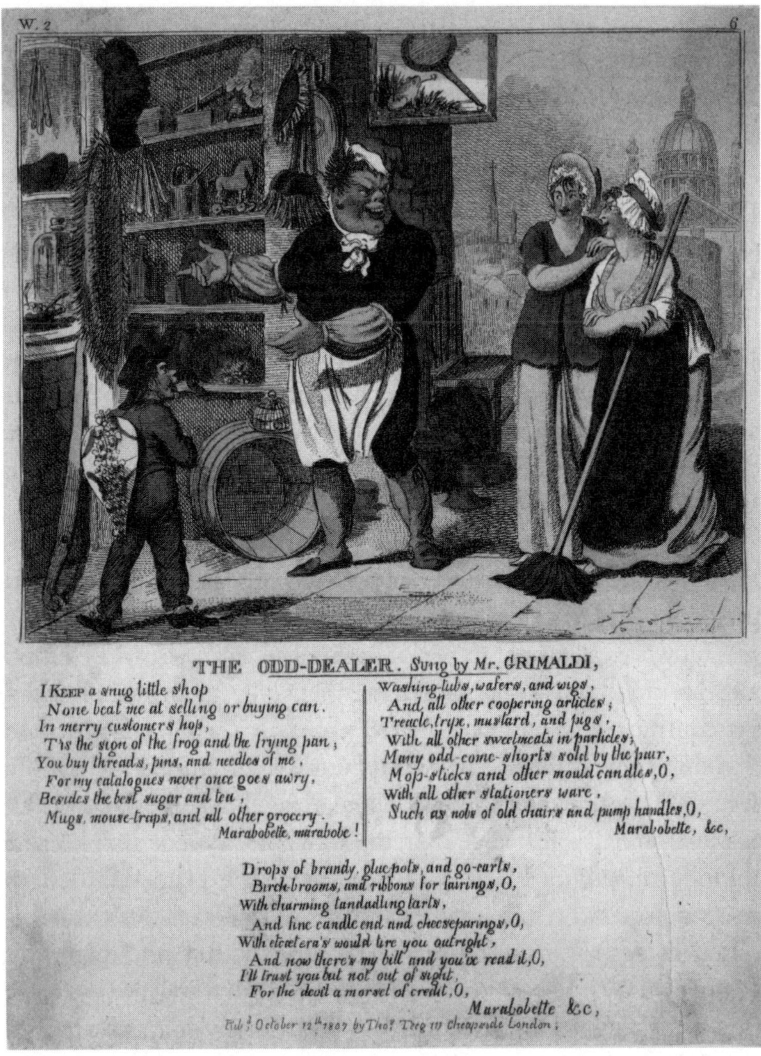

Isaac Cruikshank, 'The Odd-Dealer' (London, 1807). The satirical print and ballad satirize the petty 'odd-dealer', who sells virtually everything in his cramped display on shelves and the street, including brandy, brooms, ribbons, glue, toys and 'Besides the best sugar and tea/ Mugs, mouse-traps, and all other grocery.' Such small-scale operations would have been cornerstones of the black-market trade.

East India Company initially relied on the Dutch as its supplier, buying tea from Dutch colonies and the Amsterdam market. The government's readiness to tax tea, and thereby inflate the price, ensured consumers were dispositioned to consider cheaper suppliers. The illicit tea trade was well established by the 1730s, with contemporaries estimating that it accounted for as much as one-sixth of all tea consumed in Britain.[58] By 1746, when legal tea retailed for more than twice that of black-market tea, testimony in Parliament estimated that tea had overtaken tobacco as the most smuggled and illegally traded commodity in Britain.[59] Illegal trade in tea continued to boom after the mid-century Seven Years War, when a European peace saw a rapid expansion of overseas trade. High rates of British taxation and the availability of alternative European suppliers meant that at its peak in the 1770s, the black market in tea accounted for as much as two-thirds of the tea in Britain. Partly in consequence of the prospering black market, East India Company tea auctions, the only legal conduit for tea to enter Britain (and from there make its way to the Atlantic colonies), saw tea sales drop from an average of 7.5 million pounds in the 1768–70 period to just 3.6 million pounds in the 1781–3 period.[60]

Many of the illegal retail sales in Britain were made by coastal sellers, who had ready access to smuggled goods, and small-scale peddlers, who preferred to risk a fine than pay the fee for a licence to sell tea. However, plenty of respectable shopkeepers across the country also participated – greatly reducing their orders from wholesalers, yet continuing to sell tea.[61] As the prominent wholesaler Richard Twining publicly remarked in 1784, the gross cost imbalance between legal and black-market tea was 'obliging [the shopkeeper] to sacrifice his just profit, or his trade', forcing otherwise decent shopkeepers into illegal activity. In consequence, Twining explained, 'at length many persons who had strenuously opposed, and zealously endeavoured to destroy, this commerce are, openly, and yet reluctantly, engaged in it'.[62] Also, akin to the modern British travellers who stock up on cheaper alcohol in France before returning home, Britons in the eighteenth century stocked up on cheaper tea for themselves and friends. Emblematic of countless similar pleas to travelling friends and relatives, Lady Elizabeth Montague in 1772 wrote to her sister-in-law in Paris asking her to bring back two pounds of the best tea, complaining that it 'costs me sixteen shillings a pound in London' and boasting that she had herself had 'good luck with smuggling' in the past.[63]

Falling legal tea sales were a blow to the wavering East India Company, whose mid-century transition from a trading company to a territorial power had not been smooth. Following the Treaty of Allahabad in 1765, the company effectively gained the rights to

'Catlap For Ever, or The Smuggler's Downfal' (London, 1784). The print celebrates the Commutation Act of 1784 with Prime Minister William Pitt the Younger standing atop two tea chests, the London headquarters of the East India Company in the background, to declare to a group of cheering women that 'I secure universal approbation by reducing the price of Tea, a weed, so nourishing that it may be called the Manna of Females.'

govern and tax Bengal (an area roughly one-eighth of India), but this proved both complicated and dangerous, triggering wide-scale famine, rampant corruption, further wars and a risk of bankruptcy. Yet by this time the East India Company was, to use a modern phrase, too big to fail. As Frederick North, Lord North and prime minister, remarked during his attempts to reform it, the company was 'Too great a consequence, considered in a commercial light, not to call our attention to its welfare.'[64] The British government relied on its taxable trade, and Britons from across the country and from a wide social spectrum were invested in the company, whether it was a Newcastle widow hoping to secure her finances or an ambitious young clerk seeking employment in the company's small army of civil servants. In the first three-quarters of the eighteenth century, the company's value grew more than one-hundredfold from about £8,000 to £848,000.[65] Although difficult to estimate with a great degree of certainty, that works out to the rough equivalent of one-twelfth of Britain's gross domestic product at the time. By comparison, Apple Inc.'s headline-grabbing ascent to an estimated value of $1 trillion in August 2018 meant that it was worth the equivalent of a mere twentieth of the projected gross domestic product of the United States for the previous year.

Not surprisingly, Parliament became increasingly interventionist in the company's affairs from the 1770s, using a series of carrots and sticks in order to keep it afloat and ensure its stability.[66] One was to allow the East India Company to sell directly to the substantial American market, which in the previous decade had increasingly turned to much cheaper smuggled tea, primarily from the Dutch. The government's decision to tack a last-minute small tax on the tea, which still would have kept the East India Company's tea well below the estimated cost of smuggled tea, doomed the effort, and the first shipments to the colonies included the tea that colonists, in protest of parliamentary taxation, dumped into Boston Harbor at the Boston Tea Party in December 1773. By the 1780s smuggling had eroded the East India Company's tea sales to less than half of their height a decade earlier, putting the company at further risk. American independence irrevocably cost the company one of its largest tea markets, as the new United States raced to establish its own trading ties with Asia.[67] Parliament responded to the company's troubles in part with the Commutation Act of 1784, which reduced the 119 per cent combined taxes on tea to a mere 12.5 per cent, severely undercutting the black market and resulting in the trebling of legal tea sales. Because other European tea importers relied heavily on the British black market, the changes introduced by the Commutation Act, combined with renewed war with France, meant that the East India Company went from a 40 per cent share of Europe's Canton tea trade in 1784 to roughly a 90 per cent share less than a decade later.[68] While the black market for tea would rise again, it had all but disappeared for the time being.

IN HIS 1818 satirical print 'The T Trade in Hot Water!' George Cruikshank railed against the 'Nefarious & abominable practice of mixing teas with various cheap ingredients of the most poisonous qualities', which he claimed had led to disease and death. An angel in the London Tea House on the right sounds from her trumpet the cry of 'No Adulteration' while guilty purveyors of the false teas lament their actions as they boil in the teapot. Meanwhile, a socially diverse group of customers sing the praises of authentic tea and reliable sellers as they enter the Genuine Tea Company to make a purchase. Cruikshank's print reflects the central arguments of this chapter: the

George Cruikshank, 'The T Trade in Hot Water! or, a pretty Kettle of Fish!!!' (London, 1818).

widespread availability and economic importance of imperial goods to British consumers and the imperial economy, as well as the contemporary awareness of both. Cruikshank's print also foreshadows a key theme, explored in forthcoming chapters, that shaped Britons' engagements with the ingestibles of empire: the anxiety over authenticity (in this print's instance, concern that the black-market trade led to adulterated goods).

While such overseas luxuries as coffee, tea, sugar and tobacco were not new to the British Isles in the eighteenth century, they were new to most Britons. As a commentator remarked in a rant against taxation of basic family household goods in 1747, 'Coals, Candles Soap, Salt, Vinegar, Sugar, Tea, Tobacco, Rum Malt, Cyder, Ale, Beer' were all 'Necessaries of Life'.[69] Even the poorest of the poor and prisoners regularly consumed these goods that had formerly been the preserve of the elite. The exponential increase in British consumption of the ingestible products of imperialism had serious costs. For peoples outside of Britain, it meant great financial and political opportunities as well as dislocation, subjugation and slavery. For the British, these goods meant new relationships with the world and each other. Imperial trade became a pillar of the British state's income, resulting in conflicts to protect those interests and taxation policies designed to expand the adoption of some products into daily life. For instance, the transcendence of 'tea' from an exotic Asian beverage to a time of day and social occasion was not inevitable. Rather, along with a number of other goods, tea's widespread adoption was the consequence of a long series of choices that reflected and lastingly shaped British society and culture.

The development of enormous black markets for these goods contributed to the growing national obsession with authenticity. As the variety and quantity of goods for sale increased along with the choice of venues in which to purchase them, so too did the extent to which men and women would attempt to profit by defrauding consumers.[70] While overseas commodities such as tea, coffee and tobacco were likely the most abused goods, virtually everything was subject to forgery and adulteration – from cloth to stocks. Not surprisingly, the number of the different types of forgery offences increased during this period, as did Britons' wariness of the possibilities for deception, whether in paintings or tea. The use of the words 'authentic', 'real' and 'genuine' increased exponentially as consumers attempted to educate and protect themselves, while sellers used such words to reassure customers. Advertisements, handbills and even shop names made every effort to assert the genuine provenances of the teas, coffees and tobaccos for sale. As the subsequent chapters further reveal, widespread interest in authenticity was at the heart of how Britons engaged with the wider world and empire via food. Concerns about adulteration may have initially sparked the demand for authenticity; however, this desire evolved into something much more complex as sellers and consumers alike sought to demonstrate and ensure the genuineness of these goods. In short, the quest for authenticity ultimately enabled many of these ingestible products of imperial rule and trade, along with a host of cooked dishes, to move beyond simple sensory pleasures and become, in some circumstances, edible artefacts.

TWO

THE NEW BRITISH CONSUMER

When John Marsh reflected on his experiences as a mid-eighteenth-century schoolboy in England, food featured heavily. He recollected school dinners in vivid detail, noting specific courses, the arrangement of chairs and his favourite meals – pancakes on Shrove Tuesday, fruit pies during Advent, and ham, veal and apple pie to celebrate the anniversary of the headmaster. Yet Marsh was not simply a consumer; he was a seller, too. The senior boys at his school in the 1760s established a confectionery business in which they boiled West Indian sugar, mixed it with Spanish lemons and cooled the concoction in small paper pans to make little sweets that they sold to the other students. The children received a stark introduction to the new world of consumerism. Like many of the tens of thousands of shopkeepers across Britain at the time, the senior boys offered lines of credit when the boys' allowances ran low. When they failed to pay, they faced losing their credit, harsh interest rates and, on occasion, violence. Marsh, who enjoyed the sweets, failed to pay his debts only once but was given an extension on the grounds of good character, as his creditors recognized he was a reliable boy who would pay as soon as he was able. When Marsh and his brothers left for another school, they took the business model with them. As leader of the family business, Marsh fretted over suppliers, the price of raw materials, bad creditors and the indignity of his brother, Edward, breaking away to set up a rival business and pursue an undercutting strategy – leaving out the lemon to offer a cheaper alternative.[1]

As consumption boomed during the eighteenth century, Britons' relationships with the goods they bought, collected and displayed changed. This is not to suggest that things did not have meanings beforehand, because, quite clearly, they did. However, the scale of consumption radically altered the social and cultural landscape, making it a subject of national discussion and public concern. Food was the most conspicuous genre of consumption for several reasons. First, and most obvious, is that everyone ate, making it a shared arena for displays of wealth, taste and judgements that transcended gender, geography and social class. Second, the typical household spent roughly a third or more of its income on food, making it central to the household economy. Third, few favoured a monotonous diet, and with choice came opportunities for individual expression and the accompanying critiques.

Marsh's experiences as a consumer and seller, even if only in schoolboy enterprises driven by pennies, are a microcosm of the wider transformation in Britain fuelled by the influx of cheap foreign luxuries, particularly the edible variety. Suppliers, creditors, competition, family squabbles, marketing, credit lines and the struggle for reliable customers were all part of the drama that played out daily in Britain – from Marsh's small operation to the grandest London retail showrooms. During the eighteenth century, consumerism was sewn into the fabric of everyday life, and perishable foreign goods such as coffee, tea, sugar and tobacco worked as the needles.

Accessing the empire's ingestible goods

The question of who participated in consumerism is not easy to answer. However, it is safe to assert that more people participated in the edible aspect than in any other. Among the elite as well as the middling ranks – those British households that fell between the lesser gentry and craftsmen, and who were the driving force of consumerism – evidence for participation abounds.[2] While surviving evidence is scarce, verification of the poorest sectors of society participating also exists, most notably with regard to the consumption of the edible products of the empire. In fact, as much as 10 per cent of the household budget of the English poor was spent on sugar and tea by the end of the century, and their impoverished Scottish counterparts were not dissimilar.[3]

The engine for change was a combination of what contemporaries dubbed a desire for 'improvement' and necessity. While the eighteenth century is remembered as ushering in the industrial revolution, the impact of new tools on actual production levels was fairly modest until the following century.[4] The real change came in the form of what has been dubbed the 'industrious revolution', in which ordinary Britons drove up production largely by working harder and for longer hours.[5] Their efforts were predicated on the growing belief, rooted in the latter half of the seventeenth century, that the most effective way to betterment was to look forward, rather than backward, and through effort and ingenuity better one's nation, family, community and self.[6] While these attitudes gave rise to such noble social movements as Methodism and the abolition of slavery, they also lent themselves to the desire for immediate material betterment. In simpler terms, people sought to better their condition and demonstrate their social worth by buying things, and they worked longer and harder to do it. What most Britons wanted were the sorts of things Marsh sold as a schoolboy – small luxuries that could be divided into amounts and qualities to fit almost any budget. The favoured ingestibles of empire – coffee, tea, spices, sugar and tobacco – took centre stage. These goods' portability, durability and addictive and stimulating qualities were only part of the equation. Equally important was their foreignness, which meant they had to be purchased either in shops or other businesses such as coffeehouses, thus ensuring that consumption was public and founded on innumerable small cash (and increasingly credit) transactions. This shift proved transformative for British society.

Although seductive, a desire for improvement alone does not explain the emergence of Britain as a consumer society, not least because it relies principally on a demand-driven model, which does not sit well with the historical facts. Studies of wages and probate inventories of labourers indicate that changes in effort in early modern England were a result of rising prices of necessities and the need to earn more to survive. When prices fell, people had surplus wealth to spend on either better quality or new goods.[7] Critically, during the eighteenth century, they kept working and seeking new opportunities to increase household income even in times of prosperity. The purveyors of the empire's ingestibles, among other entrepreneurs, used the opportunity to wedge their products into the growing marketplace. Tea, for example, flourished in England as a result of a combination of factors beyond just uptick in consumer demand.

Taxation, East India Company decisions and production dynamics in China all led to a huge glut of tea by the 1740s, increasing availability while severely reducing prices.[8] Along with increased urbanization and a print culture that informed the wider public about the latest goods and how to acquire them, such external and internal factors created a perfect storm in eighteenth-century Britain for a transformation in consumer culture.

Although sometimes described as a consumer 'revolution', the process spanned generations, had roots in earlier periods and was not always linear.[9] The economic means necessary to access tea in 1688 was fundamentally different to how it was in 1788, and the two should not be muddled. A person who drank tea out of a ceramic cup and wore a printed cotton gown in 1788 might easily also be malnourished, because such goods by that time were drastically cheaper and more widely available than a century earlier.[10] What were once great luxuries had effectively become staples as the century wore on. Yet accessibility and the prevalence of such goods should not be misinterpreted as subverting consumer choice. After all, tea and coffee were not the only beverages on offer and, along with sugar, tobacco and the array of available spices, these goods offered little to the caloric intake or nutrition of the average Briton. They were nutritional luxuries – irrespective of how much Britons in the later decades declared them to be necessities. In fact, as this and the adjacent chapters demonstrate, choice increased as the century progressed. Trading networks developed to ensure that even the poorest and remotest of consumers had access to the full range of imperial goods, for which they were willing to pay a premium for perceived quality. Thus, although survival may have driven the initial increase in productivity and external forces determined which foreign goods would be cheap and plentiful, British consumers maintained their industriousness beyond times of necessity and bought the goods in abundance.

While suppliers might be elated at the spread of the empire's ingestibles across social divides, critics expressed dismay as these goods proliferated among the labouring ranks during the second half of the century. Jonas Hanway's remarks on the subject in his 1770 *Advice from a Farmer to His Daughter* are typical: 'Servants also run mad about tea; they spend a large portion of their wages in it, and squander too great a part of their time.' 'As to the poor', he continued, 'they also consume a large portion of their time; and their gains by hard labour make themselves wings and fly to *China* for this bitter draught . . . Would to God they were wise enough to spend their money in substantial food and raiment.'[11] Writing a generation later, William Cobbett similarly lamented the effects of 'good for nothing' tea among the labouring classes, bemoaning how it had supplanted hearty beer with something that 'has no *useful strength*; that it contains nothing *nutritious*'. Describing tea as 'a weaker kind of laudanum', he further complained that tea 'produce[s] want of sleep in many cases, and in all cases, to shake and weaken the nerves'. Worse still, it wasted time and money. Employing calculations that detailed the comparative costs of brewing beer and tea, which went into such minutiae as the number of fires needed to boil water, Cobbett estimated that a labouring family could save 'the sum of four pounds two shillings and two pence every year' by switching to the more nutritious beer.[12]

Consumerism deeply affected both sexes. While scholars have readily debated the differences and similarities between female and male behaviours, they are near unanimous in asserting that both sexes were avid consumers. Mistresses of middling and gentry homes were expected to manage the household, and, partly in consequence, they perceived themselves as householders in their own right, not just passing guests in a man's home. At the same time, men were also involved in household finances, purchasing goods for personal and family consumption.[13] Britons endowed these goods with a variety of meanings, personal, communal and national. Nowhere is this more evident than with the small luxuries of empire, whose acquisition required shopping – either in person, via servants or, increasingly, via mail order.

Some products were more gendered than others – such as tobacco with men and tea with women. When passing a sentence of public flogging on female thieves in 1678, a London judge associated tobacco with loose morality, railing, 'those Women, that have the impudence to smoke Tobacco, and gussle in All houses; pretend to buy Hoods and Scarfs, only to have an opportunity to steal them, turning thieves to maintain your luxury and pride'.[14] A more nuanced comment came a few decades later via a character in Mary Davys's *The Fugitive* (1705), who remarked on the gendered social expectations of these products. 'How ready are we to say that Man's a Coxcomb, that spends his Morning in Dress, at a Looking-glass, and his

Afternoons in making Visits, Drinking Tea, and criticising upon the Nicety of good Breeding,' she observed, 'and it would be every bit as ridiculous for us Women to be every Day at a Coffee-house, taking Politicks, and reading Gazettes, and at Night at a Tavern, smoking Tobacco.'[15] While an exaggeration – men regularly drank tea and women were not absent from coffeehouses – such comments echoed social practices. Nevertheless, as contemporary advertisements for tea and tobacco reflect, quality and the desire for it to reflect favourably on the holder were concerns of both sexes.

Shopping itself changed remarkably during this period. Fostering what has been described as a revolution in retailing, urban growth, combined with restrictions in traditional markets on storage, hours, prices and credit, prodded many existing and would-be sellers into physical shops.[16] Much attention has been given to how the practice of shopping changed for the upper social ranks during this period. Certainly, urban shops that catered to an elite clientele laboured to transform the acquisition of goods into a pleasurable experience with vibrant displays, comfortable seating and knowledgeable staff.[17]

Tobacco advertisement (London, 1790). The six men sit smoking and discussing the quality of the tobacco and asking where to purchase it. The host provides the answer.

Tea advertisement (London, 1808). As with the tobacco advertisement opposite, the women are depicted consuming the product (tea) and asking where to purchase it, with the host providing the name of the shop as the answer.

As early as 1701, William Burnaby's comedy *The Ladies Visiting-Day* treated elite women's shopping as a kind of luxurious education in connoisseurship and politeness. Lady Lovetoy explains how the new skills of upwardly mobile ladies included shopping and knowing to 'Buy all their Silks at *India* house, their Looking-glass at Gumly's, and all the Tea at *Phillips's*' – all recognized venues to the leisured London shopper.[18] The displays and variety of goods in London's elite shopping districts was most impressive. As one astounded visitor remarked in 1725, 'four streets – the Strand, Fleet Street, Cheapside, and Cornhill – are, I imagine, the finest in Europe.' In these shops' grand windows, he continued, 'the choicest merchandise from the four quarters of the globe is exposed to the sign of the passers-by. A stranger might spend whole days, without ever feeling bored, examining these wonderful goods.'[19]

The attractions became more elaborate as the decades progressed. Purpose-built fittings, cushioned seating and even artificial lighting became the norm at upmarket shops.[20] In such contexts, shopping was as much about the process – browsing, contemplating and imagining – as it was about acquisition. In these spaces, men and women alike learned the latest fashions and publicly displayed both their taste and their financial ability to acquire the delicacies on offer. In splendid dedicated spaces such as the Wedgwood London showroom, where the celebrated potters displayed their finest wares, education met with conspicuousness and personal indulgence. The depiction of the showroom in Rudolph Ackermann's 1809 *Microcosm of London* illustrates the grandness of shopping during this period. With wide, well-lit spaces for ease of movement, beautiful display tables and cabinets, chairs for resting and knowledgeable staff, a visit to the showroom was a shopper's delight. Importantly, as depicted in the illustration, the showroom catered to men and women, as well as to families, from the elite and middling ranks, thus highlighting how material aspirations and retail pleasures transcended both gender and generation.

While Wedgwood's showroom was especially noteworthy at the time, many of its sales techniques could be found in the tens of thousands of shops that peppered the British landscape. Display windows and defined spaces that separated the customer from the shopkeeper, for example, became increasingly common, and the surging variety of goods on the shelves suggests that shopkeepers needed to possess at least a modest knowledge of the products they offered. While some grocers operating in urban markets undoubtedly tailored their shops to attract a specific clientele, the vast majority of them had a socially diverse customer base that ranged from labourers to the ruling elite. What emerges is a portrait of shopping in these places as something of a levelling experience where

Wedgwood's London showroom, from Rudolph Ackermann's *Microcosm of London*, vol. II (1809).

men and women mingled, gossiping and discussing the news of the day. Thomas Turner's shop in East Hoathley, Sussex, was such a place.[21] It was a hub of the village. The shop itself sold a vast array of goods to the wider community, from tea kettles to coffin plates, and it served as the place where the Turners and others conducted all sorts of business, from pawnbrokering to occasional tailoring. There Turner and his wife drank tea and coffee and smoked tobacco with friends and customers, reading and discussing the latest local, national and world news.

The impact of personal credit

Credit was a pillar of the socially diverse customer base of shops that sold the ingestibles of empire. Store credit, as an alternative to cash, expanded exponentially during the eighteenth century as a result of multiple factors, most notably the ongoing shift to wage-based labour, urbanization and greater consumer desire for luxuries that could not be produced domestically. More than any other trade, grocers pioneered and regularized personal credit as a normal business function. One obvious advantage of liberal credit to a grocer was that it geographically extended his customer base. Both surviving personal accounts and shop records indicate that purveyors of the empire's ingestibles regularly operated considerable mail order services by the latter half of the eighteenth century. As described in the previous chapter, both metropolitan and provincial shops advertised in their fight to secure shares of the market outside of London. In consequence, whereas Sarah Harrison of Devonshire in her popular 1733 *Housekeeper's Pocket-Book, and Compleat Family Cook* advised rural readers to load up on key spices when in town, shoppers such as Judith Baker, a gentlewoman from Durham, shopped freely via mail order from metropolitan and regional groceries just a couple of decades later.[22]

By the second half of the century, extensive lines of personal credit had become standard practice, and surviving shop records highlight how important credit was both financially to businesses and in terms of making the ingestible products of empire widely available. The ratio of cash to credit in sales is impossible to determine on a grand scale, but the available evidence suggests that credit was crucial to any successful shopkeeper. At his shop in the Cumbrian market

Henry Heath, 'What a treat! I wish you may get it!' (London, 1829). Two companion satirical designs on one plate. On the left, a ragged and thin boy holds up a chipped plate to a portly and quizzical grocer, who stands behind his shop counter holding a bread (or butter) paddle, the boy saying, 'Two pen'orth of Scrapings and if you please, Mr Stilton, Mother says you must send it good, cos she's got Company-a coming!!'; on the right: a hopeful young girl wearing pattens leans confidently on the counter

of a general shop, declaring, 'If you please Mr Tomkins to give my Mother Change for Sixpence, and She will send you the Sixpence next week.'

town of Kirkby Stephen, Abraham Dent extended just shy of £500 in credit to customers while purchasing £677-worth of stock from suppliers. Allowing for a reasonable margin of profit and error, this would suggest that roughly half of his sales of sugar, spices, teas, coffees, tobaccos and other goods were credit transactions ranging from a few pennies to several pounds. While credit was not without the headaches of collecting, and sometimes took years to settle, it allowed him to grow his market to well beyond Kirkby Stephen's parish boundaries.[23] In larger operations, such as Alexander Hog's grocery in Nicholas Lane, London, personal credit extension ranged from a few shillings to several hundred pounds. Although risky, as customers often failed to meet Hog's Christmas Day annual payment deadline, personal credit was necessary to grow his customer base nationally. By 1788, he had firmly established himself as far afield as the Scottish market – having customers in at least eleven Scottish cities, towns and villages.[24]

Some meticulous shopkeepers logged customers' occupations in addition to descriptions of the prices and items purchased.[25] Together they highlight that credit was not the preserve of the middling or elite ranks. David Kirk's modest grocery in the small Scottish market town of Kirkcaldy at the turn of the century extended credit totalling nearly £1,000 to roughly 350 customers, who probably constituted the bulk of his customer base. The customers of John McGeorge's shop in Dumfries, Scotland, were a typically diverse group that included the households of a host of artisans, fellow shopkeepers and members of the gentry, along with those of an organist, fiddler, midwife, sergeant major, borough officer and dancing master.[26] Those grocers' lists of customers that have survived indicate that artisans and labourers regularly enjoyed the benefits of credit of several pounds – equivalent to several months' wages in some cases. For example, the grocery at the Shotts Iron Works, an emerging industrial centre halfway between Edinburgh and Glasgow, extended credit to the landed gentry and local professionals along with a long list of individuals identified as colliers, tinners, smiths, ferrymen, army sergeants and labourers.[27] David Brownlie, identified simply as a 'labourer', enjoyed a typical credit line that was in excess of £3, which was as much as three months' wages and sufficient credit to purchase 10 pounds weight of basic black tea, over 100 pounds of sugar, 3 pounds of Jamaica pepper or 24 pounds of twist tobacco at that grocery's prices. Such a diversity of customers with ample credit meant that even village shops carried a range of types and qualities of foods that rivalled metropolitan retailers. Ann Gomm's little grocery in the Cotswold town of Shipton-under-Wychwood was typical in that it offered customers a choice of at least half a dozen types of tea, three of coffee, various types and qualities of tobacco products, several types of sugar, orange peel, confectionery, chocolate and an assortment of spices that included nutmeg, Jamaica pepper, cinnamon, allspice, ground ginger and black pepper.[28] Such variety meant that she could cater to grander households that made single purchases worth several pounds as well as to labouring families who bought pennies' worth of goods at a time.

The empire's goods on display

While many of these goods have inherently desirable (and addictive) qualities, their purchase was as much to do with statements of taste and aspiration. As with the more examined porcelains and paintings of the elite, small edible luxuries were part of the complex system of goods as objects of display.[29] In short, imperial foods became part of the marketplace of culture that emerged in the eighteenth century. In an age that produced such iconic concourses for culture and money as the auctions of Christie's and Sotheby's, it is easy to be distracted by the paintings, novels, rare objects and entertainments through which British culture was created and contested. The acquisition and consumption of food as an expression of taste and culture, however, was far more prevalent.

Especially for more prosperous Britons, meals served as front-stage events in which families could display their status, both in terms of wealth and taste. In this setting, the consumption of imperial products became intrinsically linked with fashion. As the classic theory of fashion asserts, fashion is ever-changing because socio-economic groups tend to imitate those further up the ladder. This, in turn, undermines the practice's exclusivity, thus necessitating the originators to replace old fashions with new ones.[30] Thus, while merely having coffee was sufficient to impress peers and awe subordinates during the late seventeenth century, coffee soon became so common-place that consumers needed to alter their practices in order to remain fashionable.

In response, greater choice in quality and taste quickly emerged, with three total commonly available types of tea and coffee proliferating to over a dozen by mid-century. In the late seventeenth century, at a cost minimum of six shillings for a pound of the cheapest tea, price alone was sufficient to keep it somewhat exclusive. Of course, the highest quality and rarest teas could cost in excess of ten times that much, but such treats were the preserve of the wealthiest families. As prices fell and tea poured into Britain, sellers and buyers stratified the types of tea by quality and price, assigning them names and creating an array of choice. At the end of the seventeenth century, there were still only two widely recognized types of tea, but just over a decade later there were five, and by the 1730s there were at least nine commonly used names for types of tea in printed advertisements.[31]

Evidence for the widespread knowledge and acceptance of the types and values of tea is, perhaps, most apparent in the habits of the people who stole them.[32] During the late seventeenth and early eighteenth centuries, opportunistic thieves in London seemed to pilfer tea indiscriminately along with other easily pawned goods, such as spices, pocketbooks and watches. Such was the case with the apprentice William Claxton, who in 1721 conspired with his mother to rob his master. While his master was dining, Claxton raided his drawers, stealing small quantities of nutmeg, mace and chocolate along with 'half a Pound of Bohea Tea'. The scheme failed, however, when his brother hawked some of the goods to 'a Woman who told [Claxton's master] of it'. Despite his attempt to retract an earlier confession at trial, Claxton was transported for seven years to the American colonies – at the time considered a merciful alternative to hanging for felons.[33] By mid-century, thieves seemed to become more discerning by targeting the better and more expensive types of tea. Such thefts were savvy moves. After all, the 6 pounds weight of Hyson tea, generally touted as the most refined and expensive type, that Ann Smith attempted to steal in 1748 carried an estimated value of £12, whereas the £1 4*s* worth of sugar that John Smith and Joseph Blaze stole from a London shop weighed a far more cumbersome 37 pounds![34]

By the end of our period, tea itself had lost most of its exclusivity. Although some types remained valuable in their own right, they were widely available and increasingly affordable. Ann Gomm's

Cotswold grocery sold the once-limited Hyson for a mere seven shillings a pound in 1793 – not much more than the cheapest tea a century earlier. During the early nineteenth century, tea became cheaper still, with William Cobbett estimating in 1821 that a labouring family could acquire 18 pounds weight of basic tea for £4 10*s*, or less than 4*d* an ounce.[35] As a result, consumers had to further complicate the rituals of drinking hot Asian beverages if they hoped to use them to distinguish themselves.

Expressions of personal prosperity and taste through food were evident long before the eighteenth century; however, the eighteenth century witnessed both their social expansion and their more powerful establishment in the home. Visiting, the practice in which people, particularly elite and middling women, spent afternoons calling on each other, played a central role. In this way, the empire, via the consumption of its goods, entered domestic life. Although the practice of visiting took root in the seventeenth century, during the eighteenth century it became inextricably linked with tea. The two had become synonymous by mid-century, so that such expressions as 'taking tea with' and 'going for tea at' had become commonplace. Visiting turned the formerly private spaces of a home into semi-public forums in which men and women could display their social status and virtues via the ownership and correct use of fashionable objects, making eating and drinking something of a performance. In consequence, consumption of associated items for display boomed – clothes, furniture and, most notably, the favoured beverage of tea and the tools for serving it. Ownership of utensils in the forms of silver cutlery and porcelain dishes exploded among middling households in the eighteenth century, forming what historian Maxine Berg has aptly dubbed 'the grammar of the polite table'.[36] Asian porcelain flooded into British homes, with annual imports reaching two million pieces a year by the 1720s. Savvy entrepreneurs such as the Wedgwoods and Spodes soon developed a flourishing domestic industry around replicating and refining Asian porcelain.[37]

The pressure to meet social expectations and delight guests was immense. Robert Sharp, a Yorkshire village schoolmaster, finding himself the victim of consumerism, dejectedly remarked in his diary after buying a dozen china cups and saucers, a teapot, a milk jug and plates, 'but as we neither want them nor have any place to put them in for display, we have packed them in a Basket and put them in the

Garrett Closet, if this be not encouraging manufacturers I know not what is!!'[38] The truly wealthy could go a step further and create dedicated spaces for the consumption of the beverage, such as the Chinese house on a Buckinghamshire estate that Caroline Lybbe described in 1770 as 'Inside & out all in the true Chinese taste' and 'a sweet summer Tea drinking place'.[39] Even poorer shoppers occasionally selected a more expensive version of one of their staples in quantities sufficient to impress a guest. Such was probably the case of Mary Smith, a relatively poor single woman who regularly bought several ounces of black tea along with butter and sugar during her

'A Morning Visit, or the Fashionable Dresses for the Year 1777' (London, 1778).

Aaron Martinet, 'Les Dames Anglaises Après-Diné' (Paris, 1814). One of a series of drawings by a French prisoner of war and published in France, the scene depicts elite women having tea.

weekly visit to Gomm's Cotswold grocery in the 1790s. On occasion, however, she substituted a single ounce with Souchong tea or another refined type – possibly for the benefit of a special visitor or as a treat for herself. Similarly, a socially rising John Marsh celebrated his admission to the bar in 1773 by purchasing the best tea he could afford and borrowing a friend's chambers to invite and impress acquaintances and friends.[40]

How people ingested these goods mattered almost as much as the goods themselves. Politeness, which was a hallmark of eighteenth-century society, was more than a set of rules that governed behaviour. It was an evolving code of conduct through which a person's morality, social status and wealth could be judged.[41] The Earl of Chesterfield's letters to his son provide innumerable examples of how much this mattered even to the elite. The unauthorized (the letters appeared in print without Chesterfield's permission and caused a scandal at the time) guide's title page features an encapsulating quote from one of Chesterfield's letters: 'To do the honours of the table gracefully, is one of the out-lines of a well-bred man . . . and the doing of which ill is not only troublesome to ourselves but renders us disagreeable and ridiculous to others.' Throughout the letters, Chesterfield frets incessantly about how to travel, select companions and even sit and stand in company. Eating and drinking drew quite a bit of attention.

Do not be the 'awkward fellow', he cautioned, who 'drinks tea or coffee [and] scalds his mouth, and lets either the cup or saucer fall, and spills tea or coffee on his breeches'.[42]

In consequence, guidebooks, essays and advice columns on how to eat abounded. First published in 1788, in its fifth edition within seven years and in print through much of the nineteenth century, John Trusler's *Honours of the Table* was among the most popular and widely quoted.[43] An ordained Anglican priest, curate and practitioner of medicine, Trusler became a prolific writer in his later years. Residing in Bath, a national seat of fashionable politeness, Trusler turned his critical attention to food and how to eat it. Targeting the aspiring middling ranks and gentry, he emphasized the meal as a forum for politeness. 'Of all the graceful accomplishments and of every branch of polite education,' he declared in the opening lines of his guide, 'it has long been admitted, that a gentleman and lady never shew themselves to more advantage, than in acquitting themselves well in the honours of their table; that is to say, in serving their guests and treating their friends agreeable to their rank and situation in life.' What follows is an exquisitely detailed instructional manual that ranges from a fourteen-point list of expectations of servants waiting on the table to a step-by-step narration of a dinner from the perspective of the host or hostess. Seating is a mix of rank and gender, designed to provide opportunities to acknowledge socially important guests and encourage interaction across the sexes – key opportunities for young men and women aspiring to marriage. In fact, Trusler expressly states his guide is 'for the use of young people'.

In later editions, Trusler amended his guide to include carving, replete with illustrations of the various joints of meat that a host or hostess (in Trusler's world, both genders carved) might encounter. Performed in full view of guests, carving provided a critical opportunity to demonstrate one's prowess in the art of dining. As Trusler explains, 'We are always in pain for a man, who instead of cutting up a fowl genteely, is hacking for a half an hour across a bone, greasing himself, and bespattering the company with sauce.' In contrast, and with the assistance of Trusler's guide, 'where the master or mistress of a table dissects a bird with ease and grace . . . they are not only well thought of, but admired.'[44] Ever-concerned with the necessity of subtly acknowledging social rank, Trusler also promotes carving as an opportunity for the host to ensure that the most revered

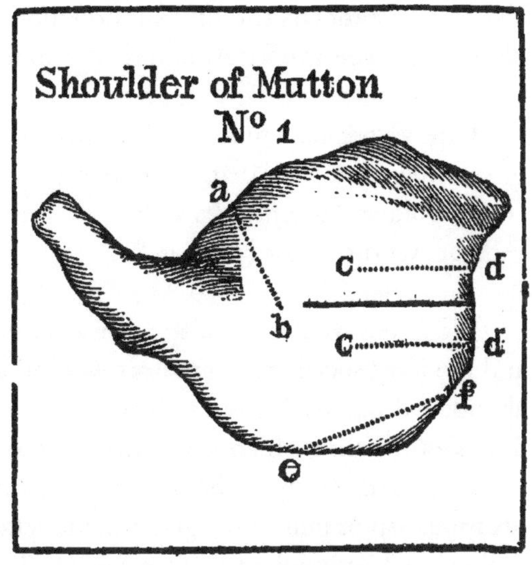

From John Trusler, *The Honours of the Table; or, Rules for Behaviour During Meals . . . For the Use of Young People* (London, 1788). Trusler's guide included dozens of similarly diagrammed illustrations for a host of roasted meats and fish.

guests are recognized by receiving the best cuts of meat. Thus the manual-like printed instructions and the simple diagrams helpfully detail both how to carve and where to find the choicest cuts. A shoulder of mutton, for example, received two diagrams and several pages of text that specified where to find 'the best fat, that which is full of kernels and best flavoured' along with advice to 'cut [it] out in this slices in the direct of *e*, *f*.'

The association of food with fashion placed it in the crosshairs of the ongoing, and furious, public debates on luxury. In what historian Frank Trentmann astutely calls the 'pendulum of consumption', possessions and the desire for comforts provoke a backlash of worries about excess and corruption. The more a society consumes, the stronger the eventual backlash. What distinguished the eighteenth century in Britain, however, was that supporters of consumption developed a widely accepted set of values of their own.[45] Defenders of consumption rooted their cases in two premises: luxuries were pleasant and, as people were willing to work harder and longer to afford the goods, all the better for the economy. Bernard Mandeville's 1705 *The Fable of the Bees; or, Private Vices, Public Benefits* set the tone. While initially scandalous, it was widely read and, although sometimes begrudgingly, recognized for its astute observations of the realities of eighteenth-century commerce and society. In Mandeville's poem, the hive is believed corrupted by a desire for possessions, and some of the bees grumble for a return to virtuous austere living.

When this happens the hive's production and prosperity swiftly plummet. The lesson for Britain is clear in the last lines:

Bare Virtue can't make Nations live
In Splendor; they, that would revive
A Golden Age, must be as free,
For Acorns, as for Honesty.[46]

While few went so far as to espouse puritanical ideals of frugality and modesty, social commentators worried about the effects of the abundance and availability of luxuries. In a letter published in the *London Chronicle*, which was among the most widely distributed newspapers in Europe at the time, a commentator lamented how the luxurious aspirations of the gentry had metastasized in lower social ranks via a description of a recent visit to a friend, who was a provincial grocer. He describes how, on the occasion of the family being invited to attend the local mayor's entertainment, his friend's 'wife and three daughters were dressed out in the most genteel and fashionable manner, and at a considerable expence ... she was determined that none of the other Shopkeepers wives and daughters should excel her and hers ... and to that purpose had consulted a great Milliner at Westminster.' Not content with lavish dresses, they had also 'been for some hours that day under the hands of a Frizeur, who had curled their hair, and raised their heads above a foot high, which resembled in some degree the caps of the grenadiers'. And to travel the mere two hundred yards to the event, he noted with disgust, they took a post-chaise. Such pretences were a social malady. 'These extravagancies were formerly confined to Courts, and the houses of the rich and the nobles,' he railed, 'but since trade and commerce have brought great riches into several cities, they have infected the citizens; and now they are spread to the country towns; nay, I am told, that they make their appearance in some villages.' Plain and neat dress, a house usefully furnished and 'a plain and simple diet' would not satisfy such women, to the inevitable ruination of their fathers and husbands.[47]

Men, too, were targets of such criticism. Fears that luxury would lead to effeminacy were pronounced throughout a period in which war was the normal state of affairs. In such times, masculinity was associated with martial qualities of physical strength, bravery and perseverance. Foreign luxuries, critics argued, eroded such traits in men by making them slighter, more delicate and preoccupied with fashion. The fop and his various incarnations became a stock figure in plays, essays and satirical prints – always a slave to fashion, physically weak and painfully effeminate.[48] Literary and visual satires throughout the century often depicted such men engaging in the delicate rituals of dining. In Isaac Cruikshank's 'Dandies at Tea' two frail yet fashionable men sit in a ramshackle London room with St Paul's Cathedral in the background, daintily sipping tea from porcelain cups at the cloth-adorned tea table – comical pretences of gentility – and politely discussing the merits of their beverage. It is not surprising that when British soldiers sought to diminish their American counterparts during the Seven Years War and American Revolution, they employed the character 'Yankee Doodle'. While later adopted by the American revolutionaries as a retort to mock British snobbery, Yankee Doodle was depicted as an effeminate dancing 'dandy' desiring to be a 'macaroni' – a reference not to the pasta but a word synonymous with the extravagant fashions of the Grand Touring male gentry; or, in Yankee Doodle's case, pathetically aspiring to be like them.

Tea is the superlative example of the diversity of roles and meanings a single commodity could hold. Despite appearing with regularity in the British Isles a few decades earlier, tea was a staple part of domestic life by the early eighteenth century. In his turn-of-the-century comedy *The Ladies Visiting-Day*, William Burnaby described elite women gossiping at home 'o'er a Dish of Tea' as being as loud as 'a Pack of Drunkards with three Bottles apiece in the Bellies'.[49] As tea drinking prevailed among middling and elite women in the early decades of the eighteenth century, the tea table became synonymous with the maliciousness of women's gossip. As Allan Ramsay described in a 1720 poem:

> A Train of Belles adorn'd with something new,
> And even of ancient Prudes there were a few,
> Who were refresh'd with Scandal and with Tea,
> Wich for a Space set them from Vapours free.[50]

Tea also attracted the ire of social reformers, including John Wesley, a founder of the Methodist movement, who described it as a frivolous luxury and recommended instead infusing water with local

Isaac Cruikshank, 'Dandies at Tea' (London, 1818).

herbs such as mint. He even devoted an entire tract to the subject in his *A Letter to a Friend Concerning Tea*, wherein he described at length his objections to it, replete with detailed mock dialogues on how to politely refuse it.[51] Others complained about the social pressure placed on the poor to spend their limited earnings on luxuries, the time and fuel wasted on preparing tea and its foreign association. Calling people 'tea-bitten', Jonas Haywood in 1768 railed that 'Many who are crying out against [the price of] wheat will give up a pound of bread, rather than a quarter of an ounce of tea.'

Carefully calculating the time, effort and money spent on tea versus on the cultivation of British land, he concluded that tea consumption made Britain a 'tributary of China for an article we can do much better without' and that tea drinking threatened the prosperity of the nation itself.[52]

Yet for other commentators on the subject throughout the century, tea consumption created an important opportunity for instruction. Writing in 1711 as *The Spectator*, the widely celebrated and cited authority of middling politeness and good taste in the period when the tea table was gaining momentum, Joseph Addison praised its uses as a gathering point for family conversation and his instruction:

> I would therefore in a very particular Manner recommend these my Speculations to all well-regulated Families, that set apart an Hour in every Morning for Tea and Bread and Butter; and would earnestly advise them for their Good to order this Paper to be punctually served up, and to be looked upon as a Part of the Tea Equipage.[53]

In Eliza Fowler Haywood's 1725 essay *The Tea-Table*, tea drinking serves as the setting for 'a conversation between some Polite Persons of both sexes, at a Lady's visiting day, wherein are represented the various foibles, and affectations, which form the Character of an accomplish'd *Beau*, or Modern *Fine Lady*'.[54] In an essay asserting the tea table's value to aspiring families, a decade later James Bland argued that the 'The Tea-Table, simply consider'd, is altogether harmless, and the right Managing [of] it is a becoming Qualification for a young Lady.'[55] In fact, he argued in a later essay, the tea table was a more advantageous investment for a family than a spinning wheel, because proficiency in polite tea drinking affords tradesmen and their wives opportunities to interact with their socially superior customers – resulting in business opportunities and economic betterment.[56]

Countless other critics agreed, and the tea table became the standard setting for imagined moral instruction, particularly of children and young adults. The illustrated *Tea-Table Dialogues*, first published in 1772, is but one example. Addressed to 'Parents and Tutors', the collection of fictional dialogues at the tea table between such tellingly named characters as 'Miss Prattle' and 'Master Thoughtful' aims to provide 'pleasurable' yet useful instruction in matters of polite conversation and the benefits of learning. What follows is a series of dialogues in which various characters discuss such topics as the virtues of the countryside, the meaning of friendship and the perils of frivolousness. The purpose of the tea table in such fictitious settings is to indicate that the characters are comfortable and natural. As 'Master Sterling' remarks, 'The pleasures of conversation principally consist in ease, freedom, and familiarity.'[57]

In this context, tea drinking emerged as a symbol of civilized domestic life. The family that drank tea together was stable, prosperous and tranquil. Exemplifying the ideal family, Thomas Rowlandson's 'The Comforts of Matrimony' depicts the husband and wife in a loving embrace at the tea table, toasting a bun, surrounded by their three healthy children and their pets and the accompaniments of middling, yet modest, living – a tea service, landscape painting, tablecloth and warm hearth. On the other hand, the upturned tea table became a stock visual cue for disruption to domestic harmony. Scenes of infidelity, domestic violence and impropriety regularly included crashing tea tables and china as symbols of artists' judgement. In a tumultuous domestic scene, James Gillray used the disturbed tea table

Thomas Rowlandson, 'The Comforts of Matrimony, a good Toast' (London, 1809).

James Gillray, 'Advantages of wearing Muslin Dresses! dedicated to the serious attention of the Fashionable Ladies of Great Britain' (London, 1802).

as part of his satirization of people's enslavement to fashion. In the print 'Advantages of wearing Muslin Dresses! dedicated to the serious attention of the Fashionable Ladies of Great Britain', a portly woman in a flimsy muslin dress and garishly feathered headdress catches fire. Mocking her size, Gillray includes a painting of an erupting volcano over the mantel. The domestic calm and civility are wrecked as her flailing overturns the tea table, sending cups, saucers and tea flying.

Coffee and the formation of public culture

Price, novelty and limited knowledge of preparation ensured that many of the commodities of imperial trade were first consumed in public spaces. Coffee is one that remained largely public throughout the eighteenth century, when its consumption became synonymous with conversation, debate, business dealings and politics in Britain and its colonies.

Compared to most other ingestible goods that became staples of the British imperial rule and trade, coffee was a relatively new product. Although the beans received occasional mention from the tenth century onwards, the familiar process of roasting and then grinding the beans into an infusion began in the fifteenth century in Arabia, from where it rapidly spread. From the start, coffee's ability to attract public discussion drew the ire of local rulers. The governor of Makkah forcibly closed the city's coffeehouses in 1511, partly due to some residents' concerns about the visible physical stimulation caused by the beverage but also due to the political intrigues of the young men who gathered there. When the governor fell from power, the coffeehouses reopened.[58] The Ottoman occupation of Yemen, the world's primary coffee producer at the time, in 1536 ensured that both the beverage and the customs surrounding its consumption soon spread around the Muslim world and beyond, provoking discourse and consternation in its wake. Within a generation, coffeehouses peppered the urban landscapes of the Middle East, North Africa and the Ottoman-controlled parts of Europe. Istanbul alone had more than six hundred coffeehouses by the 1560s, and European merchants and diplomats there adopted the habit of drinking coffee.[59] Savvy European entrepreneurs recognized a business opportunity and began importing the 'Wine of Araby' into their home countries.[60]

England was arguably the first western European country where coffee could be found commercially. Although there is considerable debate as to England's first and oldest coffeehouses, among the first mentioned is the Angel in Oxford, where the antiquarian Anthony Wood briefly mentions 'Jacob the Jew' selling coffee in 1650.[61] Perhaps the most colourful, and best documented, origin story of the coffeehouse in England is that of Daniel Edwards and his partner Pasqua Rosée.[62] Edwards, a London merchant, met Rosée, who is described in sources as ethnically Armenian or Greek and skilled in making coffee, in Anatolia sometime in the mid-seventeenth century. Identifying a business opportunity, Edwards persuaded Rosée to return with him to London as his servant. Once there, Edwards circumvented the restrictions of the Levant Company, which prohibited associated merchants like Edwards from engaging in refining and retail trades, by persuading a partner, Thomas Hodges of London's Grocers' Company, to financially back Rosée. By 1654, Rosée was in business in St Michael's Alley, near the Cornhill thoroughfare – probably using something more akin to a stall with some seating than an actual house. Although he was not Turkish, Rosée's advertising sign nevertheless featured him in Turkish dress. The local tavern owners, who took issue with the competition, objected to his right to trade on the dual grounds that he lacked an alehouse licence, which failed since Rosée did not sell ale, and because he was a foreigner, which succeeded. Not to be deterred, Edwards and Hodges quickly recruited Christopher Bowman, Hodge's former apprentice, to be Rosée's English partner. Perhaps unhappy with the various arrangements or maybe just homesick, Rosée left abruptly and is not mentioned after 1658. Now in control of the whole business, Bowman moved indoors, where customers could sit at one of eight hearths spread over four floors. The coffeehouse thrived until the Great Fire destroyed it in 1666.

Although England is historically associated with tea, seventeenth-century inhabitants expressed an overwhelming preference for coffee. By the 1660s coffeehouses and stalls could be found throughout London, as well as in a number of cities and towns throughout the British Isles (at least 83 houses by 1663). In 1670 the first coffeehouse opened in England's American colonies, in Boston – before any opened in Paris, Venice or Vienna. In England the government quickly recognized the appeal of coffee, first taxing it in 1660, but at less than half the rate of tea. This helped to drive consumption and the accompanying public political culture. As described in the previous chapter, when the East India Company developed its tea trade with China, the government showed its support through favourable taxation rates that ultimately raised the price of coffee, thus steering British consumers' love of hot caffeinated beverages irrevocably towards tea.[63] By that time, however, the coffeehouse had firmly entrenched itself into British urban public life.

As in other coffee-drinking cultures, coffee swiftly became synonymous with popular politics in England. The fashion and adventurousness of the new beverage drew younger men to gather in close company, and the caffeine stimulated their minds; the result was wide-ranging conversations on all subjects, most notably politics.[64] Coffeehouses in Cambridge were sufficiently raucous that the university banned students from visiting them without a chaperone – a rule akin to the one already established for visiting taverns.[65] In an attempt to dissuade escalating public criticism of the government, Charles II issued a royal 'Proclamation for the Suppression of Coffee-Houses' on 29 December 1675, describing them as places where the idle spread 'divers False, Malitious and Scandalous Reports' about the government 'to the Disturbance of the Peace and Quiet of the Realm'.[66] Plastered throughout London, the proclamation commanded that all coffeehouses stop selling the beverage from 10 January. The move was out of the playbook of any number of Middle Eastern rulers who attempted to quiet criticism by eliminating the drink, and, in typical fashion, it failed. Even the threat of violent punishments, including execution, three decades earlier in an Ottoman attempt to quell coffeehouse politics had failed (Charles II's proclamation vaguely threatened only 'utmost peril'), resulting in riots and, ultimately, the restoration of the coffeehouses. In England the suppression never took place. Popular outrage and divisions among Charles's ministers led to the proclamation's withdrawal two days before it was to take effect – ultimately serving to further fan the flames of political intrigue and affirm coffeehouses as leading venues for public political discussion.

Coffeehouses flourished as hubs of news and conversation, despite the continued ire of a succession of governments and increased taxation. From their earliest days, contemporary depictions invariably described coffeehouses as spaces for socialization and vigorous discussion where newspapers and other printed material could be found in abundance.[67] During the reign of Queen Anne (1702–14) there were at least five hundred across the country.[68] A generation later, there were thousands. By mid-century coffeehouses prevailed across the national landscape, weaving themselves into the social and cultural fabric of cities and towns alike. Coffeehouses, of course, offered more than just coffee. From the start, most sold a multitude of indulgent treats and nourishments. Thomas Twining, the founder of the famous tea brokering family, was the proprietor of Tom's Coffee-House in London in 1706, where he sold a range of beverages. The best rum punch to be had in London came supposedly from the Jamaica Coffee-House.[69] Nor did proprietors restrict themselves to beverages. Early on, customers could expect relatively inexpensive, fairly basic food to be available, and by the late eighteenth century, most establishments offered full meals. As the *London Pilot* pocket guide explained, 'Since the custom of giving dinners and suppers in coffee-houses has been universally adopted, there is scarcely a street in the metropolis, where the hungry passenger of moderate fortune may not live with convenience and elegance.'[70] By the end of the century, most of the larger London coffeehouses and many of the provincial ones offered rooms for travelling guests.

Coffeehouses as a whole were not exclusive spaces, although some establishments in London developed niche markets, serving a particular mercantile and/or political clientele. As John Trusler informed readers of his London guidebook, coffeehouses generally were places 'where certain questions, political, civil and moral, are discussed, and everyone may give his opinion'.[71] As early as the 1670s, self-help guides appeared to aid timid patrons. First printed in 1677, enjoying multiple editions over the next century and facing plenty of competition, *Coffee-House Jests* offered an array of 'witty jests', 'wise sayings', 'smart repartees' and 'plant tales' to engage and win the favourable attention of fellow coffee drinkers.[72]

Like their Middle Eastern counterparts, British coffeehouses predominately served as spaces of male sociability. As Richard Steele, writing as *The Spectator*, observed in 1711, 'It is very natural for a man who is not turned for mirthful meetings of men, or assemblies of the fair sex, to delight in that sort of conversation which we find in coffee-houses.'[73] Yet to treat coffeehouses as exclusively male during the eighteenth century would be as mistaken as assuming women had little interest in the affairs of state. Women, of course, worked in coffeehouses as servants from the start, just as they did in taverns and alehouses, but they were also patrons, particularly in the latter half of the century. Moreover, women routinely ran coffeehouses. As early as 1680 one 'Mrs. Cleverton, a widow' appears in the historical record

'Interior of a London-Coffee-house' (London, *c.* 1690s). A rare visual record of an early London coffeehouse, the scene depicts patrons raucously discussing the topics found in the newspapers strewn across the tables. A woman, the figure in white, orchestrates the serving of coffee by the house's servants.

with the occupation of 'keeping a Coffee-house in Bell-Savage yard on Ludgate-hill'; she fell victim to a robbery when several patrons ran off with some dishes.[74] Directories and travel guides, which were abundant in the second half of the eighteenth century, regularly mention coffeehouse proprietresses, who, like their female counterparts in a variety of retail trades, owned and operated their businesses either in conjunction with a male family member or on their own.[75]

Although hardly typical of the tens of thousands of women who operated businesses in Britain, Elizabeth Adkins was the most famous coffeehouse proprietress of the eighteenth century. Better known as the infamous Moll King, Adkins was a scandalous character who engaged in a variety of criminal activities, including prostitution and pickpocketing, and associated with the infamous London underworld boss Jonathan Wild. In 1718 she was arrested for theft and sentenced to indentured servitude in the American colonies for seven years. Upon her return, she became the proprietress of the King's Coffee-House in Covent Garden with her husband and, ultimately, independently. Although in a seemingly respectable position, she continued her criminal activities, running an elite prostitution ring and an illegal money-lending enterprise. King's was a notorious haunt for rakes, appearing in Henry Fielding's *Covent-Garden Tragedy* in 1732. In 1721 she was back in prison, where she captured the attention of Daniel Defoe, who was visiting a friend, and inspired the creation of one of his best-known characters, Moll Flanders. After leaving prison, Adkins continued in her old ways, apparently being sentenced to transportation to America again in 1734. When she died in 1747, she was still widely known, being one of the few women of the period to merit a published biography.[76] She also saved enough money from her activities, legal and otherwise, to finance her son's education at Eton College.[77]

Moll King's adventures aside, a coffeehouse was more typically what Richard Steele pronounced: 'the Place of Rendezvous to all that live near it'. Writing as *The Spectator* in 1711, Steele described in detail how his own local London coffeehouse changed throughout a typical day. 'In the Place I most usually frequent', he closely observed the middling ranks of men who made up the bulk of coffeehouse patrons, noting that 'Men differ rather in the Time of Day in which they make a Figure, than in any real Greatness above one another.' Opening at six o'clock in the morning, the coffeehouse first attracted

Illustration from the chapbook 'The Fortunes and Misfortunes of Moll Flanders', reprinted in John Ashton, *Chap-Books of the Eighteenth Century with Facsimiles, Notes, and Introduction* (1882). In the background, the left scene shows her toiling on an American plantation, while the right scene of hangings alludes to her criminality and ultimate execution.

those interested in digesting and debating the latest political news. As they set off to their shops and offices two hours later, students from the neighbouring Inns of Court arrived – 'some of whom are ready dress'd for *Westminster* . . . with Faces as busie as if they were retained in every Cause there; others come in their Night-Gowns to saunter away their Time, as if they never designed to go thither'. Next came the respectable men of business who used the coffeehouse 'to transact Affairs or enjoy Conversation'. At night, the coffeehouse became more raucous, with liquor and a rowdier clientele – when the respectable Steele told his readers that he typically returned home.[78]

Coffeehouses' relationship with the empire and imperial trade stretched well beyond their namesake beverage. They were magnets for travellers and spaces in which patrons exchanged and discussed news from far and wide. As one guide described Tom's Coffee-House on Cornhill in 1796, there 'you hear and see all the nations upon earth

– the jargon and noise'.[79] In London the wealth of choice meant that some coffeehouses served niche markets for patrons, although still welcoming a variety of customers. Child's Coffee-House, one of London's first, hosted unofficial meetings of the Fellows of the Royal Society, which funded and supported a multitude of scientific ventures intimately related to the empire – most notably the voyages of James Cook around the world. Some of the names referenced imperial victories and places. There was the General Wolfe Coffee-House in Fleet Street, named after the widely heroized British general who died while taking Quebec from the French in 1759, as well as the New England Coffee-House in London and the American Coffee-House in Bristol, which served as gathering points for American loyalist refugees during the American Revolution. Other aptly named London coffeehouses included the Africa in Leadenhall Street near the headquarters of the Royal African Company, as well as the Senegal, South Sea, Jamaica and New York coffeehouses, all of which attracted merchants engaged with overseas trade.[80]

Lloyd's Coffee-House in London exemplifies the important role coffeehouses played in gathering and spreading global news. First opened in Tower Street in 1686 by Edward Lloyd and moved to several locations before ultimately settling at the Royal Exchange on Cornhill in 1774, Lloyd's quickly became a popular haunt for shipowners and sailors, who in turn drew merchants and investors. Lloyd's soon became a place to do business buying and selling stocks in overseas ventures.[81] What ultimately distinguished Lloyd's from rivals such as Jonathan's, which became the site of the London Stock Exchange, was maritime insurance. In the coffeehouse's earliest days, Lloyd promoted maritime commercial interests by holding auctions of goods and ships and regularly announcing the latest shipping news. He soon became such a trusted source for shipping news that the Hudson's Bay Company put him on a retainer of £3 for the latest news regarding their own ships! Lloyd, his successors and his patrons experimented on multiple occasions with publishing their own newspapers, which tended to focus on shipping and commercial news. The first, a single sheet called *Lloyd's News*, launched in 1696, but *Lloyd's List*, a shipping news report, proved the most successful, starting in 1734 and remaining in print until 2013, when it became digital. *Lloyd's* was so trusted globally as a source of information that when war broke out between the British Empire and the United

States in 1812, newspapers on both sides of the Atlantic relied on its published shipping lists to keep score as to whose merchant fleet was taking the greater pounding.[82] They also started a popular newspaper in 1757, the tri-weekly *Lloyd's Evening Post*, which enjoyed national prominence until the end of the eighteenth century, when daily newspapers such as *The Times* steadily pushed the less frequently published rivals out of business.

In the 1760s Lloyd's and its interests split into Old and New Lloyd's, with the latter establishing itself under the management of a leading Lloyd's waiter with the backing of a large group of longtime patrons. Old Lloyd's bumbled along for a couple of decades, but the new version carried on the tradition of success that had made Lloyd's famous and ultimately became simply Lloyd's. The new Lloyd's moved to the Royal Exchange as the Society of Lloyd's, which offered membership by subscription. Nevertheless, its coffeehouse roots remained, with the hot beverage available on the premises for members and casual visitors alike. For London's visitors it was a sight to behold, as the *London Pilot* guidebook proclaimed:

> The whole universe, perhaps, does not produce so admirable a system of convenience, nor so striking an evidence of opulence, and national grandeur as security! Here is a constant correspondence with every seaport town in the whole inhabited world, and there ships and property on sea are insured to any amount, from one hundred pounds value, to one million, and upwards.[83]

Many of these insured ships were engaged in the African slave trade. Lengthy and fraught with dangers, including hurricanes, disease and revolts, slave trading voyages were such high-risk enterprises that the average captain rarely undertook more than three in a career. Even the ventures themselves were typically one-time partnerships designed to spread risk across a wide range of investors.[84] Insurance, therefore, was paramount, and Lloyd's patrons dominated the market of the thousands of voyages that launched from British shores and played a role in the even greater market of ships that left ports in North America and Continental Europe to purchase and transport millions of African slaves to the Americas. A dark chapter in Lloyd's history, making it a magnet for criticism of institutions' and nations' ongoing benefits from slavery, Lloyd's eighteenth-century success relied on its ability to profit from the rapidly expanding imperial and overseas trade. Its history is a stark reminder of how many Britons treated the empire as a business – a business that relied heavily on enslaved labour – much to the ire of many consumers, which the final chapter will discuss.[85]

The ingestibles of empire played a vital role in the dramatic growth in consumerism in Britain, which revolutionized how people behaved, lived and, ultimately, connected to the wider world. Addictive, easily divided, transportable, varying in quality and incapable of being produced commercially in Britain, such goods as coffee, tea, sugar and tobacco were the perfect little luxuries for all Britons, whether they were aspiring to refinement or simply seeking a small treat, irrespective of social rank or geography. Consumerism during this period was a mixture of conformity and choice. The desire to impress others and assert one's social status, wealth and knowledge required a degree of conformity to societal expectations, thereby steering consumers. Quality, rather than quantity, was paramount in this new world, and choice came in the form of both the selection of products and the retailers from which to acquire them. This mixture of conformity

Lloyd's subscription room, from Ackermann's *Microcosm of London*, vol. II (1809).

and choice is no better exemplified than by the middling and elite social convention of taking tea with visitors. While social expectations provided parameters for the event, the type and retail source of the tea, serving dishes, cutlery and furniture turned the home into a canvas on which hosts and hostesses could express themselves. Shops that dealt in these goods reshaped the national consumer landscape, serving to both satisfy and fuel consumer demand by making them easily accessible in an ever-widening range of types and qualities. The unparalleled use and social extension of personal credit by the purveyors of the empire's ingestibles ensured almost unfettered access to these goods.

Thus, through consumerism, the empire and its trade entered into the daily lives of ordinary Britons. Although the ubiquity of the empire's ingestibles meant that the significance individuals assigned these goods varied enormously, the often shared, social experience of purchasing, preparing, serving and ingesting them allowed some of the meanings to be held in common. As the following chapters reveal, these meanings included overt connections with the overseas peoples and places that produced these goods, along with the imperial links that brought them to Britain.

From Thomas Harriot's *A Briefe and True Report of the New Found Land of Virginia* (1590). The engravings, produced by Theodor de Bry, are based on the watercolours of John White, who accompanied Harriot to North America in 1585. Images such as this depicted the land as plentiful and the Algonquian natives as robust, industrious and, importantly, welcoming and peaceful.

THREE

ADVERTISING AND IMPERIALISM

Endowing objects with meanings that extend beyond their practical use is an essential part of being human. Even some of the earliest human artefacts are adorned with decorative elements that seemingly have no purpose other than to assign the object a personal or communal meaning. Flowers at early burial sites, carved bones and rocks, and ornamentation all highlight the relevance of this human practice. Exoticism plays an important role in that unusual objects' values are often tied to their rarity. Gold is a prime historical example. Novelty is also a key factor in that new items can be blank slates onto which societies can assign fresh meanings, or, especially when the objects come from other cultures, blended meanings that reflect a commodity's origins as well as its new environment.[1] Falling firmly in this category are the ingestibles of imperial rule and trade that flowed into Britain during the eighteenth century and played key roles in transforming its economy and society. While the previous two chapters explore the substantial economic and social impact that such commodities as coffee, tea, sugar and tobacco had on eighteenth-century Britain, the present chapter poses questions related to awareness. While customs ledgers, household records and shopkeepers' books demonstrate that these commodities bound Britain and its inhabitants to their empire, such records reveal little about ordinary Britons' awareness of those important relationships. In other words, when a middling woman in Oxford drank sugary tea with neighbours, was she at least generally aware of the mechanisms of imperial rule and trade that brought the beverage to her table and millions like it?

For answers, the visual historical record is more forthcoming. Like other societies across the world, the British created a substantial and diverse visual record of the overseas peoples and places they encountered. As early as 1569, natives of the Americas appeared in sculpture on the Harman Monument in Burford Church in Oxfordshire, and in the following centuries a host of paintings regularly commemorated the visits of American Indians, Africans and others – often displayed in public, including at the Royal Academy of Arts. Books, too, illustrated tales of travel and exploration with images detailing the lives and cultures of distant peoples. In fact, some of the earliest propaganda in favour of the English colonization of North America included visual images, such as the engraved versions of John White's 1585 watercolours of Algonquian people in Thomas Harriot's influential *A Briefe and True Report of the New Found Land of Virginia*. Depicting a bountiful land and compliant natives, the account helped to persuade a generation of English decision makers of the benefits of American colonization.[2]

What distinguishes the eighteenth century from previous eras in the history of the British Isles was the sheer volume and consistent application of these images. The mid-eighteenth century was a key period, as developments in printing technology intersected with the rapidly growing retail trades to bring about the advent of modern visual advertising. Cheap printed ephemera conveying images of goods, methods of production and places exploded onto the burgeoning retail scene on everything from package labels to billing stationery. While perhaps primitive in the eyes of the twenty-first-century consumer, these early advertisements have remarkably familiar attributes. They provided would-be customers visual cues for products on offer, promises of quality and fair pricing, and the exact location of where the goods or services could be found – akin to the modern billboard or magazine advertisement.

Shopkeepers who dealt in the empire's ingestibles became some of the most prolific advertisers during this period. As described in previous chapters, the portability of the goods they sold and the large numbers of shops selling them meant fierce local and national competition, resulting in innovations ranging from the liberal use of personal credit to bulk-buy deals. Advertising was a natural extension of those innovations, enabling shopkeepers to associate their individual shop with the products their customers enjoyed and thus secure market share. Not surprisingly, when visual advertising emerged as an affordable option, grocers were among the first retailers to embrace it. Repetition is at the heart of modern advertising: the relentless association of a specific item with specific images and phrases, such as the association of the adventurous Rocky Mountains with smoking a brand of cigarette, enhanced sexual appeal with a specific cologne, or nostalgia with a specific type of bottled cola.[3] Eighteenth-century retailers instinctively knew the value of consistency and embraced it, especially when it came to selling favourite ingestible products of the empire. The relentless barrage of imagery ultimately, and intentionally, contoured the meanings consumers assigned these goods. Perhaps most important, these meanings became communal, transcending social class, gender and geography. This is not to suggest that these goods' meanings became singular. The distinct combination of the warmth, taste and smell of a cup of tea on a rainy day could remind a young man of time shared with his grandmother just as much as, if not probably more than, the East India Company. However, the association of tea with imperial commerce was one that the young man, as well as millions of others in Britain, could share. The choice of such imagery by advertisers consistently informed consumers that these goods were not native to the British Isles. They arrived from overseas as a result of maritime power, colonization and African slavery, and thus consumers were overtly and repeatedly reminded that the continued enjoyment of these goods relied on the ability of Britain to assert its power overseas. For many British consumers, this was often imperialism at the point of purchase.

The emergence of visual advertising

Advertising was commonplace in the eighteenth century. Although most histories of advertising and marketing tend either to depict this period as a crude preface to the Victorian age or to dismiss it altogether, eighteenth-century advertisements were prevalent, powerful and complex. Newspapers were the primary conduit for retail advertising during the eighteenth century, with roughly half of a typical newspaper consisting of advertisements. Initially, newspaper advertising was dominated by printers selling their own products, but within a few decades newspapers carried advertisements for everything from exotic pets to employment opportunities for privateers. Advertising flourished in parallel to the rapid growth of the newspaper and periodical press, which exploded from 2.3 million copies per annum in the first decade of the eighteenth century to 12.6 million by the eve of the American Revolution.[4] By this time, newspapers carried over 333,000 advertisements each year, which accounted for well over half of most newspapers' revenues.[5] Although visually simplistic (illustrations were extremely rare), their language revealed a savviness that could rival a modern advertisement, stressing quality, urgency and opportunity.[6] Successful retailers advertised in a multitude of newspapers locally, regionally and nationally in an effort to extend market share, and many had standing advertisements that appeared in successive issues.

While newspaper advertising was an important part of the grocery trade, particularly for shops wanting either to enter or defend regional markets, it was only a small part of grocers' marketing strategies. Shops selling groceries typically cultivated a personal relationship with customers, offering liberal credit, custom orders and extensive delivery options. Thus, whereas an impersonal newspaper advertisement simply listing goods and prices might fit the needs of the London-based Original Tea-Warehouse, whose strategy was to offer wholesale prices to individual consumers nationwide and thereby undercut regional shops, such an advertisement would likely not aid a small shop in Westminster, whose primary competition was the dozen or more sellers within easy walking distance that offered more-or-less similar prices. Trade cards, which could be personalized and cheaply produced, proved more suitable to grocers' needs, and so grocers readily embraced them. Using visual imagery was not new to British retail. Elite urban shops had employed highly decorative signs in the seventeenth century, with sugar loaves acting as the most prevalent image for grocers by the end of the century. However, such signs were expensive and increasingly undesirable in urban environments because they blocked sunlight in narrow lanes and had the tendency to fall on unwary pedestrians. In consequence, most of the signs were removed during the mid-eighteenth century, often by order of local authorities, creating a golden opportunity in the history of advertising.[7]

Strictly speaking, trade cards were small cards roughly the size of a modern business card; however, the term as used here also includes a wide range of printed advertising that came in a variety of sizes, shapes and qualities, such as shop stationery and package labelling.[8] Although earlier examples survive, visual advertising truly came of age in the second half of the eighteenth century, when the growth of shops combined with advances in the printing trade to enable cheaper and more stunning productions. By emphasizing images over words, trade cards signalled the entry of advertising into visual culture. Striking images of clocks, clothing and shop interiors dominated the cards as attempts to provoke desires for particular goods and experiences. The text, which habitually gave the name and location of the shop, provided a way to satisfy that desire. Thus the trade card is akin to advertising on modern billboards, magazines or even television – in which printed words or a voiceover provide details of a product and seller against a backdrop of visual images. This is significant, because psychological studies of the impact of advertising have long demonstrated that visual imagery has a far greater impact than text alone on consumers' immediate perceptions of a product, the longevity of those views, and the quickness and extent of recall. Equally important, perceptions of products grounded in visual imagery are also the most difficult to displace.[9]

The thousand or more grocery-related trade cards that survive in archives are only a tiny slice of what circulated in the eighteenth century. Because they were disposable, the continued existence of individual cards is more by accident than design. As with most printed ephemera of the eighteenth century, consumers would have either reused them, most likely as makeshift toilet paper or kindling, or discarded them in the same way twenty-first-century consumers throw away receipts and package labels. Only later did collectors take an interest, and, as with most collectors, they chose their pieces based on pristine physical condition or association with a particular shop, rather than out of a desire to provide a comprehensive representation of visual advertising during this period. Trade cards also survived as bills and receipts in household accounts; however, detailed household accounts from this period are overwhelmingly from the elite, resulting in a potential overrepresentation of high-end shops. Partly in consequence, trade cards have been under-utilized. Of course, these are challenges historians face when using any sort of cheaply printed source material, whether it be newspapers or religious tracts: what survives is often not representative of what people actually saw and read. The answers to such challenges are careful analysis and corroborating evidence, and grocers' trade cards are receptive to both.

While the majority of surviving trade cards are from London shops, specimens from outside the metropolis abound. For example, at least four different grocers' cards from before 1830 survive from the small Oxfordshire town of Bampton. Places similarly removed from London trade, such as Banbury, Stourbridge, Milton Abbot, Scarborough, Sunderland and Welshpool, all had grocers whose cards survive.[10] Moreover, there are no significant differences between the styles of metropolitan and provincial cards, because shops regularly either bought their cards from London or from local printers who imitated the London styles. Besides, the urban/rural or metropolitan/provincial divide had limited meaning in the trade of empire-related groceries, because, as described earlier, grocers often had geographically large markets. Thus Andrew William Lee's shop in Sunderland competed with both regional and London rivals that advertised a readiness to ship their products to his area, and to remain competitive he had trade cards made for him by a London printer in 1802.[11] As a result, someone living in the smallest hamlet in the remotest county could be exposed to similar imagery as someone living in London.

Equally important, surviving trade cards came from groceries that were incredibly diverse in operational size, which further

Trade card of Andrew William Lee, Sunderland (1802).

underlines their representative value. The poorest peddlers of the empire's ingestible products most likely did not have trade cards, but visual advertisements were not the preserve of the largest shops in the wealthiest markets. Many of the grocers whose trade cards survive appeared in London and provincial trade directories, which were privately published directories of leading shops and service providers, but many others did not.

An examination of the policy registers of the Sun Fire Office, one of the largest British assurance companies of the eighteenth century, corroborates the argument that a wide variety of grocers used cards. Insurance cost as little as £1 for an annual policy covering £1,000-worth of stock and property, putting it within the reach even of modest grocers. The policies of grocers whose cards survive range enormously, from insuring a few hundred pounds' value of personal effects and stock to examples like Thomas Sedgwick's 1822 policy, which insured two buildings as well as a huge amount of stock up to the value of £4,000 on shop shelves and in a nearby warehouse.[12] Despite the volume and value of their stock, these typically were not wealthy people, as insured values of household goods, which were often included in the policy, were usually under £100. Even Sedgwick declared the value of his household goods to be a modest £200. Separate insurance riders on goods of particular value indicate that most shopkeepers considered here led a decidedly middling lifestyle, with such luxury goods as china, glass and prints but nothing extraordinary. Policies held by owners of nearby surrounding shops reveal that grocers with surviving trade cards were indistinguishable from their neighbours regarding ownership of the buildings or the value of the stock or household goods. The grocers' cards themselves show no consistent correlation between the imagery and the size of the shop. Such shops as John Bynner's grocery in Westminster (stock valued at £550) and William Baker Aird's in Soho (stock valued at £900) used cards that deployed similar Asiatic imagery, and the cards of Fortnum & Mason's grand operation in Piccadilly were not unusual, despite an 1824 policy that valued their stock at several thousand pounds.[13]

Utilizing trade cards as part of an advertising strategy would have made good business sense in the highly competitive world of the grocery trade. A retailer could spend a small fortune on producing a trade card commissioned from a well-known artist, but grocers overwhelmingly relied on stock trade cards (which differed solely in the

An undated blank trade card. This trade card, along with close approximations, was used by a number of grocers. Replete with the standard images of China and Chinese tea cultivation and consumption, the cards leave the central space open for individual grocers to either print or hand-write their details. The grasshopper was an image associated with Asian products in seventeenth- and early eighteenth-century hanging signs. Although it continued to appear on some trade cards, the grasshopper was steadily displaced.

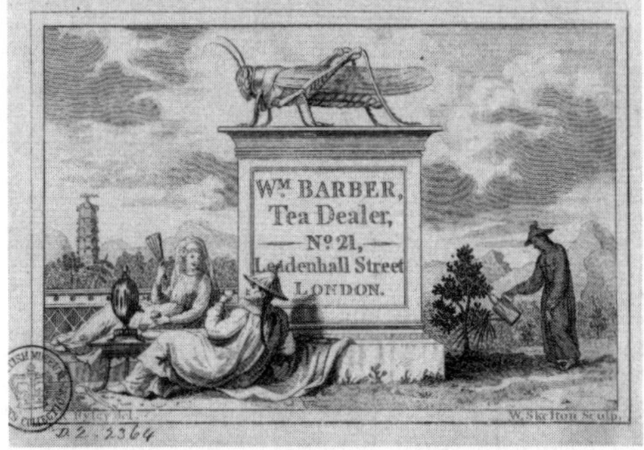

Trade card of William Barber, London (1789).

Undated trade card of C. Batten, Southampton. The image has been copied from the above design, with the primary alteration being the replacement of the grasshopper with a tea canister.

printing of the food seller's name and address) and recycled images. An example of duplication can be found in the card of William Coleman of Banbury, Oxfordshire, who, like many small shopkeepers, employed the services of an urban engraver – in this case, Price & Watson in Birmingham. The card has all of the standard imagery – a stereotypical 'Chinaman' wearing a *douli*, crates with mock-Mandarin writing, a pagoda and a faint British ship in the distant background. The origins of the image are unknown, but the same image also appeared on the trade cards of numerous other shops, including ones from Bristol, Stourbridge and Oxford. Although perhaps unintended, an important consequence was consistent visual messaging. The cards themselves were often so cheap that during the second half of the century a shopkeeper could buy either three medium-sized advertisements in a modest newspaper for fifteen shillings, or, for the same price, five hundred to one thousand individualized trade cards with a copper-plate image.[14] Newspaper advertisements would have reached a potentially larger audience, but, surrounded by dozens of other equally unenticing advertisements, they could have been easily ignored by readers who had acquired the newspaper for reasons other than to peruse retail promotions. In sharp contrast, trade cards offered the appealing opportunity to target customers directly – using the cards as receipts and packaging to remind buyers where the products were purchased or as advertisements distributed selectively to potential customers.

Besides, if grocers regularly extended credit in excess of several pounds to artisans and labourers in order to sell their goods in a highly competitive market, as described in the previous chapter, the notion of them spending just a few shillings on trade cards to promote their business is not remarkable. At the cost of as little as one-fifth of a penny, they would have been a worthwhile addition to sales, and some surviving cards that were used as bills and receipts indicate that they accompanied sales measured in shillings and pennies. The cost of the ingestible goods of imperial trade combined with the weekly and monthly quantities in which they were typically sold meant that bills of such sizes would have been fairly standard even for prosperous artisan families. Furthermore, exposure would not have been limited to patrons whose purchase merited a card, because, as we have seen, grocers often had an economically diverse

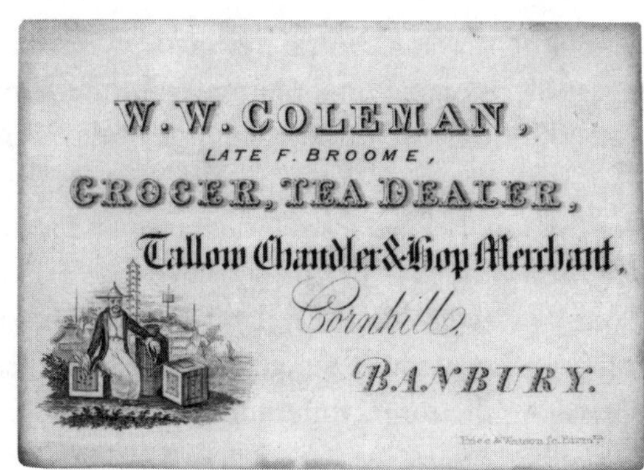

Undated trade card of W. W. Coleman, grocer and tea dealer, Banbury, Oxfordshire.

Undated trade card for F. Griszell. In the coffeehouse scene, the patrons discuss the quality of Griszell's tobacco, recommending it to each other.

customer base. Cards and packaging could easily have been viewed by poorer customers as well as the host of servants who participated in household shopping and food preparation. While women handled the bulk of shopping for household goods, grocers also catered to men, who would have shopped for their own tobacco and, to a lesser extent, coffees and teas. In consequence, trade card imagery enjoyed broad exposure that transcended geography, gender and, to some degree, social class.

The role of authenticity

Authenticity was a central message of visual advertisements for the ingestible goods of imperial trade. Adulteration and counterfeiting were rife from the earliest English trade in these commodities, at least partly because of their novelty, limited consumer knowledge and lengthy supply lines from production to consumer. In Ben Jonson's *The Alchemist*, first performed just three years after the Virginia Company established England's first successful North American colony at Jamestown, a character attests to the quality of a seller by describing the forgery methods he did *not* use:

He lets me have good Tobacco, and he do's not
Sophisticate it, with Sack-lees, or Oyl,
Nor washes it in Macadel, or Grains,
Nor buries it in Gravel, under Ground,
Wrap'd up in greasie Leather, or pis'd Clouts.

During the eighteenth century, tea was among the most adulterated and forged goods in Britain due to a combination of high taxes, great demand and the physical nature of tea itself. In fact, a 1783 House of Commons report estimated that as much as 25 per cent of the tea consumed in Britain was adulterated in some way at some point in the supply chain.[15] Whereas legal tea derived from the single source of the East India Company's trade, black-market tea had a diverse supply chain and, therefore, a potentially dubious provenance. This gave dishonest suppliers and shopkeepers ample chances to thin or wholly fabricate the teas they sold. The most common method for adulterating tea was to mix or entirely replace it with leaves that had been dried and crushed. Sloe leaves were a popular substitute for green teas, as were elder and ash leaves after they had been boiled with copper coins.[16] While such methods were not themselves dangerous, the occasional practice of introducing verdigris (a green pigment derived from applying acetic acid to copper, poisonous if ingested) was. Complaints and accusations in public and private were rife. The lines of the 'Chandler's Shop', a ballad poking fun at the infamous makeshift shops that cheated the unwary customer, never were truer:

We'll sell the very best bohea [an expensive type of tea]
And I'll chop some birch broom up, d'ye see.
We'll sell the best sugar in the land,
I'd improve it with a little sand.[17]

As a London *Times* editorial remarked in 1818, so long as the cost of tea was inflated by taxes and the East India Company's monopoly, the black market would continue, making adulteration 'inevitable'.[18]

Yet anxieties over authenticity ran much deeper than the desire not to be tricked. For many consumers, authenticity also encompassed promises of quality, as measured by the genuineness of the experience a good offered. Shopkeepers did not market the ingestible goods of empire as fantastical, made-up products from generically foreign lands. Asiatic and North American imageries were not used interchangeably as part of a casual effort to express goods' exoticism; Chinese images were confined to tea and American ones stayed with tobacco. Such attempts to market products and experiences as authentic were closely connected to what has been aptly described as the emergence of a 'culture of fact'.[19] The cultural shift was a product of the seventeenth-century's Scientific Revolution, which preferred tangible, observable data as well as public investigation and discussion, and flowed into the Enlightenment thinking that dominated British intellectual currents during the eighteenth century. The English, as well as the other inhabitants of the British Isles, moved away from explanations that showed supposition and superstition and towards systematic observations that could be measured and replicated – hallmarks of modern science. Science became intentionally accessible, with an array of societies peppering the metropolitan and provincial landscapes alike that connected great minds with great private wealth – most famously the Royal Society, founded in 1660, but also an array of smaller-scale local societies and clubs. The more established societies' transactions appeared both in dedicated printed volumes and as selected abstracts in more popular newspapers and magazines. Interest in factual

William Dent, 'Two To One, or, An attempt to Outwit the Young Pawnbroker' (London, 1793). A man carries three large tea chests marked with faux-Chinese writing while declaring, 'They wont know Sloe Leaves from Bohea [tea].'

information, or 'useful knowledge', as contemporaries called it, boomed among the reading public throughout the eighteenth century in the form of an outpouring of descriptive volumes, self-help educational literature and books from which parents could teach their children. Geography was among the most lauded subjects. As the author of the *Geography and History* 'selected by a Lady, for the Use of her own children' explained, 'I believe experience will evince that they [children] are just as capable of learning something that may be useful . . . as they are of repeating the little tales that are frequently told them for their amusement.' She continued, 'as Geography and History enlarge the mind more than any other studies, they cannot be begun too early.'[20]

In few places was the 'culture of fact' more evident than in the museums that emerged and blossomed in the second half of the eighteenth century. Artefacts both ancient and contemporary – once fantastical objects that adorned church reliquaries and private 'cabinets of curiosities' – moved to public museums, most notably the British Museum in 1753.[21] There the objects were curated into contextualized displays with accompanying 'scientific' descriptions. Opened to the public and marketed as educational experiences, the leading museums became the archives of the nation, sources of national pride and major tourist destinations. As a nineteen-year-old French visitor remarked in 1786, 'the British museum is a superb collection . . . voluntarily deposited for the instruction and gratification of the public.' 'Here, as in everything else,' he explained, 'the public spirit of the English is worthy of remark: a considerable portion of the exhibits has been voluntarily given and every day new legacies are recorded.'[22]

Most London guides included descriptions of the major museums' entrance procedures and recommended a visit.[23] The popular *Ambulator* declared that 'of all the public structures that engage the attention of the curious, the British Museum is the greatest.'[24] Besides opening their doors to a socially broad range of men, museums also catered to women and children. Carl Moritz, a German visitor to England in 1782, was impressed as much by the diversity of people he saw in the museum as he was by its exhibits. 'The visitors were of all classes and both sexes, including some of the lowest class', he noted, 'for since the Museum is the property of the nation, everyone must be allowed the right of entry.'[25] The British Museum and its chief competitor, Sir Ashton Lever's Leverian on Leicester Square, which had a wealth of ethnographic material from around the world, proved especially popular with families. As an open letter in 1777 to Lever in the *Morning Post*, thanking him for his service to the nation for 'succeeding generations', declared, 'What father would not wish his son to be contemplating the works of the Deity, in your museum, rather than spending his time in the debaucheries of the age?'[26] Caroline Lybbe Powys, the daughter of an Oxfordshire physician, visited the British Museum for the first time as a young woman in 1760. Fascinated particularly by the ethnographic and natural history exhibits, she regularly visited throughout her life and 26 years later toured the collections with her eleven-year-old daughter, an experience, along with their visit to the nearby Leverian, that 'highly entertained her'.[27]

The exhibits' appeal was their supposed grounding in reality. While museums included plenty of displays of minerals and fauna, the ethnographic collections received a disproportionate amount of space.[28] The objects on display were genuine articles that other peoples, whether past or present, used, and they told a story about their owners that museum audiences could believe. The museums exhibited tobacco pipes, porcelain tea and coffee services and a host of cooking tools and eating utensils from around the globe. Printed guidebooks, live guides and extensive labelling described the items in detail to visitors in a number of languages.[29] Above all, displays were grounded in 'facts'. As the *European Magazine* explained in a 1782 review of the Leverian, these exhibits were not designed to entice fanciful notions, for here 'all conspire to impress the mind with a conviction of the reality of things'. The magazine remarked that 'The descriptions of the enchanted palaces of the Genii, the Fairies, and the other fabulous beings of the eastern romance, though they amaze for a moment, have a sameness and an improbability that very soon disgust.' However, it continued, at the Leverian 'all is magnificence and reality. The wandering eye looks round with astonishment, and, though almost willing to doubt, is obliged to believe.' Together, these objects conspired to virtually transport visitors across the globe:

> As he [the visitor] proceeds, the objects before him make his active fancy travel from pole to pole through the torrid and through the frigid Zones. He beholds the manners of men

Frontispiece of the *Leverian Companion* (London, 1790), illustrating the Grand Saloon and Gallery of the Leverian Museum. Sir Ashton Lever welcomes a middling family to the museum, where children received discounted entrance fees and were encouraged to handle many of the objects on display. Although there were a host of private and public museums across Britain, the Leverian (1773–1806) was likely the most visited during its heyday, with the possible exception of the British Museum. The Leicester Square location become the primary depository of artefacts from the Cook voyages around the world, and, upon Lever's death, the *European Magazine* declared that he 'deserves the applause of Mankind'.

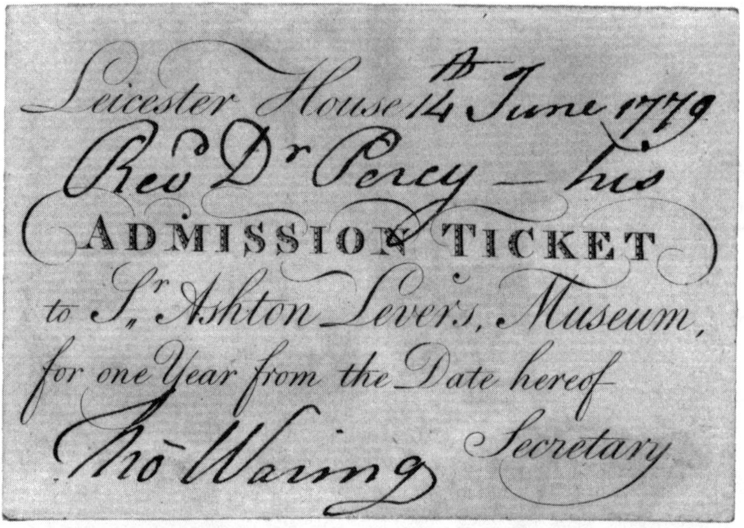

Leicester House 14th June 1779
Revd Dr Percy – his
ADMISSION TICKET
to Sr Ashton Lever's, Museum,
for one Year from the Date hereof
Thos Waring Secretary

Annual ticket to the Leverian Museum. The season-long ticket, a relatively new innovation on which institutions such as the Leverian capitalized, offered entry for a year. Because of the fragility of the paper ticket, the Leverian soon switched to copper tokens. An advertisement in the *Morning Post*, 5 July 1777, announced that annual tickets were two guineas and single tickets 5*s* 3*d*.

> in the forms of their habits; he sees the Indians rejoiced at, and dancing to, the monotonous sound of his tom tom; he sighs to recollect the prevalent power of fear and superstition over the human mind, when he views the rude deformity of an idol carved with flint, by a hand incapable of imitating the outline of nature, and that works only that it may worship.[30]

The result, a visitor declared, was a 'a *most useful* school of knowledge . . . where both our youth, and even old age, might receive instruction'.[31]

In this fact-focused context, specific designations, such as 'Turkish' and 'Plantation' coffees, 'Chinese' tea and 'Virginia' tobacco, were more than mere generic exotic dressing. They identified specific products with specific places, peoples and experiences. Akin to how museum exhibits provided context for an object by surrounding it with labels and similar items, visual advertising used visual cues to surround goods with authenticating scenes.

Imperial messages for imperial goods

Purveyors of the ingestibles of imperial rule and trade responded to consumers' concerns and expectations with consistent messaging that assured authenticity. Thus grocers' use of foreign imagery in their advertisements should be examined in this dual context: a need to authenticate the objects as well as tap into the wider public interest in the 'factual' exotics. Grocers accomplished this by associating their best-selling imperial commodities with the peoples and places from which they came. Four goods dominated the imagery of shops selling the empire's ingestibles: tobacco, tea, coffee and sugar. Unlike trade cards of other shops, which usually highlighted the products themselves or the shopping experience, the cards of shops selling these goods consistently placed greater emphasis on their products' origins and how they had reached the shop. The ultimate result was a powerful, repetitive visual message that drove home these products' associations with the empire.

The empire in North America was central to the visual imagery surrounding tobacco. Advertisements associated Virginia in particular with quality tobacco, with the slogan 'Best Virginia' serving

Trade card of S. Steel of Bedale, Yorkshire, *c*. 1778.

as the standard phrase for sellers claiming the best product. Because retailers claimed that the best tobacco came from Virginia, and Virginia was well known as a slave-holding colony, shops regularly authenticated their tobacco with images of African slavery and the plantation system in scenes that depicted the product's cultivation. In these illustrations, semi-naked African slaves harvest and load tobacco onto waiting European ships. In contrast, whites are invariably outnumbered and well-dressed, and have relaxed deportments, such as in the cards reproduced here – one from Yorkshire and the other from London. The role of the white male figure in these scenes is open to multiple interpretations, but two, which are not mutually exclusive, stand out as the most plausible. The first is that he is simply the prosperous colonial planter enjoying his product as he watches over his slaves. A second reading is that he is the British consumer, who has been transported to the imagined scene of distant Virginia via the sensory experience of smoking the genuine tobacco product. This is not unlike modern advertisements that show goods ranging from bath soap to automobiles whisking users virtually away to imagined retreats from mundane life.

The most common symbol of tobacco on trade cards was a caricatured North American Indian. Shopkeepers could not have picked a more widely recognized image for associating their product

Trade card of Edward Bury, tobacconist, London, *c.* 1780.

Trade card of Turner, tobacconist, London, *c.* 1760. The reference to the 'two Black Boys' refers to the shop's sign, not the two figures in the illustration. The image also appears on other mid-century trade cards.

with America. Although the iconic cigar store wooden statue of an American Indian would not materialize on either side of the Atlantic until the nineteenth century, tobacco had a close association in the British Isles with American Indians dating back to the early seventeenth century, when it was popularly known as the 'Indian weed'. As Britons took greater interest in the empire in the eighteenth century, American Indians featured prominently in discussions and descriptions of North America ranging from newspapers to the British Museum.[32] By mid-century, highly publicized wars in North America, in which American Indians fought as allies and enemies, had given the British a high degree of self-proclaimed familiarity with American Indian cultures. As a reader remarked in a letter to the editor of the *London Chronicle* rebuking him for the paper's simplistic explanation of the latest news from America, 'We are well enough informed too of the customs of the American Indians to want no interpreter, when we read of their taking up or burying the hatchet of war; of their tomohawking or scalping their enemies; and of planting the tree or smoking the pipe of peace.'[33] By the outbreak of the American Revolution, the caricatured American Indian had come to personify the North American colony in a number of British prints as the

Undated trade card of Sadler's, London.

American equivalent to the caricature of Britannia. Interestingly, the trade card imagery rarely links American Indians to production; instead, they typically appeared as simply enjoying tobacco either in the company of other natives or with a white planter. In fact, production-related trade cards almost invariably show only African slaves at work. Such imagery reflects popular knowledge that tobacco came from colonialism rather than trade with indigenous peoples, who never produced large quantities of tobacco for export to Britain.

As queen of the hot beverage trade, tea dominated grocers' advertisements. The associated visual imagery heavily emphasized its connection with Asiatic trade and empire. The standard image was a stereotype caricature of a 'Chinaman', often on a dock surrounded by tea caddies and crates. The crates usually had mock-Chinese writing, sometimes with intermixed boxes marked 'Tea' – to alleviate any possible confusion. Other trade cards advertising tea featured scenes of Chinese workers engaged in tea production, tea drinking and pagodas. East India House, the company's headquarters, opened in Leadenhall Street in 1729, was another symbol – even on cards of those provincial shops that would have bought their tea through brokers rather than directly from the company. The major tea brokers, who dominated the internal British trade by buying the company's tea in bulk and then selling it to small shopkeepers and regional suppliers, seem to have supplied quite a few shops with template trade cards. This made trade cards available to retailers who otherwise might not have had them – or at least not with as much visual detail – and created the beginnings of branding. One such case was the Twinings, who became major brokers and suppliers during the eighteenth century. They provided several templates over the course of the period that implored consumers to enjoy their products at the location advertised on the card.

Coffee's global associations were also apparent. However, images linked to coffee were less prevalent than those of tobacco or tea. Although British consumption of coffee exceeded that of tea in the early eighteenth century, changes to taxes designed to benefit the East India Company pushed tea drinking to the fore. By the 1740s – when trade cards with images began to take off – tea had taken an unassailable lead. By 1784 tea consumption in Britain was seventeen times that of coffee.[34] The most common image was a caricature of someone

Matthew Darly, 'The Commissioners' (London, 1778). An American Indian woman, personifying the American colonists, sits atop a pile of colonial trade goods, including barrels labelled 'tobacco' and 'indico', while the British commissioners, sent to negotiate a last-minute peace for fear of the revolution erupting into a global war with Britain's European enemies as American allies, supplicate themselves.

Trade card of George Harris, grocer and tea dealer, Bristol, 1799. A typical trade card of a tea dealer and grocer, it is full of stock images associated with the tea trade, including a pagoda, crates with mock-Chinese writing, the East India Company's London headquarters, a British ship and the stereotypical 'Chinaman' – although usually he is depicted wearing a *douli*.

from the Levant – usually a cross between an Arab and a Turk. This connected coffee with the Ottoman Empire and the Middle East – the original exporter of coffee drinking to England in the seventeenth century and initially the primary source of coffee beans. Surviving grocers' advertisements and accounts indicate that most shops offered at least two blends from mid-century onwards. The first was 'Turkish', in reference to the coffee that came from the Ottoman-controlled port of Mocha, which dominated the trade until the early decades of the eighteenth century. The second was 'Plantation', which referred to West Indian production. Some offered a third, 'Bourbon', referring to French sources, which were also in the West Indies. The extent to which these blends actually reflected their beans' origins is unclear; however, judging by the blends' roughly equivalent price and the grossly disproportionate amount of West Indian coffee in Britain in the second half of the century – in 1774 legal imports from the British West Indies were six times that of all other sources combined – it is highly likely that West Indian beans were the main ingredient in all of them.[35] Even so, images of West Indian scenes on trade cards advertising coffee were slow to displace the Levant, as it remained firmly

This 1787 example was one of several trade-card templates associated with Twinings. A blank space, in this case the inside of the archway, provides room for the cards to be tailored to include the individual proprietor's location. In the elevated centre is the British lion, and to the left and right are caricatures of someone from the Levant, representing coffee, and a 'Chinaman', representing tea.

Trade card of Ham & Thorn, tea dealers and grocers, Southend, Essex, *c.* 1800. An upmarket shop, Ham & Thorn boasted their association with the royal family.

associated with coffee in the popular imagination. Travel accounts of the Middle East invariably waxed lovingly and lengthily about coffee, and the vulgar term for coffee remained 'Mahometan Gruel' through the turn of the nineteenth century.[36] Even in the 1820s, connoisseurs continued to claim Turkish coffee's superiority, with one remarking, 'There are many substitutes for coffee which are often palmed on the public for the genuine article; but those who are accustomed to the taste and smell of the real Turkey coffee cannot easily be deceived.'[37]

Although visual advertisements rarely associated sugar directly with the empire, it nevertheless merits some discussion here. After all, sugar trumped all other imported imperial products in terms of quantity and value. As Edward Gibbon Wakefield remarked, even 'an English washerwoman cannot sit down to breakfast without tea and sugar'.[38] No definitive explanation can be given for the lack of imperial imagery on sugar advertisements, but it was most likely a result of the chronological development of sugar consumption and its function in the British diet. Thanks to medieval Mediterranean production, sugar had circulated throughout the British Isles centuries before tea, tobacco or coffee became widely available.[39] Although expensive before the eighteenth century, sugar was sufficiently common to be

Undated trade card of John Davies, London. As well as the usual tea chest and tobacco barrel, the card includes the classic three sugar loaves at centre. Despite the emphasis on coffee, tea and tobacco in visual advertising, sugar remained the primary product sold in groceries.

used as medicine and a regular cookery ingredient by the wealthy.[40] The age of the sugar market is reflected in the enduring symbol of the loaf, which was the form in which refined sugar had been transported from the Mediterranean for centuries – although during the eighteenth century sugar was sold in a variety of shapes and sizes and came from British plantations in the West Indies. In fact, the loaf had such a powerful association with sugar in the grocery trade that signs bearing three sugar loaves became a standard street marker for grocers during the seventeenth century and continued to appear on trade cards long after most of the large signs were ordered taken down.[41]

Furthermore, sugar was an ingredient that had been almost entirely adapted to British aesthetics – unlike coffee, tea and tobacco, which had been adopted and thus retained many of the characteristics of its original exporters, such as porcelain cups and pipes for consumption. Sugar was a sweetening ingredient, not a dish: a blend of sugar and chocolate, coffee or tea remained chocolate, coffee or tea.[42] In this sense, sugar was similar to imported textiles, which also became, in effect, ingredients, in this case for British clothing and soft furnishings. Trade cards for clothiers, mercers and haberdashers used images of finished products or the shops themselves rather than scenes of Indian cotton fields or Irish wool production. Moreover, sugar needed little authentication. Sugar had no complicated connoisseurship associated with it that necessitated assurances of quality and type, and it was sufficiently cheap in the eighteenth century to deter any widespread adulteration with domestic fillers by duplicitous sellers. It was rarely a target of shoplifters, unlike tea and tobacco. Sugar was sold according to weight and type of refinement, not geographical origin; 'Jamaica's Best' was not a label, and cookery books did not espouse the superiority of Antiguan sugar over its Barbadian competitor. In consequence, eighteenth-century traders did not need to rebrand or heavily advertise sugar. Customers knew it was available at any grocery, and they bought it in abundance.

Yet the late 1780s saw the beginning of a remarkable shift in sugar's visual imagery, as abolitionists increasingly sought to associate sugar and its consumption in Britain with the horrors of slavery and the slave trade. Abolitionists' highly public campaigns prevailed upon consumers to take greater interest in sugar's origins, with many advocating either abstaining from sugar or substituting East Indian sugar. Although more expensive, East Indian sugar was a product of

Bill heading for R. Martin, tea dealer and grocer, London, *c.* 1830s. The bill heading addresses consumer concerns about slavery's association with imperial groceries. To the right the 'Chinaman' holds a sign with the caption 'I am free' and, to the left, the former slave, whose chains of bondage lie severed at his feet, declares 'So am I.'

supposedly free labour and therefore, some argued, preferable to the slave-cultivated sugar of the West Indies. Shopkeepers' responses highlight how they invested the visual imagery in their advertisements with meaning and, equally important, believed that their customers did the same. As the abolitionists' campaigns gained momentum, images of slaves engaged in production of any goods rapidly declined. Some printed advertisements included 'free' sugar in the lists of goods, and others proudly noted this on their packaging and receipts. While some grocers undoubtedly acted out of conscience, such moves also represented savvy marketing. As discussed in greater detail in Chapter Six, abstaining from sugar was a highly public act in that sugar was purchased in public spaces and often consumed in company. In this context, packaging from a grocer known to sell only free sugar could serve as a visual cue to other consumers that the purchaser, although in possession of sugar, was a firm abolitionist.

Advertisements for the ingestible products of the empire also visually describe their reliance upon imperial trade and maritime power. British ships appear in a great many of the advertisements, linking such beloved products as tobacco with naval strength and commerce. The ships typically sit in the background, often as one of many visual cues. Other times, such as in Archer's mid-century trade card, the flag-adorned ships are central to the scene. They form the apex in a triangular composition – a configuration that was common in the great paintings of the day, first appearing in the religious paintings of the Renaissance and then increasingly in nationalist paintings of the eighteenth century, in which the British monarch or flag serves as the all-important apex with the cast of supporting characters at the base. The ship thus reminded the viewer of the central role of the navy and the British state in ensuring the production, trade and delivery of these beloved goods. These cards hammered home the reality that no merchant fleet, or navy to protect it, meant no such goods – at least not in the affordable quantities to which consumers had grown accustomed. This imagery contributed to what historian Margarette Lincoln has called the 'national fiction in which the sea was held to be part of their [British] being' and to the remarkable popular acceptance of the enormous expense of constructing and maintaining the Royal Navy.[43]

The importance of the subjugation of other peoples is also evident in the advertising imagery. The belief in racial hierarchy is most apparent in those cards that depicted African slavery. Such images portrayed African slaves toiling in fields and loading ships before the watchful, but almost always resting and outnumbered, white men. Elegantly dressed in European clothing and perfectly white, the white men contrast remarkably with the brutishness of the starkly black, shirtless slaves labouring in loincloths and grass skirts. A growing

Trade card for Archer's, London, *c.* 1760. The illustration was also used by several other mid-century grocers and tobacconists.

sense of British superiority is also evident in those cards that depicted the peoples of the world offering their product to Britannia in tribute – a theme that appeared with increasingly regularity in eighteenth- and early nineteenth-century advertising and then exploded during the Victorian era. The advertising imagery typically shows Britannia with her spear and shield before a racial mix of bowing people offering local goods. The image that Anthony Schick, a London grocer, affixed to his coffee-making directions is a representative example. Britannia sits in throne-like position in a nondescript foreign place, as 'natives' bow and offer her barrels of coffee in tribute; meanwhile, British ships wait in the background. The telling caption reads 'Britannia lending a helping hand to her colonies'. Similarly, the tradecard of H. Lilwall, in London's Threadneedle Street, depicts Britannia on a throne of the produce of imperial trade as a supplicant Turk, Africans and American Indians lay more goods at her feet. These images are strikingly akin to such grand spectacles as Roma Spiridione's 1778 *The East Offering its Riches to Britannia*, a rich decoration commissioned by the East India Company to adorn the ceiling of the Revenue Room of its headquarters. With an identical

Undated trade card of Chandler & Newsom, London. The image features a British ship at the apex of a triangular composition, while at the base are a slave pushing a barrel (representing coffee and tobacco) and a 'Chinaman' sitting on top of a tea chest.

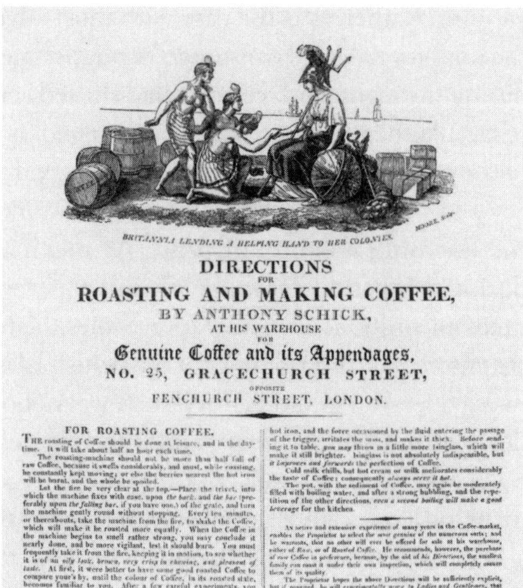

BRITANNIA LENDING A HELPING HAND TO HER COLONIES.

DIRECTIONS
FOR
ROASTING AND MAKING COFFEE,
BY ANTHONY SCHICK,
AT HIS WAREHOUSE
FOR
Genuine Coffee and its Appendages,
NO. 25, GRACECHURCH STREET,
OPPOSITE
FENCHURCH STREET, LONDON.

FOR ROASTING COFFEE.

THE roasting of Coffee should be done at leisure, and in the day-time. It will take about half an hour each time.

The roasting-machine should not be more than half full of raw Coffee, because it swells considerably, and must, while roasting, be constantly kept moving; or else the berries nearest the hot iron will be burnt, and the whole be spoiled.

Let the fire be very clear at the top.—Place the trivet, into which the machine fixes with ease, upon *the bark*, and *the bar* (preferably upon *the falling bar*, if you have one,) of the grate, and turn the machine gently round without stopping. Every ten minutes, or thereabouts, take the machine from the fire, to shake the Coffee, which will make it be roasted more equally. When the Coffee in the machine begins to smell rather strong, you may conclude it nearly done, and be more vigilant, lest it should burn. You must frequently take it from the fire, keeping it in motion, to see whether it is of an *oily look, brown, very crisp in chewing, and pleasant of taste*. At first, it were better to have some good roasted Coffee to compare your's by, until the colour of Coffee, in its roasted state, becomes familiar to you. After a few careful experiments, you

hot iron, and the force occasioned by the fluid entering the passage of the trigger, irritates the mass, and makes it thick. Before sending it to table, *you may* throw in a little more Isinglass, which will make it still brighter. Isinglass is not absolutely indispensible, but *it improves and forwards* the perfection of Coffee.

Cold milk chills, but hot cream or milk meliorates considerably the taste of Coffee; consequently *always serve it hot*.

The pot, with the sediment of Coffee, may again be moderately filled with boiling water, and after a strong bubbling, and the repetition of the other directions, *even a second boiling will make a good beverage* for the kitchen.

An active and extensive experience of many years in the Coffee-market, enables the Proprietor to select the *most genuine* of the numerous sorts; and he warrants, that no other will ever be offered for sale at his warehouse, either of *Raw*, or of *Roasted Coffee*. He recommends, however, the purchase of raw Coffee in preference, because, by the aid of *his Directions*, the smallest family can roast it under their own inspection, which will completely assure them of its quality.

The Proprietor hopes the above Directions will be sufficiently explicit, but if required, he will *experimentally prove* to *Ladies and Gentlemen*, that

Heading of 'Directions for Roasting and Making Coffee' from Anthony Schick, London, 1812. The image was followed by directions for making the 'best' coffee, and would have accompanied packages of it. In the illustration Britannia is on a West Indian island, signalled by the bowing 'natives', and is 'lending a helping hand to her colonies', according to the caption.

message of the benefits of empire and superiority of Britain, the only significant difference is the artists' mediums: cheap copper plates versus opulent oils.

THE ADVERTISING IMAGERY surrounding imperial commerce's leading groceries consistently and steadily reminded consumers that they were reaping the rewards of imperial rule and trade. Consumers' purchases directly supported the empire and indelibly tied them to it. Scenes such as African slaves harvesting tobacco, although simplified, were neither fanciful nor sanitized to show slaves' contentment. Advertisers showed little restraint, choosing to preference authenticity and accuracy and thus both draw upon and further inform widespread understandings of how these goods were cultivated and transported. In consequence, these goods were not depicted as gifts from the gods or magical places. Instead, the imagery that adorned shop receipts, packaging and advertisements attempted to provide authentic accounts of the plants, peoples and places from which the goods came, as well as the vital British ships that secured their safe and inexpensive arrival in Britain. In so doing, they represented the British Empire as an empire of peoples connected by trade and goods.

Of course, the sharp disposition in favour of authenticity in the visual imagery of advertising these goods did not take place in a vacuum. Rather, as is the case with most advertising then and now, the imagery reflected consumers' aspirations and expectations, which during the eighteenth century had shifted acutely towards a culture of fact. Authenticity and accuracy mattered, as reflected in the growth of the public importance of science, the greater emphasis on numeracy and the flood of information that saturated British society via the booming medium of print. As much as novelists prospered during this period, far more ink and paper were spent on the hundreds of millions of newspaper copies, histories and geographies that flowed into every corner of the British Isles. Whether the humble newspaper or a grand history, such works bombarded readers with descriptive accounts, maps, tables and figures related to the empire. Such developments were critical to the emergence of the Enlightenment in Britain, which, as the second part of this book argues, played a key role in how many Britons related to the food they prepared and consumed.

The advertising imagery associated with these products left little doubt as to who was believed to be in control of the relationships. There was an overt racial hierarchy at work. The images also highlighted an important multiracial element of imperial commerce and

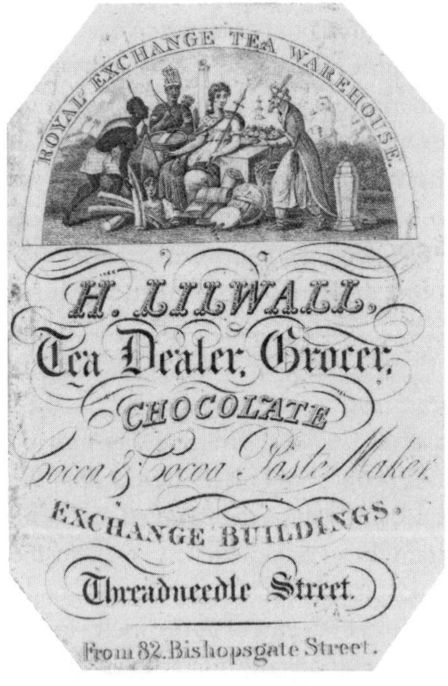

Undated trade card of H. Lilwall, London. Britannia sits on a throne of imperial goods as the empire's subjects and trading partners present her with its rewards, ingestible and otherwise.

Spiridione Roma, *The East Offering its Riches to Britannia*, 1778, oil on canvas. The vast painting, which features a supplicated India offering its Asiatic goods (including tea) to Britannia, was commissioned by the East India Company to adorn the ceiling of the Revenue Room of its headquarters. A British ship sails in the background.

rule. While the Europeans, whether in Britain or a colony, reaped the bulk of the rewards, they relied on others for production and trade. This imbalance of power ultimately prompted considerable reflection about difference in the world's societies and their varying merits, and, as explored in the second part of this book, these differences were explored through food.

PART II

DEFINING, REPRODUCING *AND* DEBATING

FOUR
DEFINING A BRITISH CUISINE

On the eve of Chester's music festival in September 1814, the local newspaper singled out the city's culinary talents in an article anticipating the celebration: 'Apollo, Epicurus, and Thespis, have by turns ruled the roast, and the culinary gale which fills the streets at evening with the perfumes of the kitchen, might induce a passing stranger, to imagine that cookery was the chief employment of our industrious citizens!'[1] Such a claim was almost unthinkable a century earlier, when British cookery was unglamorous and went largely uncelebrated in the public eye.

The massive influx of the ingestible goods of imperial commerce was part of a larger reformation in British food, affecting not only what Britons ate but, as explored in this and the other chapters in Part Two, also how they discussed and understood eating. Although examples of the inhabitants of the British Isles linking food and culture can be identified far into the past, what transpired during the eighteenth century marked an important departure because the discussions were national, with participants and an audience that transcended region, social class and gender. Thanks to the power of print and the growing interest in cookery, couples in mid-century Kingston in Kent and Kingston in Devon could sit down to almost identical meals as they read the same newspaper stories. Critically, the growth of consumption empowered largely disenfranchised groups, particularly women, by providing them with increased choice, and opportunities for expression. The growth of print culture and reading provided a forum for national discussions. Although men participated, the acquisition and preparation of food remained a predominately female affair throughout the eighteenth century, and through those activities women found outlets to express views and interact with wider society on a number of cultural, social and political topics, including morality, the Enlightenment and imperialism.

The present chapter focuses on the national discourse on cookery and the emergence of British cuisine as part of a conscious set of cultural and social ideals. While a chapter on the formation of a national cuisine might at first appear to be a deviation from the central themes of a book about food and empire, this chapter is a necessary detour. First, it provides an important opportunity to establish how essential the acquisition, preparation and consumption of food was to how eighteenth-century Britons understood themselves and their society. Second, it further highlights how interwoven eating was with consumer culture. While the previous chapters emphasized individual commodities, this chapter lays the groundwork for the equally significant practices of preparation. Finally, the chapter underlines the dynamism of the discourse surrounding eating. Although the practices of the elite retained an allure for socially ambitious Britons, the articulation of British culture could be incredibly democratic. Women, including servants and members of the lower-middling ranks, publicly mediated the widely expressed anxieties surrounding consumption, offering solutions that defined the nation's aspirational eating habits, and created the framework for a national cuisine. Understanding the critical roles that eating practices played in Britons' understandings of themselves, as individuals and as a society, ultimately provides indispensable context for understanding how the British, in turn, applied this framework to their rapidly expanding empire.

Why cookery mattered

Britain during the long eighteenth century was an emerging nation, not just with regard to projecting economic and political power across the globe but in terms of establishing its cultural identity. The Act of Union in 1707 linked the future of Scotland to England and Wales. For the effectively junior partners of Scotland and Wales, whose economies and populations paled in comparison to England's, the power imbalance was profound. Yet England, too, was emerging from generations of foreign influence. The restoration of the Stuart monarchy in 1660 ushered in a host of French customs and fashions, including plenty that surrounded food; the accession of the Dutch William of Orange to the thrones of England, Ireland and Scotland in 1689 continued the pattern, as did the accession fifteen years later of the German George I, who did not bother to learn much English and spent much of his time in his native Hanover. Only when George I's great-grandson was crowned George III in 1761 did the British again have a native-born king, a fact not lost on the new ruler, who in his accession speech rejoiced: 'Born and educated in this country, I glory in the name of Briton.'[2] Partly in consequence, the selection, preparation and consumption of food among the English and British elite closely followed continental European cookery – an established vogue often imitated by the aspirational ranks. Leading cooks were typically French, trained by a Frenchman, or masquerading as one or the other, and late seventeenth- and early eighteenth-century printed cookbooks were overwhelmingly compilations of continental recipes and techniques written for specialists.

By the end of the long eighteenth century, Britain's situation had changed remarkably. The British Empire was the world's preeminent imperial power, and the majority of its territorial inhabitants were no longer British-born. Alongside the growth of the British state, economy and empire during the eighteenth century was an equally momentous newfound desire to assert British greatness through the arts and sciences. The Royal Society, British Museum and Royal Academy of Arts all began and flourished during the long eighteenth century – institutions in which Britons sought to establish their own body of knowledge, skills and styles in the face of their engagement with an ever-widening world.[3] The modern social sciences tell us that investigations, comparisons and, ultimately, judgements of others have consequences for how the examiners understand themselves. So, too, was it for the British, whose desire to understand their civilization's place in their rapidly expanding world meant a host of comparisons with both overseas peoples and the continental Europeans whose cultural practices had reigned over the British elite for generations. The onslaught of information and new goods that flowed into Britain was unprecedented, as was their accessibility. Sifting through all of this was a monumental task that gave birth to the likes of the revered Adam Smith and Samuel Johnson. No less important to contemporaries, however, were the likes of Hannah Glasse and

Elizabeth Raffald, humble cookbook authors who were arguably more widely known and more immediately influential in how Britons negotiated their changing worlds.

The acquisition, preparation and consumption of food is a kind of language in which participants express themselves and interpret others.[4] In this sense, the formation of a national cuisine is a national discourse, full of reflections, trepidations and aspirations. The emergence of a national style of cookery in Britain in the latter half of the eighteenth century was not unlike the postcolonial experiences that followed the retreat of the European empires two centuries later.[5] Widely hailed by contemporaries as both an art and a science, cookery was an increasingly evident part of Britons' assertions of cultural prominence during the eighteenth century. While definitions of both 'national' and 'cuisine' vary, a useful sociological approach is to look for the following in discussions about food: a language of tradition, validation of home cooking, appeal of regional dishes, nostalgia for locally produced foods and recipes, reflections on authenticity, naturalization of foreign foods and, perhaps most importantly, a desire to treat food as a way to commune.[6] Discussions about food and cookery in Britain during this period developed all of these traits.

Critically, discussions (both contemporary and historical) about food, cookery and culture are as much about perceptions as practices, with the former often being more important than the latter. In other words, how many of Oxford's inhabitants ate a dish described as 'Oxford Pudding' in Ann Shackleford's *The Modern Art of Cookery Improved* is not imperative. The recipe itself, consisting of widely available ingredients – sugar, currants, lemon peel, eggs, flour, nutmeg and butter – that were mixed and boiled, hardly stands out from the array of other similar puddings on offer in either her cookery book or competing works.[7] More important is that she and her fellow authors increasingly gave these recipes regional and national designations. These were no longer simply 'pudding'. They had a geographic designation and with it an imagined context. Assigning geographic or ethnic labels to dishes for consumption across a wide area is akin to how the newspapers and periodical press in eighteenth-century Britain created a sense of national community. For example, via the press, readers in Bristol knew, or least assumed they knew, how the inhabitants of Glasgow responded to news of the outbreak of war with the American colonies in the summer of 1775 or the birth of Princess Charlotte in 1796.

The power of such imagined communities has long attracted the notice of scholars interested in the ties that bind people who have no physical contact, coalescing into social classes, ethnicities and nationalities.[8] Food, or at least the discussions surrounding its acquisition, preparation and consumption, was part of this cultural development. The emergence of a consciously British way of cookery reflected both national pride and widespread anxiety about the future and Britain's place in it. Forged in a context of rapid imperial expansion that led to encounters with new civilizations and near-constant conflict with old European rivals and indigenous peoples, British cuisine was at once a mix of foreign ingredients and techniques and a widely proclaimed, unique style.

Asserting civility through cookery

Considerations of the quality, style and diversity of cookery found in eighteenth-century Britain were linked closely with wider deliberations on human civilization. In these discussions, food, from its methods of production to the manner in which it was consumed, became a means for assessing the state of British society as well as other societies that Britons were encountering via their expanding empire. The Enlightenment provided the predominant intellectual framework for these discussions, particularly what later became known as the Scottish Enlightenment, whose leading figures sought to explain the socio-economic evolution of societies from hunter-gatherers to emerging industrial societies of Europe. Discussed in more detail in the following chapter, the subject was of national interest and embraced by the reading public. The Scots philosophers (the Scottish Enlightenment label came later) led the effort to rationalize the great diversity of societies around the world and explain why some appeared far more advanced than others. Critically, the British also adopted and adapted this thinking to consider their own society. The eighteenth century for Britain was a period of enormous change, a key component of which was the rise of the country as a global power. Questions about what facilitated this rise and whether or not it would last were natural, and the British sought answers through examinations of historical and contemporary practices and behaviours, food being a leading subject. What they sought most was evidence of progress – that British society was ascending, rather than in decline – and they found it in British cookery. Although Britain was not short of attention-grabbing commentators who bemoaned the state of society, the overall societal outlook in almost any given area during the century was one of optimism, particularly from the mid-century mark.[9] Discussions of the state of British cookery reflected and reinforced this disposition.

The British during the eighteenth century were acutely aware of their 'primitive' pasts. The classical works of Caesar, Polybius, Thucydides and Tacitus were part of a standard curriculum for elite and middling boys and sufficiently widely read that newspapers editors assumed their broad audiences were at least familiar with them. Passages in these works made clear that the peoples of central and northern Europe were once designated 'primitive' in the same ways as Europeans branded the indigenous peoples they had encountered in sub-Saharan Africa, the Americas and the South Pacific.[10] Antiquarianism, the forerunner to archaeology, also flourished during this period and provided material evidence to support the ancient texts' descriptions.[11]

Commentators widely used cookery to highlight the states of historical societies in the British Isles. In his lauded 1771 *An Introduction to the History of Great Britain and Ireland*, James Macpherson described ancient Britons' cookery in detail. He described its baseness, noting that 'The dishes at those [celebratory] feasts were not numerous, and there was little variety in the cookery.' Such minimalism carried over to eating, Macpherson continued, remarking that 'The utensils used upon these occasions were few in number and simple in their fashion', with spits and large earthen pots being 'the whole furniture of the kitchen' and guests having to arrive with their own knives and forks, should they desire them.[12]

Scotland's more recent past drew particular attention – sometimes employed by critics to denigrate the Scots but at other times used to highlight Scotland's recent, rapid progress up the ladder of civilization. Similar to a host of other historians, Hugo Arnot in his 1779 *History of Edinburgh*, printed by leading publishers William Creech in Edinburgh and John Murray in London, dismissed medieval Scots' cookery, depicting it as reflecting the poor state of Scotland's civilization at the time. In a paragraph detailing the lack of iron production in medieval Scotland, Arnot shifted seamlessly to cookery, describing how 'in their military excursions, they [the Scots] carried along with them no provision of bread or wine, no pots and pans; for that they boiled the cattle in their hides'. When they hastily abandoned their camps, he continued, the English found in them few edibles besides meat, as well as cauldrons made of stretched hides 'with the hairs still on them . . . filled with water, and the flesh put in them, ready to be boiled' and shoes 'made of raw leather, with the hair still on them'. By the end of the sixteenth century, Arnot later explained, 'the manner of living among the Scots had greatly improved.' When the English investigated the Scots' camps following the English victory at the Battle of Pinkie, they found a variety of foods, including cheese, butter, oatmeal, wheat bread, ale and wine, 'and, in some of the tents, silver-plate and chalices'. 'Still, however,' Arnot concluded, 'their manner of living makes a wretched figure, when compared to modern refinement.'[13]

The British rejection of these old ways in favour of refinement was a source of pride that extended well beyond the circle of cooks labouring in kitchens. After all, as Alexander Gerard, professor of moral philosophy at the University of Aberdeen, espoused in his influential *Essay on Taste* (1756), discernment in nature, art and science was the hallmark of an advanced civilization. Thus, 'savages appear perfectly indifferent' to 'many actions reckoned either virtuous or vicious by civilized nations'.[14] In this context, cookery served as a significant tool for British claims to cultural progress and superiority. For instance, in his book-length abridgement of the leading works on society, John Adams included a chapter 'On Refinement of Cookery'. In it, he employed the evolution of roasting meats to describe social progress. He first explained that 'The hospitality of the Anglo-Saxons was sometimes exerted in roasting an ox whole.' This was because 'Barbarous nations, being great eaters, are fond of large joints of meat'; however, Adams observed, 'Great joints are left off gradually, as people become more and more delicate in eating.' Thus, he continued, 'in France, great joints are less in use than formerly; and in England, the enormous sirloin, formerly the pride of the nation, is now in polite families banished to the side-board.'[15]

In this context of evaluating and categorizing societies, the British were unsurprisingly sensitive to foreign opinions about their cookery. This was no more so than with the French, whom the British treated as rivals in every arena and whose widely accepted greater refinement in cookery challenged British notions of their own cultural superiority. French cookery, whether in the form of French cooks in elite homes or terminology in recipes, prevailed among the elite and aspiring middling British sorts to varying degrees. For those unable to afford a personal cook trained in Continental cuisine, there were a host of alternatives. Urban inhabitants had the option of eating out, but others could simply make the dishes themselves, as French dishes and techniques abounded in the mid-century cookery books that targeted professional and middling families alike. In 1748 John Bell, one of the leading publishers in London, printed the *French Family Cook: Being a Complete System of French Cookery*. Unlike previous translations of French works, professional cooks were not the focus; instead, the book targeted 'Persons of moderate Fortune and Condition' and 'all who are concerned in the Superintendence of a Family'. Throughout the collection of translated recipes and careful instructions, the book emphasized affordability with such promises of dishes 'calculated to grace a Table at a small Expence' and advice on how to produce seasonal offerings 'at the most moderate [expense] possible'.[16]

Continental European, particularly French, influence remained a sore point throughout the eighteenth century. As John Thacker, who cooked for the dean of Durham Cathedral and, on occasion, the 'residence of the College of Durham', complained in his mid-century *Art of Cookery*, even original English recipes were laced with faux-French terminology – such as 'fricasey' and 'a-la-mode', which over time lost their connection to the French method (and spelling) – simply 'to excite Curiosity' in British audiences. As for foreign cooks, Thacker assured his readers that he had worked with many but had never encountered 'a Foreigner who had so sound and good a Way of working as an old English Cook'.[17] Such bravado played out during wartime, when British commentators derided their French enemies via cookery-laced language. As a reader remarked in a letter in the London newspaper *The Gazetteer*, lamenting British setbacks against the American-allied French in 1779, had the late William Pitt (a key figure in Britain's victory in the Seven Years War a generation earlier) been at the helm, 'he would not have suffered the French soupmmaigres to insult the English beef-eaters'.[18]

Widely reprinted disparaging comments from French visitors haunted the British. One of several of Pierre-Jean Grosley's remarks from his translated and widely circulated account of his mid-century visit to London represents the host of derogatory French comments about British cookery that appeared in newspapers, magazines and travel accounts. 'I had heard a great deal of excellence of the meat which is eaten in England,' he sneered, 'but, after having used it in all the different shapes in which it is served up to tables, that is to say, both roast and boiled I could find in it neither the consistence, the juice, or the exquisiteness, of that of France.'[19] Some British commentators attempted to dismiss such remarks as obvious French bias, such as when the *Salisbury and Winchester Journal* reported on 'An amusing instance of national pride [that] occurred a day or two ago'. According to the newspaper,

> A French gentleman, of the true Bounaparte school of antipathy to England, was expressing his disgust at English buildings, English institutions, English cookery, English manner, &c. when an Englishman present . . . observed, 'At least you will allow our pavements are good.' 'No,' exclaimed the Frenchman, 'I hate them: they are so smooth and level that one knows not whether one is walking or sliding.'[20]

Nevertheless such derogatory remarks clearly stung.

Foreign acknowledgement of the quality of British food made national news. As a widely reprinted story in the *Derby Mercury*, which first circulated in the London papers, smugly announced in 1762, 'The French shall no longer be the only *Legislateurs de la Cuisine*, for the English Nation will soon share that Honour.' 'Mr. Tron, formerly chief Cook to the Cardinal de Bernis, and now chief Cook to one of the Princes of the Blood,' the story continued with a swelling of national pride, 'is actually set out for London, to learn the English Method of Cookery; so that if Food gives different Spirits (as Hippocrates has proved) our Nation, by eating like them, may gain a little of their Resolution.'[21] No victory was too small. Even the matter of French consumption of Cheshire cheese was a subject of comment, at least in the producing region's newspaper, which proclaimed in 1818 that the lately increased price of Cheshire cheese was a result of its exportation to France, where 'Cheshire Cheese is now considered as necessary an appendage to a French dinner table, as it is to an English one – with this difference, that our Gallic neighbour's eat much more of it.'[22] Supposedly unbiased third-party accounts that expressed a preference for British cookery were causes for jubilation. A nationally circulated newspaper story printed in the *Yorkshire Gazette* gleefully reported shortly after the cheese story that 'The French Papers, are reviewing the travels of the Persian Ambassador, Mirza Abdeel Khan, in Europe.' 'It appears that he visited England and France *incognito*, twelve years ago', the report continued, and 'The Parisian critics are extremely angry with his Excellency, for preferring English ladies and English cookery to French.'[23]

Concerns and anxieties

While many Britons took pleasure in the recent refinement of their nation's cookery and reflected with national pride on the diversity, quality and abundance of edible delights on offer, others used the opportunity to express a range of concerns. As one derisively remarked, 'had the English continued as Pagans, they would have invented a new deity to preside over cookery.'[24] As discussed in Part One, the consumption of the empire's ingestible goods was no small part of the debates on luxury that raged throughout the eighteenth century. Similarly, cookery was a magnet for critics who were less sanguine about the upswing in popular consumption and its impact on the nation's health.

Numerous respected figures engaged with the day's pressing questions about human social development discussed luxury, but few directly addressed the role of food more critically than Henry Home, Lord Kames. A judge and one of the most prominent figures of the Scottish Enlightenment, Kames wrote extensively about the development of human societies in his acclaimed *Sketches of the History of Man* (1774). For Kames, luxury in general and edible luxuries specifically posed a clear danger to Britain's recent ascent as a global power:

> In every great state, where the people, by prosperity and opulence, are sunk into voluptuousness, we hear daily complaints of depopulation. Cookery depopulates like a pestilence; because when it becomes an art, it brings within the compass of one stomach what is sufficient for ten in days of temperance.

According to Kames, abundance, quality and tastiness enticed people to eat more, making them obese and, in turn, lazy. France had long experienced this, he continued, but now the 'like is observable in Britain'. In fact, he claimed, 'Cookery and coaches have reduced the military spirit of the English nobility and gentry, to a languid state: the former, by overloading the body, has infected them with dispiriting ailments; the latter, by fostering ease and indolence, have banished labour, the only antidote for such ailments.' Such an environment, he railed, was 'weakening the power of procreation', because such luxurious outlets 'weaken . . . the appetite for procreation' among men, while obesity and the lack of physical movement made the women 'ill qualified for the severe labour of child-bearing'. 'A barren woman among the labouring poor', he mused, 'is a wonder.'[25] Kames's remarks were not isolated. Rather, they reflected deep national concerns about the longevity of British global power and the internal cultural threats to it. Over four decades earlier in a diatribe worthy of Kames, the *Caledonian Mercury* worried what would become of the nation's economy when the cost of luxurious cookery and edible foreign delicacies meant that funds 'sufficient to have kept an old English Squire with all his Hospitality, [were] scarce enough to defray the Expences in the Kitchen of a *modern tradesman*'.[26]

As Britain's imperial power grew, Britons increasingly asked the question of *how long will this last?*, wondering if the nation's downfall would be as rapid as its rise and looking to the past for clues. Not surprisingly, contemporary concerns about consumption and cookery were evident in Britons' readings of the past. Edward Gibbon's *The History of the Decline and Fall of the Roman Empire* (1776–88) emerged as the seminal work on the subject, but he was not alone in holding luxury accountable for the demise of once-great civilizations.[27] Gibbon regularly pointed to the contagiousness of luxury, even asserting that Attila accepted peace with Rome in 452 and withdrew his Hun army partly due to the debilitating effects of Italian cookery. The Huns' 'martial spirit was relaxed by the wealth and indolence of [the] warm climate' they found upon their invasion of Italy, Gibbon explained. Their 'ordinary food consisted of milk and raw flesh', he continued, but in Italy, they 'indulged themselves too freely in the use of bread, of wine, and of meat, prepared and seasoned by the arts of cookery'.[28] Edward Montagu's account blamed Asian luxuries for the decline of the Roman Empire. 'Ornamented couches, the rich carpets, the embroidered hangings and other expensive productions the looms of Asia', he argued, had led to 'heighten the mirth and indulgence of the table'. As a result of the 'expence and luxury of the table', he scornfully concluded, a 'cook, who by their frugal and temperate ancestors, was looked upon, from his very office, as the vilest slave in the houshold, was now esteemed an officer of mighty consequence, and cookery was erected into an art'.[29] The ancient Athenians were little better, with one British critic claiming that cookery had risen to such prestige that men received the freedom of the city solely because 'their father had been eminent in the art of cookery, and was famous for having introduced new sauces'.[30] The application of such lessons to Britain, where tavern chefs were becoming celebrities, required little deductive effort on the part of readers.

A favoured literary tool of the social critics of the period was the 'accidentally discovered' private letter from a visiting non-European to friends and family at home. While few readers likely accepted such letters as authentic, the critiques were common, appearing in newspapers, magazines and pamphlets with claimed authors ranging from South Pacific Islanders to Cherokee Indians. Such letters attempted to view British culture through a global lens, and food featured regularly. A typical example is a fictitious letter from a 'Persian', written anonymously by Sir George Lyttelton in 1761. In the letter home, the author remarks incredulously that 'I have seen a poor country gentleman sit down to one of these fine dinners . . . yet, for fear of being counted unpolite, not daring to refuse anything that was off'd him; but cramming and sweating with the struggle between his aversion and civility.' The occasional delicacy or luxurious meal for a celebratory event was acceptable and the custom of the author's culture, but the English practice went too far, to the detriment of the nation. 'Why then, said I, this continual extravagance?' he demanded. 'Why is this number of victims daily sacrificed to the daemon of luxury? How is it worth a man's while to undo himself, perhaps to undo his country, that his board may be grac'd with patties of perigord, when his guests had rather have the fowl from his barn-door?'[31]

Critics routinely responded to the perceived infiltration of unnecessarily fussy foreign cookery and manners of eating with nostalgic laments that idealized a simpler and more wholesome recent past. When discussing the job of cooks in 1747, even the *London Tradesman*, a careers guidebook intended 'for the information of parents, and the instruction of youth in their choice of business', offered a rare editorial on the state of the profession. By mid-century, it explained, any would-be cook was expected to be versed in French culinary skills. Mourning the loss of simplicity in English cookery, it remarked, 'We have of late Years refined ourselves out of that simple Taste, and conformed our Palates to Meats and Drinks dressed after the *French* fashion: The natural Taste of Fish or Flesh is become nauseous to our fashionable Stomach.' 'In the Days of good Queen Elizabeth', the guidebook continued, English cookery was not 'a Science or a Mistery' and 'required no Conjuration to please the Palate'. A fish tasted like a fish. Worse still, the English were not content with the concealing effects of French sauces: 'We abhor that any thing should appear on our Tables in its native Properties . . . [and so] all the Earth, from both the Poles, the most distant and different Climates, must be ransacked for spices, Pickles and Sauces, not to relish but to disguise our Food.' Rancorous commentary aside, the guidebook nevertheless advised acquiescence to anyone pursuing cookery as a profession: 'But it is to no purpose to preach against Luxury and French cookery; they have too powerful a Party in the nation: We must take the Cooks as they are, not as they ought be.' After all, the *London Tradesman* offered in a conclusion that returned to the purpose of the publication, 'cooks skilled in French cookery could earn a hundred pounds a year – only half that if versed in English cookery only'.[32]

Celebrations and commemorations drew particular attention. An especially sorrowful essay on the refinement of British food came in the form of a letter from 'An Old Fellow', first printed in the *London Magazine* in 1773. In his observance of New Year's celebrations, he bemoaned that 'Times, Sir, have changed.' 'In such a day as this', he reminisced, 'an English kitchen used to be the palace of Plenty, Jollity, and Good-eating. Every thing was plain and plenty. Here stood the large, plump juicy buttocks of English roast beef, and there smiled the frothy tankards of English beer.' Alas, he woefully continued, 'Now mark the picture of the present time: instead of that firm roast-beef, that fragrant pudding, our tables groan with the luxuries of France and India. Here a lean fricassee rises in the room of our majestic ribs; and there a scoundrel syllabub occupies the place of our well-beloved home-brewed.' Such a travesty, he declared, was

James Gillray, 'A keen-sighted Politician warming his Imagination' (London, 1795). In the print 'Lord-Pogy' (William Grenville, Secretary of State for Foreign Affairs) warms himself as he reads. On the mantel is a book titled *Court Cookery*.

simply anti-British. By adopting frivolous foreign cookery, people were 'forgetting that good-eating and good porter are the two great supporters of Magna Charta and the British constitution, we open our hearts and our mouths to new fashions in cookery, which will one day lead us into ruin'.[33] In contrast, celebrations that did not sink to adopt the frivolity and adulteration of foreign-tinged modern cookery earned public praise, such as in a reader's leader to the *Oxford Journal* that complimented a recent commemoration feast at the university's Corpus Christi College, 'where, upon six long tables, were displayed, neither borrowed magnificence nor foreign cookery, but a truly collegiate entertainment, whose characteristics were elegance without ostentation, and liberality without extravagance'.[34]

In this context of adulation of the simplicity of British cookery, the whole concept of cookery could be associated with falseness and obfuscation. With increasing frequency in the latter half of the eighteenth century, the terms 'political cookery' and 'state cookery' became synonymous with attempts to manipulate facts into favourable claims. In Parliament, Edmund Burke chastised a fellow MP for reconstituting earlier propositions into seemingly fresh arguments by declaring, '[I] disliked the hash; such French cookery was disagreeable to [my] stomach.'[35] Similarly, William Windham, Member of Parliament for St Mawes, remarked in his attempt before the House of Commons to cut through the government's misleading accounts of the state of the nation's military as it renewed its war with France in 1803, 'Why,

Isaac Robert Cruikshank, 'The Master Cook and his Black Scullion composing a Royal Hash' (London, 1820). A group of corrupt politicians under the Devil's direction manipulate a dish (a metaphor for an unsavoury bill) through cookery to make it palatable – 'a Dainty Dish to set before a King', as one of the characters describes it. Through the steam, George IV's face appears and declares, 'The Odour of this Cookery is exquisite!'

after all the State cookery, after stewing down pounds of beef, with dozens of chickens, a ham, and other ingredients, it turns out that the regular army has only acquired an addition of six thousand men to the former establishment.'[36] Such accusations extended to lawyers, newspaper editors and almost anyone thought to be dressing the facts in the manner ornate cooks dressed food. At the 1799 trial of Elizabeth Jones, indicted on the felonious crime of stealing two watch chains and twenty yards of silk, William Henbethel, the supposed victim, fell apart under tough questioning. The accusations, it turned out, were a sham and a conspiracy against poor Jones, who, it seems, has spurned Henbethel's romantic advances. Or, as the question put to Henbethel pointedly claimed, 'I believe there has been a little bit of cookery in this business; do you know any one of the witnesses, who has been prompting the others what to say; have they not been instructing each other what to say?' Jones was acquitted.[37]

A new genre of cookery books

The British consumer faced difficult terrain by mid-century when navigating the selection, acquisition, preparation and eating of food. Foreign ingredients and cookery offered consumers fresh opportunities to appear fashionable but invited disdain over accusations of luxury and unnecessary complication. Meanwhile, growing literacy, print culture and social interaction gave a bully pulpit to all manner of critics and blurred the distinctions between domestic and public spaces. Worse still, the public discourse on society and civilization (and where the British fitted within the global hierarchy) heavily emphasized the importance of food, thus reminding Britons that what they ate and how they ate it reflected not only themselves, but their nation.

The popular response was to embrace a new genre of cookery book that took hold in the second half of the eighteenth century. These widely appealing household guides gained national prominence by successfully negotiating the pitfalls of frivolity without alienating those who aspired to be fashionable. Dominated by the very women who were emerging as important actors in the rise of consumerism in Britain, these books set the standards for a British approach to food and the parameters for a national cuisine, and they solidified the association between the quality of the food on the table and the moral quality of a household. These were not simply printed collections of recipes; rather, they were purposefully constructed guides to both the social and technical mazes of cookery in Britain.

The lives of Hannah Glasse and Elizabeth Raffald, whose names are associated with two of the most successful cookery books of the era, *The Art of Cookery Made Plain and Easy* and *The Experienced English Housekeeper* respectively, highlight the entrepreneurial spirit and often humble origins of the women who shaped British cookery. Born out of wedlock in London, Glasse was raised by her father's middling Northumberland family before she married a junior officer in the British Army. The couple suffered financially from a series of poor business ventures, and by the 1740s, Glasse, then a widow in London, was a dressmaker with one of her daughters. One enterprise that proved successful was her cookery book, which appeared in 1747 and remained in continuous print for over a century, enjoying dozens of editions. Initially supported by a subscription – a tactic often employed when the author lacked the personal means or commercial backing to publish something – Glasse's book soon attracted national attention as part of the emerging market of cookery books that targeted female readers and middling households.[38] Elizabeth Raffald was a Yorkshire housekeeper who married the estate's head gardener in 1763 and left service. She and her husband supported themselves through a number of ventures, including offering cookery lessons to the local urban gentry, opening a grocery, publishing a trade directory and operating the Exchange Coffee House in Manchester.[39]

Although Glasse and Raffald launched their own books, they became household names through the marketing efforts of male publishers, who recognized the new genre for its commercial potential. Bankruptcy forced Glasse to sell the rights to her book in 1754, and then it truly flourished. Leading London publishers including Thomas Longman, William Strahan and John Almon vied for the rights to print new editions of her book, placing it in the same publishing houses that produced Adam Smith's *Wealth of Nations* and Edward Gibbon's *Decline and Fall of the Roman Empire*. Similarly, although Raffald published the first edition of her book in Manchester in 1769, her book rose to national prominence after her death in 1781 under the stewardship of a series of leading metropolitan publishers that included the likes of Richard Baldwin, a

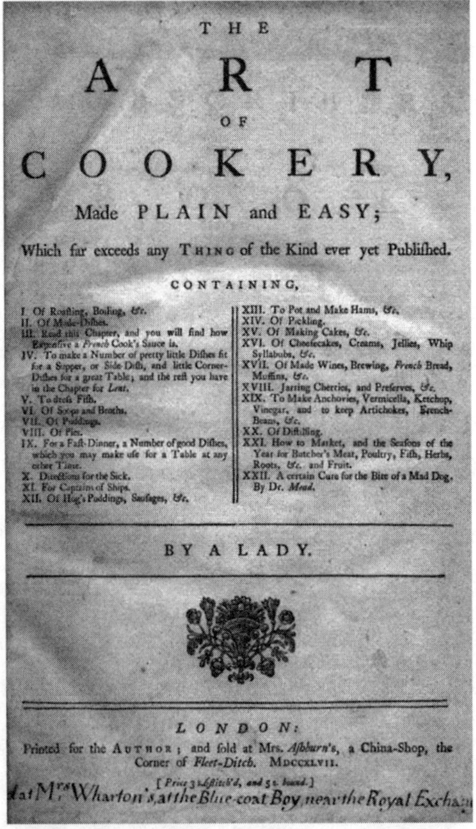

THE

ART

OF

COOKERY,

Made PLAIN and EASY;

Which far exceeds any THING of the Kind ever yet Publiſhed.

CONTAINING,

I. Of Roaſting, Boiling, &c.
II. Of Made-Diſhes.
III. Read this Chapter, and you will find how Expenſive a *French* Cook's Sauce is.
IV. To make a Number of pretty little Diſhes fit for a Supper, or Side-Diſh, and little Corner-Diſhes for a great Table; and the reſt you have in the Chapter for *Lent*.
V. To dreſs Fiſh.
VI. Of Soops and Broths.
VII. Of Puddings.
VIII. Of Pies.
IX. For a Faſt-Dinner, a Number of good Diſhes, which you may make uſe for a Table at any other Time.
X. Directions for the Sick.
XI. For Captains of Ships.
XII. Of Hog's Puddings, Sauſages, &c.
XIII. To Pot and Make Hams, &c.
XIV. Of Pickling.
XV. Of Making Cakes, &c.
XVI. Of Cheeſecakes, Creams, Jellies, Whip Syllabubs, &c.
XVII. Of Made Wines, Brewing, *French* Bread, Muffins, &c.
XVIII. Jarring Cherries, and Preſerves, &c.
XIX. To Make Anchovies, Vermicella, Ketchup, Vinegar, and to keep Artichokes, French-Beans, &c.
XX. Of Diſtilling.
XXI. How to Market, and the Seaſons of the Year for Butcher's Meat, Poultry, Fiſh, Herbs, Roots, &c. and Fruit.
XXII. A certain Cure for the Bite of a Mad Dog. By Dr. *Mead*.

BY A LADY.

LONDON:

Printed for the AUTHOR; and ſold at Mrs. *Aſhburn's*, a China-Shop, the Corner of *Fleet-Ditch*. MDCCXLVII.

[*Price* 3s. *ſtitch'd, and* 5s. *bound.*]

at Mrs Wharton's, at the Blue-coat Boy, near the Royal Excha

Title page to Hannah Glasse's *The Art of Cookery, Made Plain and Easy* (1747). The first edition lists the author as 'By a Lady'; Glasse's name did not appear on the book until after her death in 1770.

member of the prominent Baldwin family who published newspapers, magazines and leading authors.

One might interpret Glasse and Raffald as victims of men who used their privilege to exploit the women's labours for considerable profit. However, such a narrow understanding misses the cultural importance of their books. By the 1780s virtually all of the major London publishers included a cookery book on their lists, and, while one can only guess at a total production number during the eighteenth century, conservative estimates are for over half a million copies – the majority of which appeared in the last three decades.[40] The likes of Glasse, Raffald and other female authors had the impetus to reshape the cookery book genre, but the London publishers contrived to multiply their importance exponentially by turning them into household names and something akin to commercial brands. First, the publishers printed a steady and lucrative stream of revised editions, thus keeping the brand fresh. Second, they emphasized the authors more than the authors had themselves. Glasse, for example, never gave her name on the editions she produced, instead publishing them anonymously as 'By a Lady'. The London publishers personalized the book by listing her as the author, thus making her a household name only after her death in 1770. Henceforth, Glasse's name was featured prominently in order to associate it with the book. In the case of Raffald, the publishers went even further by adding a portrait of her. The portrait was highly unlikely one of Raffald, primarily because it changed noticeably over time. At first, Raffald was an older woman, who then became decidedly younger and eventually took on a youthful appearance. The latest editions, printed by different publishers, were a mix of images. Marketing presumably played a role as publishers vacillated between promoting the book as sage wisdom from an elderly woman, guidance from an older aunt and advice for young housewives and housekeepers from a peer.

From Elizabeth Raffald, *The Experienced English Housekeeper, For the Use and Ease of Ladies, Housekeepers, Cooks, &c.*, 8th edition (1782).

From Elizabeth Raffald, *The Experienced English Housekeeper, For the Use and Ease of Ladies, Housekeepers, Cooks, &c.* (1803).

Crucially, the success of Glasse, Raffald and women like them compelled male cooks to conform to their style, thus driving the genre. For instance, James Scatcherd, who published the *European Magazine* and whose authors included Samuel Johnson, enlisted John Farley and the duo of Francis Collingwood and John Woollams, the renowned chefs of the famed London Tavern and the Crown and Anchor, respectively, to publish two of the first celebrity-chef cookbooks, complete with favourable prefacing portraits.[41] These venues were the height of London dining. After dining at the London Tavern, William Hickey reflected in his memoirs that the experience 'surpassed every other tavern we went to. The dinner excellent, served in a style of magnificence peculiar to that house, wines all their best.' The rival Crown and Anchor boasted a huge ballroom for grand entertainments, where Charles James Fox celebrated his birthday in 1798, entertaining 2,000 guests.[42] Importantly, the cookery books attributed to their elite cooks were not professional instruction manuals. Instead, Collingham and Woollams openly revered the likes of Glasse and Raffald as inspirations, freely noting that they had adopted and adapted the women's recipes – an unimaginable admission just a few decades earlier. 'It will from

John Farley, *The London Art of Cookery* (1783). The image below Farley's portrait is of the celebrated London Tavern.

hence follow', they explained after praising a number of female authors by name, 'that we do not presume to arrogate to ourselves the Reputation of having ushered into the World a Work entirely new, which indeed cannot be expected.'[43] Farley's best-selling book, first published in 1783, consciously modelled its organizational structure on other domestic guides and stated its intended broad appeal plainly in the preface:

> As this Work is intended for the Use of all Ranks in general, not only for those who have attained a tolerable Knowledge of Cookery, but also for those who are but young in Experience, we have occasionally given the most simple with the most sumptuous Dishes, and thereby directed them how properly to decorate the Table of either the Peer or the Mechanic.

The extent to which the celebrity cooks contributed to the books that carried their names is questionable, particularly in Farley's case.[44] However, in this regard they differed little from many of the other commercially successful books in the genre, whose original female authors had a direct connection to only the first few editions. Regardless, there was little grumbling at the time on the subject, and, in the case of Farley, the London Tavern proudly endorsed the work, selling copies on its premises.

As with the sale of any product, the new cookery books' success relied on their ability to identify, address and appeal to a broad base of customers. Manuscript recipe collections had circulated privately among women for hundreds of years, but the shift to revising and printing these collections as household advice books for public consumption was a decidedly mid-eighteenth-century phenomenon. Partly, this change reflected the demographics within the cookery profession. As in other parts of Europe, the growth of the middling ranks in Britain meant a greater demand for household cooks; and male cooks, as in almost all professions, were far more expensive than their female counterparts, typically with salaries three or four times higher.[45] Women continued to do the bulk of the grunt work both in domestic and public kitchens, but women also increasingly managed the operations as housekeepers, grocers, food-cart owners and coffeehouse proprietresses.

However, and more important to the subject of the present book, the new cookery books' success reflects the emergence of a national

Francis Collingwood and John Woollams, 'Principal Cooks at the Crown and Anchor Tavern in the Strand, late from the London Tavern', frontispiece for *The Universal Cook, and City and Country Housekeeper* (1792).

consumer culture shaped by both food and women's participation. This consciously included aspiring households from manufacturing trades. For example, an earthenware decorator working at Worcester & Bow or a skilled cutler could purchase any one of the books for one or two days' wages.[46] Anticipating such an audience, William Augustus Henderson pledged in his *Housekeeper's Instructor; or, Universal Family Cook*, 'The Receipts for each article are formed on so easy and cheap a Plan, as to be within the Purchase of all Ranks of People.'[47] Similarly, books advertised themselves to servants wanting to advance themselves, which made sense considering that advertisements for housekeepers and female cooks expected applicants to be literate and trained.[48] As the opening line of an advertisement in *The Times* in 1811 makes clear, the employer expected the female cook to have the skills of a man: 'WOMAN COOK. – WANTED, for a Family, a complete WOMAN COOK, who has been brought up under Men Cooks, and understands Foreign cookery.'[49]

Nevertheless, the middling ranks likely consumed the great majority of the books. The men and women who bought them were the same people who transformed tea into the favoured domestic beverage and made it synonymous with polite socialization. They shrewdly used credit to source the empire's ingestibles from both local and national suppliers and acquired the latest utensils and drinking vessels to stage their sitting rooms as expressions of taste and wealth. They were from the broadening middling ranks who found themselves running households with servants for the first time, as well as members of the gentry who found themselves under increased scrutiny and wanted to appear fashionable. In short, the books sought to reach the great swathes of people who found themselves wrapped up in eighteenth-century consumer society. Buying, preparing and eating food was something people did already; the new cookery books, like the guides to manners and advertisements discussed earlier, advised on how to accomplish these tasks well and to their advantage.

As with any self-help genre, the issue of prescription versus practice with regard to the new cookery books is a topic worth exploring.[50] Undoubtedly, these books were somewhat idealistic. The illustrations showed calm, well-dressed mistresses and well-groomed and industrious servants, and everyone was physically fit and attractive. Nothing was burnt, and the work and dining spaces were immaculate. Moreover, like today, owning a cookery book was not the same thing

Eliza Fowler Haywood, *A New Present for a Servant Maid: Containing Rules for her Moral Conduct both with Respect to Herself and her Superiors.* The engraving was produced for the new 1771 edition of the book. In it, a servant consults a cookery book.

as cooking from it, and modern homes are littered with cookery books whose recipes remain untried. In fact, one woman's recent crusade to cook through an entire book of well-known recipes was so unorthodox that it became the subject of a popular blog, book and film.[51] Unfortunately, we have limited archaeological evidence of how users engaged with the books. The sheer volume of cheap copies and ever-renewing editions in circulation meant that they were not particularly valuable as second-hand books, and, like similar materials, rarely merited mention in auctions or probate records. Moreover, collectors and archivists could afford to be highly selective, typically choosing copies in pristine condition and without the historically useful handwritten annotations and thumbed pages sometimes found in limited editions of expensive books. Some evidence of practice is found in diaries and letters, such as the private correspondence of the novelist and playwright Fanny Burney, who treated Glasse's book as the standard of British cookery, citing it by page number and edition in her diary critique of a friend's dinner.[52] Samuel Johnson and his dinner party agreed that Glasse's book was the best available.[53] Unfortunately, the men and women whose diaries and private correspondence survive are exceptional in their own right, and few among them delved into the tedium of which cookery book or recipe they used on a given day. Some bills of fare have survived from a handful of elite households, but these are hardly representative of the wider population's habits.[54]

Still, these books clearly were intended to be used, not simply admired. Authors professed an ardent desire to employ an accessible written style for the benefit of the less literate and novice alike. Glasse set the precedent, explaining in her preface the reasons for her departure from the professional language of other cookery books: 'If I have not wrote in the high, polite Stile, I hope I shall be forgiven; for my Intention is to instruct the lower Sort, and therefore must treat them in their own Way.' 'So in many other Things in Cookery', she continued, 'the great Cooks have such a high Way of expressing themselves, that the poor Girls are at a Loss to know what they mean.' In short, as Glasse pledged in her preface, anyone can cook if armed with her book.

> As I have both seen, and found by Experience, that the Generality of Servants are greatly wanting in that Point [cookery], therefore I have taken upon me to instruct them in the best Manner I am capable; and, I dare say, that every Servant who can but read will be capable of making a tolerable good Cook, and those who have the least Notion of Cookery, can't miss of being very good ones.[55]

The 'great cooks' themselves adapted. As Richard Briggs, a well-known London cook and then principal cook at the famed Temple Coffee-House, assured readers in his 1788 *The English Art of Cookery, According to the Present Practice*, fashionable cookery need not be complicated. 'I have bestowed every Pain to render them [recipes] easily practicable, and adapted to the Capacities of those who may be ordered to use them,' he pledged. After all, Briggs concluded, 'To waste Language and high terms on such Subjects, appears to me to render the Art of Cookery embarrassing, and to throw Difficulties in the Way of the Learner.'[56]

The books were both plainly organized and comprehensive. Lengthy tables of contents broken into subsections defined by areas of household management were standard by the 1780s, and, from mid-century onwards, detailed indexes prevailed, enabling the user to reference a particular recipe among the hundreds on offer with ease. The recipes themselves were subdivided into styles of cookery or the main feature of a dish, such as vegetables, fish or poultry. Each recipe received its own name and corresponding page number within the subsection. The books advertised themselves as being comprehensive, almost invariably using such phrases as 'complete system of cookery' or 'cookery in all its various branches', and they offered reservoirs of useful advice to make good on such promises. The level of detail and comprehensiveness in the instructions was nothing short of impressive. As Martha Bradley explained in the opening lines of her 1770 *The British Housewife*, 'We are to conduct the Cook and the Housekeeper throughout the year, and we begin with the first month.'[57] Bills of fare, complete with illustrations to demonstrate, in the words of Glasse, how 'the Manner of the dishes are to be placed upon the Table, in the present Taste', were regularly included, particularly when increased competition in the 1780s led to the addition of more images. For instance, Charlotte Mason's *Lady's Assistant* prepared the user for every occasion, providing 'one hundred and fifty select bills of fare, properly disposed for family dinners of five dishes, to two courses of eleven and fifteen with upwards of fifty bills of fare for suppers, from five dishes to nineteen'. Most cookery books also included seasonal guides for shopping, advice on selecting the best produce and meat, useful numerical tables for quick calculations, directions for carving, labelled butcher's illustrations of animals, basic medical remedies and advice on managing servants.

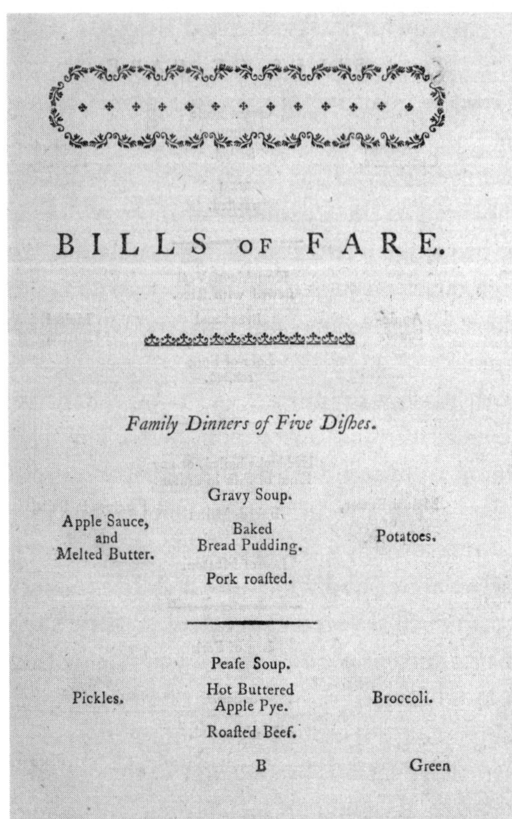

BILLS OF FARE.

Family Dinners of Five Diſhes.

Gravy Soup.

Apple Sauce, and Melted Butter. — Baked Bread Pudding. — Potatoes.

Pork roaſted.

Peaſe Soup.

Pickles. — Hot Buttered Apple Pye. — Broccoli.

Roaſted Beef.

B — Green

Bill of fare for a family dinner of five dishes, from Charlotte Mason, *The Lady's Assistant*, 6th edition (1787).

Whether or not people who kept a copy of Mason's cookery book diligently employed its instructions to make 'Hams, the Yorkshire Way' is not essential to the primary subject of this chapter or the book as a whole. The primary issue here is that of perception – the formation of an ideal and the desire and expectation to pursue it. By 1800 fewer than 2,000 steam engines were produced, they were fraught with problems, and they made little initial cumulative impact on the economy.[58] However, each represented an investment in an ideal, and the discussions surrounding them produced the perception that Britain was industrializing, which in turn prompted clamorous debates and vociferous responses – not unlike the public and private discussions surrounding the changing British diet in the eighteenth century. Thus cookery books could be purchased and read out of aspiration – not unlike the modern reader who thumbs through an illustrated cookery book looking for inspiration, idealizing the perfect Christmas dinner, reminiscing nostalgically about a

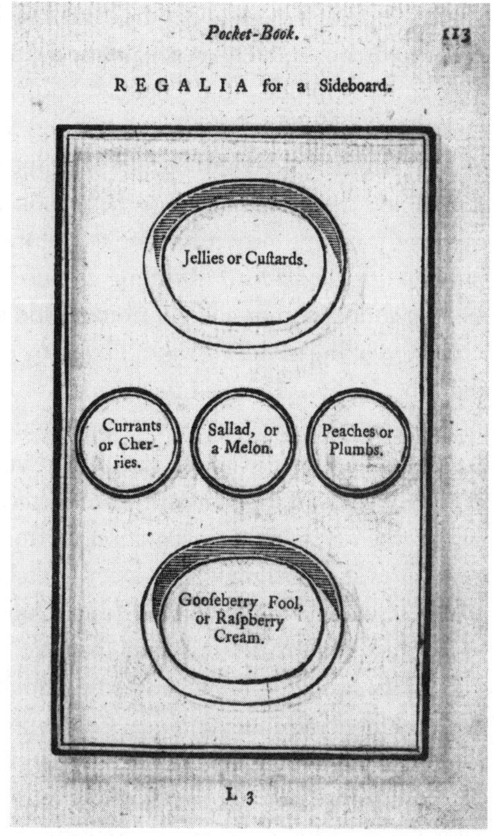

Bill of fare entitled 'Regalia for a Sideboard' in Sarah Harrison, *The House-Keeper's Pocket-Book, and Compleat Family Cook*, 6th edition (1757).

favourite childhood treat or imagining an exotic foreign dish. Certainly, enough Britons engaged with these cookery books that their turns of phrase entered the mainstream, and references to them appeared even in unrelated contexts. As with her most successful counterparts, Glasse's phraseology entered into mainstream English. 'Made plain and easy', from the title of her cookery book, became a stock phrase in everything from political negotiations to printed instructions of all types. When remarking on politics and finances in 1802, *The Times* advised that 'Speculists of every denomination would do well to attend to the sure system of Mrs. Glass's [*sic*] Cookery, who begins her receipt for dressing a favourite fish with "*first catch your Chub*."'[59]

Inventing British cookery

Ultimately, these books created a sense of community through their ubiquity and style. Scholars have emphasized the connecting power of print in an age of great cultural and social change.[60] Yet the focus has been predominately on the political discourse found in newspapers and pamphlets, and cookery books have been largely, and undeservedly, absent from the discussion. Food has been a binding force in families and communities since the dawn of humanity. Print culture and the proliferation of these cookery books added a virtual layer to the community, recording traditions, standardizing practices and creating identities.[61] Running a household for the first time or moving to London or a larger home could be intimidating. The enlargement of the middling ranks, changing expectations of the gentry and urbanization all meant that many women did not have the same experiences and local networks as in generations past. As Mason explained, her book would be useful 'particularly to the younger part of my sex, who, on their entering into life, may not have those advantages which arise from instruction or from practice, and who are sometimes at a loss how to conduct their table with that decency and propriety, which are much to be desired, not only in making dinners for company, but in a family way likewise'. Of course, older women sometimes needed a refresher, and no doubt these books appealed to a multigenerational audience. As the preface to Mrs Frazer's *The Practice of Cookery, Pastry, Pickling, Preserving, &c.* remarked, 'if they [recipes] can in any degree contribute to the improvement of the young, or as a help and remembrancer to those of riper years and experience, she [the author] will think her labor amply rewarded.'[62]

The women, and sometimes men, who used these books essentially were inviting strangers into their homes and entrusting them with their family's health and their own self-esteem. Accordingly, a degree of confidence was essential, and the books established this by familiarizing the authors. The tools available included authors' portraits, illustrations of familiar kitchen scenes, descriptions of authors' backgrounds and highly personalized prefaces. Female authors in particular regularly asserted that the recipes came from their own vast experiences, either in running households of their own or in service as housekeepers and cooks. As Sarah Harrison pledged to her readers as early as 1733, 'the Contents are wholly furnish'd from my own Experience, and therefore ladies may depend more safely upon them.' Three-quarters of a century later, the message of comfort had not changed. Maria Rundell remarked in the first edition of what would become one of the most successful cookery books of the nineteenth century that her recipes and advice could be relied upon, because 'the following directions were intended for the conduct of the families of the authoress's own daughters, and for the arrangement of their table, so as to unite a good figure with proper economy'.[63] Successful authors thus invited readers into the comfort of their own kitchens, like extended family or seasoned mentors, to provide tested advice and intimate knowledge. Partly in consequence, the most successful cookery books and household guides, which enjoyed lifetime print runs in the tens of thousands and new and reprinted editions that spanned generations, had an incredible cultural influence. Together, these cookery books and the discussions surrounding them laid a foundation for a British cuisine that embodied the values of the eighteenth century's emerging middle class yet proved sufficiently timeless to enable future generations to build upon them.

Simplicity was at the heart of the culinary style. Yet this was not simplicity rooted in austerity or artlessness; rather, it was engrained in an adulation for uncomplicatedness and unpretentiousness to the point of being a moral quality. Authors regularly lambasted the British elite and those who aped them for latching on to French cuisine for the sake of fashion. As Glasse remarked in her book's preface, 'Such is the blind Folly of this Age, that they would rather be impos'd on by a French Booby, than give Encouragement to a good English Cook.' Commentators ridiculed foreign cuisine not so much for its lack of appeal to the palate, but for its unnecessary complexity and ostentatiousness. In consequence, virtually all of the popular books discussed here openly adopted and adapted French recipes, terminology and techniques, but not without some premeditation and the occasional justification. As Raffald noted in her preface, 'though I have given some of my Dishes French Names, as they are only known by those Names, yet they will not be found very Expensive, nor add Compositions but as plain as the Nature of the Dish will admit of'. In consequence, such terms as *en daube*, *à la braize* and *fricassée* lost much of their original meanings, as well as spelling, in British cookery during the second half of the century. For example, while *fricassée* referred to the Continental European technique (practised under this term in England for centuries) of sautéing meat, typically chicken, in oil at low temperatures and then braising it in a sauce, new cookery books adapted it into 'fricasey' and included frying almost anything, including eggs.[64]

Economy was imperative. In its various forms and meanings, economy was at the forefront of both private and public discussions in Britain. The national economy and the government's role in nurturing it was a subject of unending and intense debate – both in Parliament and the press – that drew in Britons of all ranks and genders. After all, disagreements on how to regulate the economy toppled governments and sparked protests in the American colonies that led to rebellion. In consequence, tables and charts filled the pages of the burgeoning British press, detailing agricultural prices, troop movements, government expenditures and budgets. The public desire to understand and use this information resulted in increased literacy and numeracy among the population as a whole.[65] Such interest spilled into people's private lives, particularly among those who aspired to make the most of their newfound or dwindling discretionary income. Surviving private journals, diaries and correspondence are packed with details of expenditures and budgetary lists to the point that their absence is unconventional.

Not surprisingly, 'economy' increasingly took on a meaning of efficiency, especially in reference to the household economy. Women, whether as mistresses or housekeepers, demonstrated their virtues by managing the household economy in such a way as to discourage waste and frivolity and make the most of the resources available. As meals were frontstage activities in which a husband, wider family and guests participated, the management of food was a critical opportunity to demonstrate the quality of a household's economy and, by implication, the worthiness of the woman who ran it. Such economy-conscious titles as *The Prudent Housewife* and *The Frugal Housewife* peppered the lists of books.[66] As Harrison commented in the first edition of her 1733 book, 'How lightly soever Men esteem those Feminine Arts of Government which are practiced in the Regulation of an Houshold, I may venture to assert, that they are of much more intrinsick Value than some admired Branches of Literature'. 'For, to say the Truth,' she continued, 'what can be really of greater Use, than by Prudence and good Management to supply a Family with all things that are convenient, from a Fortune which, without such Care, would scarce afford common Necessaries?'[67] Two generations later, Charlotte Mason concurred by remarking, 'It is certain, that a woman never appears to greater advantage than at the head of a Well-Regulated table; which should be always so supplied, that the unexpected visit of a friend, or even a stranger, should occasion no inconvenience or confusion.' 'A table may be so conducted', she concluded, 'as to be the credit to the taste and management of the mistress.'[68]

Frugality, however, did not necessarily mean austerity, and so cookery and presentation needed to incorporate fashion. Cookery books thus positioned themselves as guides through that confusing maze, offering the assurance of the latest recipes and techniques via regularly updated editions while avoiding a level of ostentatiousness that would invite criticism. Balance, with the aim of value for money, was key. In his 1768 cookery book intended 'for the use of families', James Jenks offered socially aspiring readers an entire section on 'The Art of dressing Common Provisions in the genteelest and least expensive manner'.[69] After lambasting her competition for unnecessary 'ostentation, hurry, or bustle' as well as 'extravagant and useless steps', the Edinburgh-based Mrs Frazer nevertheless assured her readers that she had included plenty of dishes that were 'presently in vogue'.[70] Although employing the title *Domestic Economy* for his book, Maximilian Hazlemore promised his readers elegance and taste within its pages. 'I have carefully excluded all extravagant, and almost impractical [recipes]', he explained, and 'the most frugal and least dishes have generally been preferred'. Nevertheless, he promised, 'care has been taken that nothing should be omitted that might gratify the appetite of the epicure'.[71] And sometimes less was more in the way of fashion. As Maria Rundell explained to her readers enduring the inflation of the Napoleonic Wars, 'Generally speaking, dinners are far less sumptuous than formerly, when half a dozen dishes were supplied for what one now costs; consequently those whose fortunes are not great, and who wish to make a genteel appearance without extravagance, regulate their table accordingly.' Therefore, she continued, in the present age, 'It is not the multiplicity of things, but the choice, the dressing and the neat pleasing look of the whole, which gives respectability to her who presides.'[72]

As a genre, the books also promoted conformity in British cookery. To a great extent, this was purposeful. The authors were, after all, writing guidebooks to assist readers with limited knowledge of the subjects of cookery and household management. In a marketing strategy worthy of a modern agency, the authors created demand by fuelling anxiety. They promoted the view that a badly run household, defined by a lack of adherence to the standards established in the cookery books, reflected a moral failing within the mistress or housekeeper – a situation that invited ridicule. Buying and adhering to a reputable book's household guidance was the way to protect oneself, and one's family, from shame. Moreover, authors assumed an authoritative tone, supported by claims of decades of experience and associations with famous eating venues, and explicitly in the linguistic tone of the writing. Through their instructions, the books set standards for such food-related topics as the number of dishes in a course, the number of courses in a meal, which dishes belonged to a particular season and, via shopping guides, what constituted quality ingredients. They also defined what was unnecessarily ostentatious and what was prudently frugal, yet fashionable.

Less intentionally, they lent uniformity to British cookery by replacing manuscript collections and narrowing the definitions of familiar dishes. This is a natural development that has affected a multitude of cultures around the world following the widespread adoption of new communication technologies, such as print or radio – leading to standardization in spelling, dialect, pronunciation and, in the case of food, cookery. In eighteenth-century Britain, a comparatively similar group of printed cookery books rapidly replaced a much more diverse body of manuscripts – a process that would continue in Britain and be repeated globally. For example, a wide diversity of recipes for Christmas puddings almost certainly existed throughout Britain in the oral traditions and manuscript collections that preceded the new household cookery books. The new books, however, demonstrate a great deal of consistency, resulting in something akin to what might appear on a British table today. Not only did such books define how a Christmas pudding should look and taste, they propped it up as the expected Yuletide treat that would spread across the British Empire. Moreover, to reach the widest audiences possible, cookery books typically targeted audiences in the 'town and country', blending urban and rural and inevitably lessening regional differences.[73]

The rampant reprinting of other authors' recipes only exacerbated this. While plagiarism or intellectual property theft is perhaps too harsh an accusation given the eighteenth-century context, in which most newspapers were cut-and-paste collections of circulating news, the level of repetition is staggering, to the point that many cookery books by the end of the century were primarily curated collections of borrowed recipes. The fact that most of the editions of successful cookery books appeared after the authors' deaths, yet included all sorts of 'new' recipes and bills of fare, only worsened matters. Some authors, such as Mary Cole, took offence. 'I should before have observed, that in reading the various books upon this subject which have been printed, I soon perceived that every subsequent writer had borrowed very largely from those who had preceded,' she complained in a rare personalized attack against her competition. Even 'Mrs. Glasse's book contains the best receipts which she could discover in the four esteemed works of this kind then extant', Cole noted, and 'Mrs. Mason, Mrs. Raffald, and Mr. Farley, have pursued similar steps; but have not, like myself, candidly acknowledged their obligations.'[74] Yet Cole was almost singular in her degree of public outrage, and to expect cookery books to adhere to levels of intellectual ownership akin to scientific discovery is unfair. As a genre, the traditional manuscript recipe collections from which the new printed cookery books emerged were about borrowing, trading and improving; thus many of these collections were living works, recording the knowledge, aspirations and experiences of multiple generations and families. While claims of originality were part of the marketing scheme, authors did not rely heavily upon them, choosing instead to assert their worth as prudent selectors of worthy recipes from the overwhelming number in circulation.

Ironically, the authors themselves heavily promoted regional variations and cookery, thus fostering a sense of regional diversity as part of British identity. Although references to British place names were comparatively few in the books published before mid-century, they abounded afterward, increasing as the decades progressed. Glasse, for example, by her 1751 edition offered many, including four types of regionally named pie – Cheshire, Devonshire, Shropshire and Yorkshire. Cleland, based in Edinburgh, acted similarly with Oxford sausages, Irish pancakes, Norfolk dumplings and Bath buns, to name just a few.[75] By the 1770s, such recipes as Oxford pudding, Shrewsbury cakes and Norfolk dumplings had become classics that could be found in most of the popular cookery books with relatively little variation between the recipes. Regionalism surged as the century wore on, with books adding regional techniques. Hazlemore, for example, included the usual array of named dishes, openly noting his sources for some of them, such as Cheshire pork pie, which he borrowed from Glasse, Mason and Farley, and he added 'Chickens after the Scottish manner' and 'Soup sante the English way'. Books further highlighted variation by grouping similar recipes together (either in the indexes or within the pages themselves). Mason's *Lady's Assistant*, for example, includes recipes for common, Worcestershire, New England and Scotch pancakes by the 1778 edition. The differences were slight, as the primary ingredients were flour, eggs and milk. Her New England pancakes, for example, added only cinnamon. The English, Scottish and Welsh versions of cheese on toasted bread, or rarebit (referred to at the time as 'rabbit'), became standard by the 1790s, and typically appeared one after the other in books for easy comparison.

Scottish cookery, in particular, enjoyed a newfound appreciation. During much of the eighteenth century, and earlier, it had been derided. In his published tour through Britain in the 1720s, for example, Daniel Defoe representatively indexed the experience of Scots cookery under 'cookery, *very nasty*'.[76] During the second half of the century, this changed. A multitude of reasons are credited for this shift in English attitudes expressed in general towards Scots – greater economic cooperation, the virtual elimination of Jacobitism and its threat to the Union, generations of integration of Scots into the political and military establishment and the prominence of the Scottish Enlightenment, among others.[77] Of relevance here is that English softening towards the Scots included a recognition of the merits of Scottish culture, including food. As Samuel Johnson observed of Scottish food in the published account of his trip through Scotland in the 1770s, the differences from English food were not altogether great, and nor were the amount or quality of their tableware. The contrast appeared in 'Their more elaborate cookery, or made dishes'. Rather than chastise the dishes for their alien taste, Johnson open-mindedly recognized his own bias and judged them by their merits. 'An Englishman at the first taste is not likely to approve' of the dishes, he remarked, 'but the culinary compositions of every country are often such as become grateful to other nations only by degrees'.[78] William Guthrie, in his *New Geographical, Historical, and Commercial Grammar*, attributed the improvement in traditional Scottish highland cookery to a combination of a love of tradition and new economic prosperity. Highland Scots 'affect a fondness for the memory and language of their forefathers beyond, perhaps, any people in the world . . . [and] they retain it abroad as well as home', he observed. In consequence, he continued, 'They are fond of the antient Scotch dishes, such as the hoggice [haggis].' 'These dishes, in their original dressing, were savoury and nutritive for keen appetites', Guthrie explained, 'but the modern improvements that have been made in the Scotch cookery, have rendered them agreeable to the most delicate palates.'[79] By the 1780s, Scottish recipes abound in cookery books, including 'Scotch barley soup', 'Scotch collops', 'Scotch pancakes', 'Scotch soup', 'Scotch chickens' and 'Scotch cocky-leaky'. Recipes for haggis appeared, too, with two different methods offered in the 1778 edition of Glasse's celebrated book.

Scottish cultural festivities, such as those celebrating St Andrew, Scotland's patron saint, and the poet Robert Burns, proliferated throughout Britain in the early nineteenth century. Public accounts of the festivities almost inevitably detailed the traditional food on offer. As the *Morning Post* noted in its description of London's St Andrew's Day festivities of 1815, 'Profound respect was paid to St. Andrew's favourite fare, the Sawney Haggis and Highland Whiskey . . . [as is] usual with the Sons of Caledonia on such occasions.'[80] The poet Robert Burns's famed 'Address to a Haggis', which features in modern Burns Night celebrations, was a firm fixture from the start. The tradition began in 1801 when a group of Burns's friends gathered in memoriam at his former home in Alloway five years after his death, and the event soon became a celebration of the poet and Scottish culture, with an emphasis on traditional cookery, across the country and beyond. As the *Carlisle Patriot* observed in its coverage of the occasion in 1817, 'we were happy to observe some highly appropriate dishes, particularly "the chieftain o' the puding race" – a gude Scottish haggis' – a line taken from Burns's poem.[81]

When George IV visited Scotland in 1822, the first visit by a reigning monarch in almost two centuries, the organizer, Sir Walter Scott, ensured that the experience was an orchestrated cultural immersion. While much has been made about the visit's elevation of tartan into Scotland's national, rather than Highland, identity – the king wore and later had a portrait of himself made in a tartan kilt – at the time the food drew more attention in the press.[82] In a verse stylized as lines from a Burns poem, the *London Examiner* proclaimed upon news of the king's arrival in Scotland, 'Let his glorious Kingship dine, On gude sheep heads and haggis fine; Gie him whisky 'stead o' wine'.[83] A number of Scots-authored cookery books, which differed little from their English-authored counterparts, had enjoyed national audiences for decades. However, in the context of the king's visit, some took on airs of cultural celebrations, such Margaret Dods's *The Cook and Housewife's Manual*, which dedicated thirteen pages to 'Scotch National Dishes'. Dods, the principal cook at the Cleikum Inn, St Ronan's, drew national attention when her book was sold throughout Britain and published simultaneously in Edinburgh and London. In a widely reprinted review, *The Scotsman* fawned over the book, praising the preface 'written in the style of the prefaces to the Waverly novels' and the inclusion of 'the leading *national dishes* of Scotland, beginning with the venerable *haggis*'.[84]

THREE KEY THEMES run through the national discourse on cookery during this period, whether discussions took place in the kitchen or the press. First, practices of preparation gave food meaning. In other words, how something was prepared mattered as much as the ingredients. Second, British cookery was asserted to be unique. Cooks and commentators alike went to great pains to describe the distinctive aspects of British cookery and highlight differences with their Continental counterparts, stressing adaptation over wholesale adoption. British cookery, they continually emphasized, was not fussy or pretentious; rather, as reflected in the title of Glasse's hugely successful book, British cookery was *Plain and Easy*. Third, British cookery was refined and evidence of an 'improving', or progressing, society. While plenty of commentators lamented the extent of the refinement and feared the eroding effects of such luxury on British society, virtually all agreed it possessed a degree of sophistication that highlighted the British as a civilized people.

The extent to which locals ate the regionally named dishes ascribed to them is debatable. Cooking a wheat-flour batter with the fat drippings of roasting meats, for example, was hardly novel or unique to any particular place in Britain (or Europe). Versions of it, sometimes referred to as 'dripping pudding' (in reference to the fat drippings used to cook the batter), abound in a host of different sources. Nevertheless, in 1747 it became 'Yorkshire Pudding' thanks to Hannah Glasse, a Londoner, who published the recipe in the first edition of her seminal cookery book – a label that stuck and forever linked it to the culture of the north of England. This was not unlike the appropriation of tartan and other selected and romanticized aspects of Highland culture, including the consumption of haggis, for the whole of Scotland following George IV's 1822 visit. Future visitors expected Yorkshire eateries to offer the puddings promoted in cookery books, just as they expected to encounter tartan-wearing Scots as they crossed the border, and plenty of entrepreneurial locals were willing to oblige. Such invented traditions had important consequences. They celebrated regional differences, imagined or real, as a key component of British identity. Regionally ascribed dishes offered opportunities for an imagined epicurean tour of Britain, just as publicized recipes for members of the royal family gave Britons a virtual taste of the monarchic life, bringing people closer together. Critically, Britons did not limit their emphasis on food as a reflection of culture to deliberations on their own society. These discussions shaped how Britons understood and engaged with other peoples, which ultimately had significant consequences for those who were connected to the empire through rule and trade.

FIVE
AN EDIBLE MAP OF MANKIND

Refined cookery was a hallmark of civilized living in eighteenth-century Britain. Simultaneously embracing a number of polite society's key attributes – taste, connoisseurship, economy and display – cookery, and Britons' fascination with it, transformed tables into arenas where elite and middling men and women brandished their skills. As this book has argued throughout its pages, the selection of ingredients, choice of dishes, vessels for serving, decor of the venue and manner of eating all served as opportunities for men and women to project a desired image – and to assess each other. As explored in the previous chapter, Britons did this in critiques of their own society, using food as a bellwether for both the nation's moral health and its forward progress on the path of civilization. In this context, a generation of cookery book authors became cultural arbiters, defining an ideal of Britishness through the ordinary acts of eating.

If the processes of acquiring, preparing and eating food can characterize an individual, its extension to an entire culture is not a stretch. As the 'Hypochondriack' explained in the *London Magazine* in 1779, 'Amongst the arts by which civilization is marked, that of cookery, or the preparation of victuals for the table, is one of the most conspicuous.' 'The art of cookery', he explained, 'marks civilization'. Thus, he continued, 'In the most savage situation mankind devour their meat raw, and go naked; and from this state of brutality there is an ascent by innumerable gradations to the luxury and elegance of a company of ladies and gentlemen of high rank sitting at a dinner in London or Paris.'[1]

As a shared human experience, the preparation and consumption of food provided useful points for social and cultural comparisons at a critical time when the British were scrambling to make sense of the vastly different peoples to which imperial expansion had exposed them. In the space of a couple of generations, the British Empire had exploded from a collection of English colonies and trading outposts into a vast trading network and territory over which a white, largely British-born minority attempted to rule. Operating in parallel, and at times in tandem, with imperial expansion was an explosion in print culture, which ensured that descriptions of alien peoples and places became part of the daily diet of information that bombarded ordinary and elite Britons alike. The nation's efforts to explore, discuss and then rationalize the information into an applicable system of human taxonomy was profound and at the heart of the Enlightenment experience in Britain. Their enquiries contributed immeasurably to the foundation of such lasting institutions as the British Museum and the creation of the social sciences. Although later dubbed the 'Scottish Enlightenment' for the predominately Scots philosophers and universities that led it, this was a national public discourse that British society embraced as its own. The most eloquent and influential attempts to explain human difference during this period became the foundation of Britain's most pronounced and lasting expression of the Enlightenment – what Edmund Burke famously dubbed 'the great map of mankind'.[2]

Practices of cookery played a critical role by providing travellers, commentators, philosophers and audiences with an accessible way to understand and present cultural differences. After all, everyone acquires, prepares and eats food. In this context, techniques of preparation, ingredients, displays and manners of eating all became viable subjects of consideration equal to such topics as roads and architecture. An examination of British cookery also highlights the extent to which Scottish Enlightenment principles and interest in foreign cultures penetrated Britons' lives and routines. Cookery book prefaces aimed at middling housewives and their servants sometimes read like philosophical tracts, with replicated foreign dishes providing opportunities for Britons at home to tour virtually the wider empire and world. The table thus could provide a multi-sensory educational experience akin to visiting one of the museums that emerged during this period. Combined, these commentaries and experiences made

Burke's map of mankind edible. Although not without exceptions, what emerged was a society that was inherently interested in difference and anxious to explore, if not sometimes celebrate, human diversity. The British were also increasingly comfortable with assumptions of their superiority, embracing cultural differences as intellectual curiosities rather than opportunities for self-improvement. This was a world they wanted to understand, primarily because they sought to dominate it.

The taxonomy of human societies

While the rapid expansion of the British Empire profoundly affected the cosmologies of the foreign peoples over whom it claimed dominion, the impact for Britons at home was also significant as they adjusted to their changing world. The intellectual backbone of these reflections was the Scottish Enlightenment. While the wider European Enlightenment is difficult to characterize as consistent, the Scottish Enlightenment was comparatively coherent. It was led by a mixture of Scots academics, clergymen and jurists who were connected to each other primarily through the flourishing Scottish universities, and whose students could be found throughout the British Empire.[3]

Union with England in 1707 created a new world for Scots, transforming their political, economic and intellectual culture. Two aspects are of particular importance here. First, a key response to the transfer of political power to London was a greater emphasis on Scotland, which had four universities versus England's two, as an intellectual hub. Second, integration into the empire opened up a wealth of opportunities, with Scots disproportionately participating in colonial migration, imperial governance and the military. Before 1707, the Scots' involvement with the New World was minimal. Scotland had no successful colonies of its own, and its transatlantic commerce had to contend with English protectionism. In consequence, during the seventeenth century, English emigration to the Americas exceeded Scottish fiftyfold.[4] The Act of Union in 1707 gave the Scots unrestricted access to the old English Empire, and through investment, manpower and migration, they made it a truly 'British' enterprise.[5] Between 1763 and 1775 alone, 3 per cent of the Scottish population emigrated to North America.[6] Large numbers of Scots held colonial posts throughout the empire, and they maintained both their memberships in the prominent Edinburgh clubs that were the hubs of the Enlightenment in Scotland as well as their correspondence with leading intellectual figures.[7] As in the rest of Britain, interaction with the empire meant exposure to the great diversity of cultures over whom it claimed dominion and with whom it traded. Prominent intellectual leaders responded by categorizing, sorting and systematizing the information. Using methods that paved the way for the modern social sciences, the Scots philosophers examined European accounts of peoples and civilizations, both past and present, in an attempt to explain how societies develop (and why they do so at varying rates). Predominately devout members of the Church of Scotland, most assumed that the peoples of the world originated in a single, common creation.[8] This shared beginning made the variations in human societies particularly intriguing and in need of explanation.

Crucially, the Scots philosophers designed their work for broad audiences, turning what often began as lectures for students into commercial enterprises.[9] The major London publishers produced books that garnered substantial profits for them and their authors, with such leading figures as William Robertson said to have earned 'no less than 4,500 Sterling' for one of his histories.[10] This was a hefty sum in that a household could be considered middling with an annual income of £50 and potentially in the lesser gentry at £200.[11] The books appeared in subscription libraries and book club holdings, were digested in magazines and newspapers, and earned high praise from reviewers. Human socio-economic development was a hot topic of the day, particularly in the second half of the century. Accounts of indigenous peoples packed British print culture, and the reading public yearned for someone to make sense of them. As the *Monthly Review* declared in the opening lines of its assessment of Adam Smith's *Moral Sentiments* in 1759:

> Of all the various enquiries that have exercised the thoughts of speculative men, there are scarce any which afford more genuine or lasting pleasure, to persons of a truly liberal and inquisitive turn, than those which have Man for their object. Indeed, what can be more worthy to be studied, and distinctly known?[12]

To add relevance and appeal to their theories, the Scots and their followers increasingly mined travel accounts and private correspondence for information about the world's peoples to use as illustrative examples. William Robertson even attempted a modern survey of colonial officials and traders in North America.[13]

The Scottish Enlightenment's discourse on human socio-economic development played out before the public via the press, especially during the second half of the century, when the Enlightenment, print culture and British Empire simultaneously flourished. Newspapers and magazines liberally and proudly extracted, summarized and discussed the accounts, consciously presenting the philosophical works as accessible to all reading Britons, who were diverse in social standing, gender and geography by mid-century.[14] And while some publications clumsily attempted to engage female readers through such narrow topics as the *Leeds Mercury*'s regular

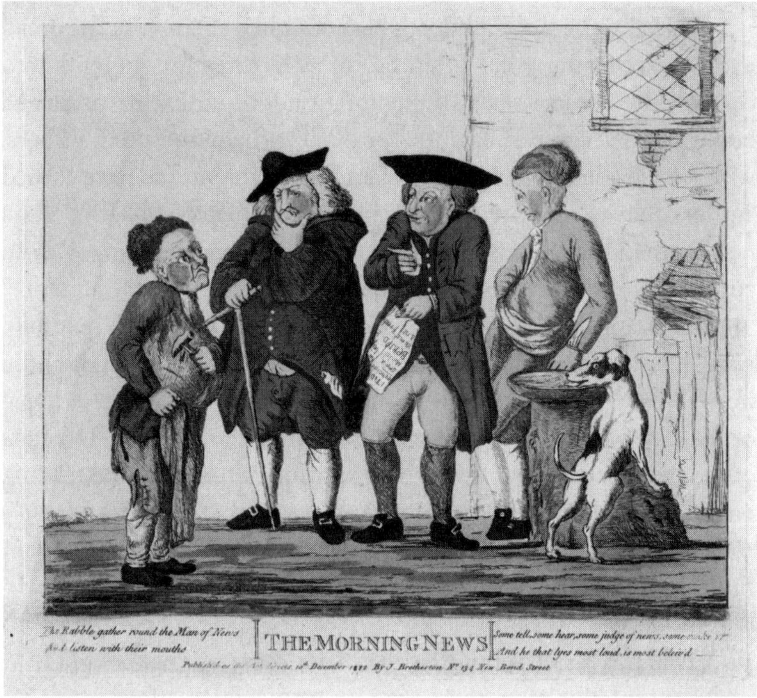

Henry Bunbury, 'The Morning News' (London, 1772). The caption reads: 'The Rabble gather round the Man of News and listen with their mouths. Some tell, some hear, some judge of news, some make it, And he that lyes the most is most believed.' Depicting men from the overtly labouring ranks, the print highlights the socio-economic diversity of readers.

'The Dress of the Month', most increasingly included women in broader topics about morality, natural philosophy and politics, such as the *Edinburgh Magazine*'s 'illustrations of the first principles of philosophy, for the use of ladies' in March 1759.[15] In consequence, the British reading public, like Burke, largely embraced the ideas.

Importantly, human taxonomy was no parlour game. The authors intended their conclusions to be 'useful knowledge' – a hallmark term applied to everything from cookery books to agriculture. British audiences would not suffer the flowery language and counterintuitive proposals of Jean-Jacques Rousseau and other proponents of the idealized 'noble savage' during the French Enlightenment. As the *London Chronicle* representatively sneered in a review of Rousseau's translated *Social Contract* in 1762:

> the meanest Christian must make a better patriot, and a much more social human being, than the model of perfection which John James [*sic*] exhibits in his Natural Man, who runs wild and naked in the woods upon his hands and legs, eats acorns, shuns his species, [except] only when the spirit of copulation moves him, and lives and dies among his brother-brutes.

For more on the noble savage, the paper mockingly advised readers to 'see the *Dissertation on the Causes of Inequality of Mankind* by this same John James Rousseau, designed by nature to howl in a wilderness, but converted by force and pernicious influence of the social contract, into a citizen of Geneva'.[16] The consequences were ultimately severe, particularly for those peoples identified as being in the lowest states of civilization.[17]

Working from the assumption that humanity had a common starting point, leading Scots philosophers and those who engaged with them often drew conclusions that explained Europeans' transcendence as evidence of both their cultural superiority and greater natural intelligence. As William Robertson remarked in an often-cited passage from his *History of America*, 'we may conclude, that the intellectual powers of man in the savage state are destitute of their proper object, and cannot acquire any considerable degree of vigour or enlargements.'[18] In other words, Robertson questioned whether or not so-called savages, such as the indigenous peoples of North America, could be raised to civility within a lifetime. Cultural practice, he and others argued, had physiological consequences. For example, many held that primitive savages could digest raw meat; whereas a middling woman in London, whose digestive tract was accustomed to cooked foods served in sanitary conditions, could not endure such a diet. At the same time, the savage would struggle to digest, let alone appreciate, the elaborate dishes found in an elite London home, with their spices, sauces and global ingredients. As a Leeds newspaper explained to its readers in 1768, following the sensational story of 'the savage girl' found living wild in the woods in France, 'Her stomach and constitution having been constantly accustomed to raw food, full of its natural juice, could by no means endure our artificial kinds of food, rendered by cookery, according to the opinion of several physicians, much more difficult of digestion.'[19] To be fair, Enlightenment figures throughout Europe raised similar questions about the rate at which a primitive person or society might be brought to European standards of civilization, and many reached different conclusions to Robertson, who himself had a complicated view of imperialism, writing about its horrors at least as much as its benefits.[20] Nevertheless, statements such as Robertson's fit the agenda of later expansionists who often saw native peoples as obstacles to remove rather than integrate with or leave alone.

Cookery played a key role as part of the criteria used to classify and rank societies. After all, cookery is a universal practice among human societies, and the acquisition, preparation and consumption of food was a favoured tool for measuring social differences within Britain. As described in the previous chapter, tea visits and dinners had transformed parts of middling and elite homes into public arenas in which hosts and guests alike displayed their position through their selection of teas, porcelain cups and table manners. Extending such evaluative judgements to foreign societies was not surprising. Food was an especially important part of the Scots' conjectural histories, in which they theorized how human societies evolved from hunting communities into complex, sedentary societies.[21] Such icons of the Scottish Enlightenment as Adam Ferguson, Adam Smith, John Millar and Lord Kames all included food production as a driving force of socio-economic change. Although differing on many points, they generally agreed that hunter-gatherers became commercial societies through various stages in which the concept of private property was invented to enhance and control food production – evolution and expansion of which paved the way to modern, urban commercial societies such as found in eighteenth-century Britain. In these societies, luxuries proliferated and the arts, including cookery, flourished.

Food and the taxonomy at work

While the classification of foreign societies according to quasi-scientific criteria was evident in a wide variety of print genres, the most ubiquitous was the travel account. Published travel accounts flourished during this period as an increasing number of travellers found a fertile market in British readers anxious to make sense of their rapidly expanding world. The accounts appeared throughout print culture – on their own, in digest volumes, and as individual and serialized extracts in magazines and newspapers. Travel accounts were the most popular genre in lending libraries, where a modest annual subscription gave middling and elite men and women access to otherwise costly volumes. These libraries dotted the imperial landscape by the second half of the century, appearing in provincial and colonial cities and towns through the British Empire. Even Quebec City, despite being a remnant of New France and boasting a population that barely exceeded 10,000 people, opened a library to great fanfare in 1779.[22] The Bristol Library's surviving borrowing records offer a rare look at the reading habits of the men and women who paid the one-guinea annual membership fee and underline the popularity of travel accounts. Borrowing of travel accounts and histories outpaced that of theological volumes by ten-to-one.[23] In fact, three of the five most-borrowed books were travel accounts.

Accounts of foreign peoples and places found further audiences via book clubs, which exploded to number in their thousands by the end of the century.[24] In these groups, members pooled their resources and selected titles by ballot, often using review magazines as catalogues. These clubs became features of provincial towns, where they were open to local 'respectable' members of society, often regardless of gender. At the end of the eighteenth century, Joshua Toulmin boasted in his history of Taunton that the Somerset market town had four book clubs, one of which was exclusively for women.[25] When John Marsh, a minor member of the provincial urban gentry, and a group of friends founded a small book society in Chichester in 1789, accounts and histories of foreign places were the first books they selected. Little changed after the society added women to its membership a dozen years later, as it continued to choose a disproportionate number of foreign accounts.[26]

The purpose of most accounts was to instruct as well as entertain, and so authors throughout Europe often adopted a style aimed to transport the reader virtually to alien places. For example, in typical fashion the author of a description of Arabia instructs that 'To paint to himself these deserts, the reader must imagine a sky almost perpetually inflamed, and without clouds, immense and boundless plains . . . where the eye frequently meets nothing but an extensive and uniform horizon.'[27] Readers took the calls to exercise their imaginations to heart, as William Cowper revealed in a private letter written after reading James Cook's account of his first voyage to the South Pacific: 'My imagination is so captivated upon these occasions, that I seem to partake with the navigators, in all dangers they encountered. I lose my anchor; my main-sail is rent into shreds; I kill a shark, and by signs converse with a Patagonian, and all this without moving from the fire-side.'[28] The importance of this linguistic style and the reception of it should not be discounted. This was a period which took the force of the imagination seriously – as having the power to compel action, shape perception and cause affliction in the form of mental disorders. As James Murray later remarked in the preface to his *Travels of the Imagination*, 'Things are no less real, because the fancy colours them, and this journey is not the less true, because the imagination has a had a share in it;– and there is not a sentimental journey extant that would have existed, if fancy had not woven a thread in the web of sentiments.'[29] Travel accounts thus became the ordinary person's tour of the world, and, though virtual, the experiences and conclusions taken from them mattered.

Food and travel went hand in hand then just as much as they do today. Eighteenth-century travellers not surprisingly sought new and authentic experiences, of which eating was a central part. European Grand Tour journals abound with detailed descriptions of seemingly every morsel of food that was consumed during the journeys.[30] The published accounts of places further afield almost invariably included detailed descriptions of the cookery and eating habits of the observed peoples. These published descriptions often possessed a quasi-scientific tone. From this perspective, cookery observers treated cookery on a par with architecture and transportation infrastructure.

The acute coverage of American Indians in the British press during the Seven Years War, which focused disproportionately on the brutality of their style of warfare, demolished any hope that the indigenous inhabitants of North America would be widely accepted as noble savages.[31] Instead, due in part to the stereotypes perpetuated by the Scottish Enlightenment and its adherents, the American Indians came to personify the crudest, basest form of human society. As the *Annual Register* remarked in 1777 – in the wake of public outcry over Britain's employment of American Indians against the rebelling American colonists as being beyond the rules of civilized warfare – primitive life was not ideal:

> Poets, philosophers, and politicians, had in vain exerted their genius, wisdom, and talents, to describe or discover the state of simplicity, innocence, and nature, the origin of society, and the source of laws . . . That age, which was supposed to be golden, we now behold; and discover it affords only a state of weakness, imperfection, and wretchedness, equally void of innocence, and incapable of happiness.

'If we find man without property, and feeding on acorns,' the *Annual Register* continued in condemning fashion, 'we also find him a sullen, suspicious, solitary, and unhappy being; a creature endued with a few goods, and cursed with numberless ill qualities; unjust and cruel from nature and habit, treacherous on system, implacable in revenge, and incapable of gratitude, friendship, or natural affection.'[32] Thus comparing someone to an American Indian became an insult of the person's claim to civility. For instance, when reporting on a brutal murder of a young woman 'at the little Public House at Kill y cwm' in Wales in 1772, *Jackson's Oxford Journal* remarked: 'We shudder at the Barbarity of Indians, who roast their Prisoners alive; but the detestable, the hellish Brutality of these Villains is far more horrible.'[33]

Not surprisingly, therefore, the cookery of American Indians was a subject of universal ridicule in accounts that described it, solidifying their position at the bottom of the British perceived hierarchy of civilizations.[34] As with their weaponry, language and architecture, British commentators had virtually nothing positive to offer with regard to their cookery. In his compilation work *The History of America*, William Russell explained in typical fashion that 'The art of cookery is in small repute among savages [American Indians]: the question with them is to eat; to satisfy the stomach, and all the cravings of hunger, not how to tickle the palate or provoke the appetite.'[35] Available descriptions direct from those observers on the ground offered little alternative. Robert Beverley's evaluation of Virginia natives in his history of the colony included a section 'Of their Cookery and Food' in which he dismissed it as having 'nothing commendable in it, but that it is perform'd with little trouble'. He further informed his readers of their willingness to eat virtually anything, the absence of spices and the lack of diversity in beverages. Equally important, he asserted that eating was not a social occasion for the American Indians since they ate at no set times, had few utensils and 'seldom or never, sit more than two together [at meals]'.[36] In what was probably the most cited English-language account of American Indians of the century, Cadwallader Colden, a graduate of the University of Edinburgh and Enlightenment figure who served as lieutenant governor of colonial New York, underlined such sentiments, remarking that

> their Food and Cookery is not agreeable to our delicate Palates. Their Men value themselves, in having all Kind of Food in equal Esteem. A Mohawk Sachem told me with a Kind of Pride, That a Man eats every Thing without Distinction, Bears, Cats, Dogs, Snakes, Frogs, &c. Intimating, that it is Womanish, to have any Delicacy in the Choice of Food.[37]

Even Henry Timberlake, who had lived among the Cherokee, guided them on trips to Britain and openly opposed the brutal imagery often used to describe them, provided an unfavourable account of Cherokee meals. Although he 'could not much commend their cookery', it was their manners that most offended him: 'What contributed greatly to render this feast disgusting, was eating without knives and forks, and being obliged to grope from dish to dish in the dark.'[38] Opinions about American Indian primitiveness and their base cookery did not seem to change significantly by the end of the century. Describing the native peoples living in Canada, the *Juvenile Library*, an 1800 encyclopedia-like collection of 'every useful subject', was particularly dismissive. Denigrating them as beggars, thieves and liars, the account's final insult and effort to demonstrate their base primitiveness focused on cookery. According to the account, these peoples ate most foods raw, 'except for the occasion they have bought brass pots' from Europeans; the only other mode of heating was hot stones, which led to dirt and sand in the food – something the primitive American Indians did not seem to mind.[39]

The cookery and eating styles of other so-called primitive societies fared little better. Besides ridiculing the nomadic lifestyle and personal hygiene of the peoples of Kamtschatka, or 'Tartars', travel accounts regularly took aim at their cookery. One traveller complained that it 'creates such a stench as is intolerable to those who are not accustomed to it'.[40] Another remarked that the 'prodigious quantity of meats and badness of the cookery, were equally amazing'.[41] Rawness, or absence of cookery, was taken as evidence of primitiveness. 'They eat, generally speaking, all their food raw, insomuch that the blood of the flesh they devour runs out of their mouths,' noted one aghast traveller, who then surmised wryly that 'It may be easily imagined that their cookery requires no great apparatus.'[42] Descriptions of indigenous cookery in the Philippines mixed with assertions of the natives' lazy indifference: 'They can be active enough as they generally please but are generally lazy, and will seldom work unless they are compelled by hunger . . . The common people live principally on rice, sago, and small fish; while those in better circumstances eat buffaloe beef and fowls with their rice, but their cookery is very indifferent.'[43] Colonists and travellers also quickly dismissed any potential benefits of Aboriginal Australian cookery, just as they discounted the peoples themselves. When describing an encounter at Botany Bay, Arthur Phillip remarked in his account of one individual who saw the British boiling meat: 'It is probable he might profit by what he saw; and as the natives of this coast have no other mode of dressing their food than by broiling, a new plan of cookery could not be a small acquisition to them.'[44]

Even abolitionists did little to rehabilitate views of sub-Saharan African cookery. In her popular *Sketches of Human Manners*, Priscilla Wakefield drew from the 'writings of travellers of reputation' to inform middling families about the 'customs of the inhabitants of the different parts of the world'. 'Africa', she informed readers, 'is the least civilized of any of the four quarters of the world.' As evidence, she described the simplistic circumstances of Abba, a fictional villager of the 'Mandingoes' (Mandinka), a people in Senegambia. Abba's basic mud hut is equipped with 'nothing more than a bullock's hide, spread over a hurdle of canes . . . [and] two or three low, wooden stools'. For cooking there is only 'a stone jar for water; some earthen pots for dressing their food; and a few wooden bowls and calabashes, or drinking cups, made of the dried skins of wild gourds'. To emphasize that Abba is not poor, Wakefield remarked that 'not even that of the dooty, or chief magistrate, was distinguished by any ornament, or variety of utensils.' Yet these primitive conditions were sufficient for someone such as Abba. 'Indifferent as these accommodations may appear to those who are accustomed to the many conveniences used in a European house,' Wakefield explained, 'neither Abba nor his mother had a wish for anything beyond what they enjoyed.'[45]

Civilizations that won the admiration of the British did so in part for their civility in eating. The Society Islanders, particularly the Tahitians, received great praise from travellers and domestic commentators alike. In some ways, the Tahitians played the role of noble savages in the late eighteenth-century British world view. Accounts depicted them as living in Eden-like tranquillity that harked to simpler times and underlined the undesirable by-products of life in modern civilizations.[46] Few of the many accounts of the Society Islands, whether first-hand or secondary compilations, failed to mention cookery, and virtually none were entirely unfavourable. In his compilation work *Elements of Geography, and of Natural History*, John Walker freely admitted that Tahitian methods of roasting meats were 'found superior to the cookery of Europe'.[47] After providing explicit details of the methods and ingredients used, another account declared that Captain Samuel Wallis in his trip around the world on the *Dolphin* found 'that this method of cookery exceeds every other he has known, the meat being extremely tender, and full of gravy'.[48] John Hawkesworth's 1773 account of the first Cook voyage, which was probably the most popular travel account of the century, described the variety of sauces found in Tahitian cookery – some of which the Europeans preferred to their own.[49] Not surprisingly, when Omai, the island's most famous visitor, toured Britain in celebrity style in the 1770s, honoured guests were anxious to try the renowned cuisine. On one occasion he even hosted a Tahitian-styled barbecue along with Joseph Banks, a voyager to the South Pacific and future president of the Royal Society, who narrated the event.[50] Although the term 'barbecue', in various forms, as it relates to cooked meats dates at least to the late seventeenth century in Jamaica, barbecuing appears in British cookery books as a cooking technique in the 1770s, when it became associated with the South Pacific manner of cooking of pork, thanks to descriptions of the technique in travel accounts and demonstrations by Omai in Britain.[51]

Tahitian cleanliness, discrimination and selectivity – hallmarks of a civilized society – were central in portrayals of food selection and eating rituals. James Cook offered a typical, widely reprinted description of a meal:

> When we came to the chief's house, we found the cloth laid; that is, green leaves were strewed thick on the floor. Round them we seated ourselves ... The table was garnished round with hot bread-fruit, and plantains, and a quantity of cocoa-nuts brought for drink ... and it must be owned, in favour of their cookery, that victuals were never cleaner, nor better dressed.[52]

Accounts also described Tahitians' diets as differing according to social rank. Borrowing liberally from various travel accounts, a 1790 'universal geography' explained that 'With respect to the food of the inhabitants of this island, there is great difference according to their rank. Vegetables compose the chief part of the diet of common people, whilst those of exalted rank feed on the flesh of hogs, dogs, and fowls, and gormandize to excess.'[53] Mealtime rituals were described as varying according to custom, social rank and gender in that the elite had attendants, women were excluded (except as servants), and various rituals of hygiene and social deference were followed meticulously.[54]

In the cases of civilizations that the British recognized as much older and equally, if not more, complex than their own, printed descriptions of cookery reflected and informed assumptions of elaborate social hierarchies and luxuries. William Chambers's 1757 *Designs of Chinese Buildings, Furniture, Dresses, Machines, and Utensils* looked at design as a reflection of Chinese sophistication, examining the grand buildings as well as the more commonplace eating utensils.[55] The compilation *A Summary of Universal History* remarked that 'Chinese cookery is in general good', detailing the liquor, diversity of ingredients and sauces in a paragraph that runs into a discussion of Chinese roads, which it called 'among the wonders of China'.[56] A lack of transitions between architecture, engineering and cookery as subjects was typical rather than exceptional, thus further underlining the argument that the inclusion of a discussion of cookery was not so much for novelty as it was to provide evidence for classification. The 1777 edition of Edward Terry's *A Voyage to East India* placed his section 'Of their Diet, and their Cookery' in between sections on architecture and 'the Civilities of this People'.[57] In other instances, technology, decor and cookery are blended in the same paragraph, such as in *A Summary of Universal History*'s comments on the Japanese:

> They are good arithmeticians; better printers than their neighbours; inferior to them in their use of gun-powder, but superior in those works which may be termed upholstery . . . Their cookery is good, and often very delicate. They have a convenient method of enlarging and contracting their apartments, by means of folding screens.[58]

The tastiness of these societies' cookery received mixed reviews, but in general their cookery's complexity and the manner in which they consumed their food was regarded as on a par with even the most civilized Europeans. The diversity of dishes, spices, utensils and etiquette were all praised even when they were remarkably different from what might be found in Europe. As John Henry Grose remarked in his 1757 account, 'They [Indians] have also almost as many names for their dishes as the European cookery.'[59] Perhaps most telling of Europeans' predisposition to accept the cookery of 'civilized' societies as equal to their own was their willingness to praise it even when they did not care for it. Tastiness was more often remarked on as a casual observation, rather than part of the evaluative criteria. In so doing, they recognized what modern anthropologists have concluded: taste was a product of one's historical environment and personal preference.[60] Instead, ingredients, preparation methods, utensils and rituals were all worthy of detailed consideration when categorizing a culture's development. As Lady Montagu noted in her reflection on her travels in the Ottoman Empire: 'I am a very good judge of their eating, having lived three weeks in the house of an Effendi, who gave us very magnificent dinners,' she explained. 'The first week they pleased me extremely,' she continued, 'but, I own, I then began to grow weary of their table, and desired our own cook might add a dish or two after our manner. But I attribute this to custom, and am very much inclined to believe that an Indian, who had never tasted of either, would prefer their cookery to ours.'[61] British commentators made similar observations about Chinese cookery in other accounts, such as this comment in a 1761 compilation of Asian travels:

> Though provisions are so very plenty here, the Europeans find not only the want of bread and wine, but a difficulty in relishing their cookery, which is very different from ours. Father Borri not unjust observes, that our manner of dressing victuals would be as disagreeable to a native of Cochin-China; as an instance of which prejudice as was present when the governor of Cochin-China was at a table, to which several very nice dishes were served up in the European taste, none of which could agree with his palate.[62]

Such understanding and forgiveness were not afforded to the American Indians or sub-Saharan Africans, for whom observations both informed, reflected and reinforced existing assumptions.

Cooking up the empire

More than ever, food and conversation went hand in hand during the eighteenth century. Whether in the public space of a coffeehouse or the semi-public space of domestic parlours and tea tables, the selection, preparation, presentation and eating of food became a vehicle for displaying prosperity and sophistication. Tableware, decorations and the choice of foods all mattered as aspiring Britons merged food with fashion. In this context, the food itself took on elements of material culture, serving as items for display and conversation. As discussed already, individual goods, such as coffee or tea, are prominent examples of this. Yet Britons' engagement with the empire's edibles did not stop there. Rather, they extended to prepared dishes that attempted to replicate the cuisines of peoples from around the globe. Of course, working to impress dinner guests with new or exotic dishes was hardly new. Medieval cooks famously celebrated their lords with an array of dramatic dishes intended to astonish and delight guests. Parades of peacocks, swans and grand sugar sculptures festooned the tables of the nobility. What distinguished the eighteenth century was that exotic dishes from around the globe became accessible further down the social scale and that they often acted as edible artefacts, representing the peoples and places from which the dishes supposedly originated. Such practices ultimately further highlight the widespread connections between domestic life and interest in the world outside of Europe that was increasingly linked to the British Empire.

Dining practices of the day fostered conversation. Popular guides for middling and elite households prescribed practices that encouraged intimacy between guests and focused on the offered dishes. At dinner parties, the practice of seating guests according to social rank was blended during the second half of the century with the new approach of female-male-female seating in which the men helped to serve the adjacent women. As John Trusler remarked in his widely distributed and copied treatise *The Honours of the Table, or, Rules for Behaviour during Meals*, 'Custom . . . has lately introduced a new mode of seating. A gentleman and a lady sitting alternately round the table, and this, for the better convenience of a lady's being attended to, and served by the gentleman next her.'[63] This 'promiscuous seating',

'A Fox-Hunting Breakfast' (London, 1777). The scene shows men at an early breakfast preparing for a fox hunt. Coffee would have been included as part of the usual fare.

James Gillray, 'Matrimonial-Harmonics' (London, 1805). Suffering the tedium of matrimonial life, a man sits reading a newspaper while his wife screeches a song on the piano. Meanwhile a dog barks, a cat yowls and a baby cries. Before the hearth sits the expected tea service – a pillar of a leisured domestic life.

Trusler explained, encouraged polite conversation, and no subject was easier than the food at hand. The rules of the number of courses or dishes in a course were not hard and fast; however, serving multiple dishes in each course was the common practice, and guests were expected to try a little of everything.

The selection of food reflected the hosts. After all, as the popular cookery books of the day made clear, the managing of the household's table was envisaged to be a partnership between the mistress and housekeeper. Even among the gentry, mistresses were expected to direct the household's resources by procuring provisions, monitoring stocks and selecting the main dishes.[64] The books' subtitles often reflected this arrangement, such as Martha Bradley's *The British Housewife: or, the Cook, Housekeeper's, and Gardiner's Companion* and Robert Abbot's aptly titled *The Housekeeper's Valuable Present: or, Lady's Closet Companion*.[65] Editions of Hannah Glasse's *Art of Cookery Made Plain and Easy* and William Augustus Henderson's *Housekeeper's Instructor* even included prescriptive illustrations of mistresses sharing the books with their housekeepers.[66]

In consequence, guests had the opportunity to discuss the various dishes as they served each other and themselves and were almost

Frontispiece to Hannah Glasse, *The Art of Cookery Made Plain and Easy*, new edition (1777?). The caption reads: 'The Fair, who's Wise and oft consults our BOOK, And thence directions gives her Prudent Cook, With CHOCIEST VIANDS, has her Table Crown'd, And *Health*, with *Frugal Ellegance* is found.'

guaranteed to end up with at least some of even the most alien dishes on their plates. Serving a dish 'in the Chinese style' would not have been lost on guests; in fact, its primary purpose would have been to titillate diners into a conversation in the same way a carefully selected object displayed in a case or on a table might. While there are few records of actual conversations about the food at a particular setting, the consumption of food as an obvious opportunity for conversation is unmistakably evident in satirical prints, plays and novels. Academics offer rare glimpses into how dishes sparked conversation, as the dons of Oxford colleges tediously recorded their dinner conversations via the wagers they laid, which included challenges about ingredients, dish names and what might be served on a given night. In one episode, a Mr Gent bet a Dr Stapylton two bottles of port, the standard wager at University College, that the 'Mango pickle is chiefly brought from the East Indies'. Gent won the wager, indicating the college fellowship benefited from the more expensive genuine article, rather than the mock version then circulating in cookery books that substituted cucumbers for mangos.[67]

Foreign dishes, particularly those from beyond Europe, should be considered among the genres of original and replicated foreign objects – porcelain, furniture, fine art and so on – that flourished in eighteenth-century Britain. When viewed from this perspective, their purpose and importance are better understood. When it came to decor, replication was a key component of eighteenth-century British fashion. The Grand Tour flooded elite homes with French and Italian designs, further encouraging the popular fascination with cultures beyond Britain's shores. Like its less expensive cousin, tea, Chinese wallpaper first appeared towards the end of the seventeenth century, but it became more popular in the years that followed. By the end of the century, one could find the genuine article in elite homes across London, including the banker Thomas Coutts's drawing room in the Strand, where it still hangs.[68] Elizabeth Montagu decorated a room in Chinese wallpaper in her famous Portman

Frontispiece to William Augustus Henderson, *The Housekeeper's Instructor; or, Universal Family Cook* (1793). The accompanying explanation reads 'A Lady presenting her Servant with the UNIVERSAL FAMILY COOK who diffident of her own knowledge has recourse to that Work for Information. On the right hand a Person Instructing a Young Man in the ART of CARVING by referring to a Print on that Subject.'

Square house, completed in 1781, which she sometimes referred to as 'the Empire of China'.[69] Stoneleigh Abbey in Warwickshire, which later became the fictional setting for Jane Austen's *Mansfield Park*, had a room fitted in the 1760s with an Indian cabinet, bamboo chairs, seventeen Indian prints and a host of other Asiatic-themed objects.[70] While such spaces were the preserve of the elite, plenty of middling and labouring households had access to such goods, albeit on a lesser scale. Imports of Asian porcelain, furniture, fabrics and other baubles flowed into Britain by the millions – to such an extent that savvy Asian producers created specialized designs and production lines specifically for European markets.[71] Perhaps even savvier were the British business men and women who saw the opportunity to market replicas that captured the exoticism of the original with design modifications – such as handles, sizes and favoured colours – for the British market.[72] Thomas Chippendale and Josiah Wedgwood, for example, built fortunes and became household names that have endured for centuries by replicating and innovatively modifying Asian furniture and tableware for the aspiring middling social ranks of Britain and its colonies.

Such objects potentially carried a diversity of meanings. While consumers likely purchased Asian porcelain because they found it

James Gillray, 'Tea Just Over, or the Game of Consequences Just Begun' (London, *c.* 1801). The comical scene depicts a provincial evening party in which men and women freely mingle, converse and flirt.

aesthetically pleasing, the appeal of such objects can also be tied to their association with the foreign peoples that produced them. After all, objects as representatives of peoples and places were the basis of the modern museum movement, which developed and flourished in eighteenth-century Britain. As already discussed, such places were major attractions packed with ethnographic objects from across the globe. Often organized according to the socio-economic categories established in the Scottish Enlightenment, the museums were a material map of mankind.[73] Thus a country house with a room decorated in a South Asian style or a record of someone eating an Asian meal might be mistakenly dismissed as devoid of meaning – as merely isolated choices and random preferences. Context, however, offers an important vantage point. A Briton who bought Indian knick-knacks or ate bowls of curry would likely also have belonged to book clubs that favoured foreign travel accounts and geographies, visited museums with the world's cultures on display, attended celebrations marking imperial victories, fasted and prayed for imperial successes, worked in manufacturing districts that produced goods for export to the colonies, visited shops that employed visual images of the empire, discussed imperial politics in coffeehouses and at tea tables, and followed the latest news and commentary on imperial affairs in any one of the millions of newspaper copies churned out annually.

Interest in ethnographic objects was such that a commercial market for them developed. While never as abundant as Asian porcelain or Chippendale's replica designs, ethnographic art and other objects regularly appeared in upmarket auction houses, including the new houses of Christie's and Sotheby's. Prices were not extravagant. American Indian tomahawks, Chinese chopsticks, African drums and South Pacific grass skirts were on offer for prices well under a pound.[74] As with grocers' sales tactics with such overseas goods as coffee, tea and tobacco, auctioneers made promises of authenticity with such words as 'genuine', 'true' and 'real'. Of course, whether or not the 'Nest with the egg of the Sea-Swallow, as cut from a rock in an Island of West Borneo, *used by the Chinese in their rich soups*' sold at an auction in 1786 was indeed the genuine article, rather than something found in a chestnut tree in Surrey, is impossible to verify.[75] Yet someone was willing to pay the not insignificant sum of eight shillings for the privilege of possessing it, suggesting that the buyer wanted to believe in its authenticity and that the object carried a greater meaning than a crude mass of twigs. It was a conversation piece in a domestic setting that connected alien cultures via domestic cookery.

Nowhere is the use of cookery to engage with other cultures more evident than in the new genre of cookery books that blossomed during the eighteenth century. Printed cookbooks at the start of the eighteenth century were expensive, few in number and overwhelmingly produced as technical books written by professional male chefs for other professionals. In contrast, as discussed in detail in the previous chapters, female authors dominated the new genre of cookery books, which targeted middling women and their servants. These inexpensive, highly successful books conquered the cookery book market, flooding into hundreds of thousands of British homes from the 1730s onwards. In fact, they were so successful that renowned male chefs openly imitated their style. By the end of the century, virtually every major publishing house boasted at least one of these books on its list, and the most successful books had become brands in their own right, with multiple, extensively revised editions spanning decades. These books ultimately defined the ideal of British cookery by guiding users through its increasingly diverse and complicated sea. As Sarah Harrison pledged in the preface to the sixth edition of her *House-Keeper's Pocket-Book, and Compleat Family Cook*, 'the Design of the Undertaking is to inform such House-keepers, as are not in the higher Rank of Fortune, how to Eat, or Entertain Company, in the most elegant Manner, at a reasonable Expence.'[76]

Keen to assert the value of their craft and acutely aware that food served as both facilitator and subject of conversation, the authors and their publishers offered commentary rich in context. Broadly adopting the Scottish Enlightenment's discussion of socio-economic evolution, they universally agreed that cookery was both an art and a science, evolving over generations and serving as evidence for a society's rank among nations. The near-ubiquitous inclusion of 'art' in the title of so many of cookery books was itself a conscious assertion of the importance of food preparation in assessing the developmental status of a society. And, as with other art forms, taste was something that could be expressed by both the artist and the consumer.

In fact, many of the comments found in the books' prefaces would not be out of place in a dissertation by Adam Smith. Henderson's popular *Housekeeper's Instructor; or, Universal Family Cook*, offers a typical speculation on the rise of modern cookery in Britain:

> In the primitive ages of the world, when the preservation of human existence was supported only by the simple and spontaneous productions of Nature, Mankind were totally unacquainted with every mode which has been since discovered and adopted for the gratification of sensual indulgence. As time advanced, the people became more dispersed, and nations were formed in different parts of the known world, so improvement took place as well in the Art of Cookery, as in the common transactions of life. Every age contributed, by additional invention, to the increase of this material and gratifying enjoyment, till at length those articles, which were simply used in their natural state, became refined, and were rendered, by art, not only pleasing, but deliciously grateful to the palate.[77]

Cookery books, along with a host of social commentators, philosophers and critics, hammered home the lesson that cookery, like other arts and sciences, was a learned skill reflecting the degree of sophistication of both the individual and wider society. As Francis Collingwood and John Woollams, of the widely esteemed Crown and Anchor Tavern in the Strand, proclaimed in their popular *The Universal Cook, and City and Country Housekeeper*, 'Cookery is become a Science, that every Age has contributed its Mite to the Improvement of this Art, which seems now to have reached a very high Degree of Perfection.'[78]

In consequence, foreign dishes from societies deemed on a par with Britain in refinement soon appeared. Like travel accounts, they provided Britons a safe and titillating way to explore the variety of peoples about whom they were reading in the press and whose material objects might be viewed in any number of public museums or private collections. Recipes for non-British dishes in British cookery books abounded during the second half of the eighteenth century. Like its competitors, each new edition of Glasse's seminal *Art of Cookery* offered a new array of foreign-associated dishes, including such delights as 'Hamburgh sausages', German 'sour-crout', 'Chickens and turkies dressed after the Dutch way' and 'fricasey of calves feet and chaldron, after the Italian way'. Among these were also a host of non-European dishes, which by the 1778 edition included recipes for curry, 'pellow', 'India pickle', 'turtle dressed the

West India way', 'mutton kebobbed', 'Carolina Rice pudding' and 'Carolina Snow-Balls'.[79] John Farley's popular *London Art of Cookery* offered these and more, such as Indian 'Piccalillo', 'Indian bamboo imitated', 'oatmeal pudding after the New England manner' and 'New England Hams'.[80] Other recipes commonly on offer in cookery books included 'American Pot-ash Cakes or Biscuits', 'A Turk's cake', 'New England Pancakes', 'pickles the Indian way', 'West Indian pepper pot', 'Mutton the Turkish way', 'China Chilo', 'Mullagatawny, or Currie-Soup' and many others.[81]

Crucially, in all of these recipes, authenticity – or at least the pretence to it – was paramount. Phrases such as 'the West Indian way', 'the Turkish way', 'as in China', 'as found in New England' and 'as made in India' were standard in foreign recipes. Even when they drew from predominately British ingredients, their authors still claimed the final result would be authentic. Although the recipes varied between authors, and even between editions of the same book, authors stressed the authenticity of their recipes.[82] For example, recipes in Glasse's *Art of Cookery* for pilau, or 'pellow', changed over time, yet each was introduced as the 'Indian way' or 'the true Indian way'. Moreover, and in contrast to other recipes, instructions for recreating non-European dishes almost never emphasized the scrumptiousness of a dish. In fact, many travel authors had long complained about the lacking tastiness of those overseas cuisines that later appeared in the cookery books. Just as in museum displays of foreign artefacts, the primary intended wonder and enjoyment of an exhibited item was not its innate beauty but rather its authentic association with another culture. In such contexts, these dishes operated as edible artefacts.

As a result, context served as an important way to enhance these dishes' authenticity. Cookery book recipes often included explicit serving instructions. New overseas ingredients regularly came with descriptions of their origins and production methods. In the 1758 *The British Housewife*, the Bath-based Martha Bradley provided information on a large number of spices, from which later competitors generously borrowed. Often these descriptions focused on production, such as her explanation that ginger was cultivated in the East Indies and America but that 'The Finest is brought from Calecut in the East-Indies', and that to preserve it 'They dig it up in Autumn, and, after washing it, spread it on a Kind of thin Hurdles, supported on Tressels. When the Air comes to it, it quickly dries. The best is such as is soundest, and of the yellowest Colour within.' In other instances she offered the geopolitics that surrounded a commodity's trade, assuming that her readers would take an interest. In describing cinnamon, for example, she not only related its East Indian origins but explained that 'The Dutch supply all Europe with Cinnamon, which they have in the Islands of Ceylon in such Abundance that they burn a great deal annually to keep up the Price.'[83] Charlotte Mason's creation of something akin to a spice glossary in her *Ladies' Assistant*, in which she provided paragraph-long descriptions of spices such as cinnamon, nutmeg, mace, Jamaica pepper, turmeric and cloves, became increasingly common in the second half of the century. From it readers received a mini-lesson in imperial history and geopolitics, learning which products slaves cultivated, which had been transplanted to the Americas from Asia and Africa, how indigenous peoples used them and which competing empires controlled their trade. While such commentary may seem out of place in a cookery book aimed primarily at middling women, it was typical of printed literature designed for similar audiences. *The Young Lady's Geography*, for example, included no fewer than a dozen references to tobacco, primarily in descriptions of how it was produced and the advantage it gives to British commerce.[84]

The arrangement of the table provided further context. Table decorations and the design of particular dishes gave further opportunities for hosts to display an interest in imperial topics and distant places to provoke conversation. Table decor was an important part of shared meals and revealed hosts' tastes. Accompanying dishes mattered, and so recipes for curry, for example, came with detailed instructions for preparing rice specifically for that dish.[85] The selection of utensils also could provide further authenticity to an experience and they became subjects for discussion. A national debate about the best vessels for tea lasted for decades in which men and women deliberated over whether or not tea tasted better in authentic Asian chinaware or the British-made equivalent. Claiming not to support the 'prejudice' itself, *The New London Cookery and Complete Domestic Guide* remarked: 'It is asserted by some female connoisseurs in tea, and perhaps it would be more difficult to disprove than to account for the fact, that tea tastes much better from Indian than British china.'[86] The dishes themselves also served as decorations that reflected imperial themes. In the wake of James Cook's voyages to the Pacific, the Manchester-based Elizabeth Raffald offered a recipe for a 'floating Desert Island' complete with gravel walks of shot comfits, eryngo root structures and islanders.[87] An alternative was a large confectionary 'Chinese Temple or Obelisk', which Farley assured 'will be a beautiful corner for a large table'.[88] 'These ornamental decorations', explained William Augustus Henderson following his own 1793 recipe for a 'Chinese Temple', 'are calculated to embellish grand entertainments, and it is certain they have all a very pleasing effect on the sight.'[89] Potentially several feet in size, such decorations were undoubtedly conversation starters.

The emergence of these dishes in British cookery ultimately points to the growing popular interest in the empire and the peoples connected to it. As numerous scholars have persuasively demonstrated, the mid-century decades marked the development of a sustained, widespread interest in imperial matters in the public printed discourse of the press.[90] Overseas activities loomed large in newspapers and pamphlets of the day, informing audiences with reports, maps and commentary of distant events' relevance to readers at home. As Thomas Turner, a Sussex shopkeeper who traded in the ingestibles of empire, representatively remarked in his diary after reading the *London Gazette*'s account of the capture of Quebec in 1759:

> In the even[ing] I read the extraordinary Gazette for Wednesday, which gives an account of our army in America, under the command of General Wolf, beating the French army under General Montcalm (near the city of Quebec) wherein both generals were killed . . . as also the surrender of the city of Quebec, with the articles of capitulation. Oh, what pleasure it is to every true Briton to see with what success it pleases Almighty God to bless His Majesty's arms with, they having success at this time in Europe, Asia, Africa and America.[91]

Changes in cookery reveal the depth of the shift towards being a globally aware and interested society. The discourse on empire did not end with reading a newspaper at breakfast; it could literally be breakfast. Popular domestic guides attached the most universal of household activities, cooking, to overseas interests. Many cookery books even included mini-imperial histories in descriptions of the ingredients, such as in Martha Bradley's account of 'Cayan Pepper' in her *The British Housewife*: 'we imported this from the Negroes of our Plantations. The Fruit is common in Africa, and they having been accustomed to eat it there, shewed our People the Way in America, and they have taught us.'

The timing of the widespread appearance of these recipes also points to their connection to the wider public discourse on empire. Before mid-century, virtually no recipes, with the exception of instructions for tea and coffee, were widely associated with regions outside Europe. This was not for lack of contact – the East India Company's servants had been returning to England for a century and a half and travel accounts had described overseas dishes in vivid detail for some time – nor for lack of cookery books. Although the number of cookery book titles grew exponentially in the latter part of the mid-century period, a few titles in the genre of inexpensive works on cookery aimed at the middling ranks had been available beforehand. For instance, Sarah Harrison's cookery book first appeared in 1733, but it was not until the eighth edition in 1764 that non-European recipes appeared. Only after the nationally celebrated Cook voyages to the South Pacific, and numerous favourable descriptions of Tahitian barbecues in both the travel and newspaper press accounts, did 'barbicued pig' (the Tahitian meat of choice) appear in cookery books.[92] Moreover, before the American Revolution, when the British began to think of the colonists less as fellow nationals and more as foreigners, there is not a single dish with a colonial North American designation, such as 'Carolina rice pudding' or 'New England pancakes'.[93] Until then, rice pudding and pancakes were merely rice pudding and pancakes.

How many families feasted on Farley's 'Chinese Temple' is impossible to determine, not least because few detailed records of people's daily lives during the eighteenth century survive, and few among them thoroughly record what they ate. Most of the recipes included here were not overly complicated or expensive, and the spices used appear regularly in grocers' advertisements and stock records. As more spices became more widely available, the recipes incorporated them. Moreover, the recipes came in a variety of forms in an array of competing books. There was more than one recipe for New England pancakes, and they appeared in multiple cookery books over a period of years. Unfortunately, while menus first appeared in

Paris at the end of the eighteenth century, the practice would not make its way to Britain until much later.[94] In consequence, while the London Tavern in 1782 hosted the widely reported celebrations of the East Indian Company directors following news of victories over the Dutch in Asia and Admiral George Brydges Rodney after his victory over the French in the West Indies, we do not know if its famous cook prepared East or West Indian dishes from recipes in his popular cookery book to commemorate the occasions.[95]

Curry offers the best case study for the actual consumption of replicated dishes, because it was universally associated with India and was a distinct dish. Curry itself, or at least in the incarnation that the British consumed in Asia and Britain, was an anglicized cousin to what Indians ate.[96] Nevertheless, in eighteenth-century Britain, its claim to be a 'true' Indian dish went unquestioned. Scholars tend to place the emergence of widespread consumption of curry in Britain in the mid-nineteenth century, but evidence points to an earlier date of the second half of the eighteenth century.[97] The first published cookery book recipe for curry appeared in 1747 in the inaugural edition of Glasse's *Art of Cookery* under the title 'To make a Currey the Indian Way' – one of at least four different recipes that would appear in editions of her popular cookery book by 1800.[98] In the second half of the century, recipes appeared regularly in popular cookery books under headings that claimed to offer similar authenticity, although, ironically, curry was decreasingly served in British households in India.[99] That these works claimed 'plain and easy' recipes for use by middling and elite women and their servants suggests that curry was neither too exotic nor too complicated to prepare. Although addressed 'to all the Good House-wives of Great-Britain' and designed to appeal to rural households, the 1764 edition of Sarah Harrison's cookery book included a unique recipe for 'Currie, an East-India Dish' – suggesting both the ease of the recipe and widespread availability of the needed ingredients.[100] Mary Cole likewise included a curry recipe in a collection she assured readers was devoid of 'all extravagant, and almost impracticable receipts'.[101] Authors whose credentials included working in great households or well-known venues also incorporated curry recipes into their cookery books, which in the case of the latter were often sold on the premises. Determining whether or not the Cleikum Inn in Edinburgh or the Crown and Anchor tavern in London served the curry from the principal cooks' published cookery books may be impossible. However, at the very least the Norris Street Coffee-House in London was advertising curry by 1773 in language that suggests an existing market that was familiar with the product. Their customers could either enjoy the freshly prepared dish or purchase it as 'True Indian Curey Paste' to take home. The coffeehouse even offered delivery 'at the shortest Notice to any Part of the Town'. Rice was included.[102]

Variations in the printed recipes also suggest that curry was widely available and increasingly popular in the second half of the century. Printed recipes initially limited the animal flesh ingredient to rabbit, but soon they called for fowl, chicken, veal, cod, turkey, sausages and even lobster – all the while, of course, claiming authenticity. Recipes differed too on the use of cream, lemons, eggs, cucumbers and other ingredients. In his *The Art of Cookery and Pastry Made Easy and Familiar*, James Skeat simply told readers that 'you may put in what best suits your fancy.'[103] By the end of the century, curry was sufficiently popular that a recipe circulated that offered an 'easier, and much approved' method for cutting both the preparation time and the by then growing ingredient list by half.[104]

Perhaps the best evidence for the consumption of curry at home was the appearance in Britain of the spice blend 'curry powder' in the late eighteenth century, which suggests a sellers' response to market demand. Glasse's 1747 recipe calls merely for pepper and coriander in the way of spices, but in the 1760s and '70s, the spice list grew to include a combination of coriander, bay leaf, cayenne and turmeric. Elizabeth Austen, a cousin of the novelist Jane, bought curry powder as early as 1775, and by the mid-1780s, 'curry powder' had all but replaced the old combination of spices in cookery books.[105] An advertisement for curry powder at Sorlie's Perfumery Warehouse in Piccadilly assured potential customers that 'any person can make up a dish of Curry' with the easy-to-use powder and thus enjoy 'The celebrated East-India Dishes, and most sumptuous Sauces'. The assumption in cookery books was that curry powder could be readily purchased, just like any other spice, although at least one provincial cookery book gave instructions on how to make the blend as late as 1795.[106] Nor was it particularly expensive. When John Stevens and Benjamin Weston were indicted in 1803 for stealing a full pound weight of the powder, the contents were valued at a mere three shillings – significantly less than many other spices.[107] With such easy instructions and ingredients at hand, Margaret Dods of Edinburgh in her 1826 cookery book said of curry: 'This common favourite dish is at once economic, convenient at table, and of easy preparation.'[108]

While plenty of eateries offered curry, the Hindoostane Coffee-House was likely the first to specialize in it. Established in the fashionable Portman Square, on the corner of George and Charles streets in London, in 1810, the case of the Hindoostane Coffee-House further highlights foreign dishes' edible connections to their originating cultures – true or imagined. The proprietor was Sake Dean Mahomed, an Indian from a prominent family who served in the East India Company's army before making his way at the age of 24 to Britain, where he lived for a further half-century and pursued a variety of careers, including author and professional shampooer. The Hindoostane Coffee-House did not cater to the thousands of relatively poor Indian servants and sailors then living in London; rather, it sought the custom of elite and middling Londoners yearning to remember service in India or desiring something new. Mahomed provided more than just curry and other Indian dishes: he offered an East Asian experience by decorating the establishment with bamboo-cane sofas and prints and paintings of Asian landscapes. Customers could also enjoy fragrant hookahs (some even called it the Hookah Club), for which Mahomed offered his proprietary blend of shisha. Mahomed met with quick success, advertising in *The Times* and doubling the Hindoostane's size by taking over the neighbouring property. His prosperity, however, was for reasons unknown short-lived. Within a few years, he had declared bankruptcy – a common occurrence for him – and had established himself as manager of a Brighton bath house. The Hindoostane Coffee-House, however, continued under new British management for another two decades.[109]

DURING THE EIGHTEENTH century, cookery in Britain was both a tool for measuring non-European societies and a mechanism for exploring them. The travel accounts that judged foreign cookery and the domestic guides that provided recipes for reproducing it reveal the interconnected, but distinct, urges of the day to discover the new and then classify it in a quasi-scientific manner. The British world was expanding rapidly, and one of the ways Britons attempted to understand it was to highlight the universal commonalities of humanity, such as eating, and then make distinctions between individual cultures. The process almost invariably reinforced assumptions of British civility and the accepted hierarchy of human civilization. Asian Indians had the cuisine of a civilized society; American Indians did not. Therefore, cookery books boasted numerous recipes 'in the Indian way' but not a single one 'in the Cherokee way'. American colonists, while similar to their European cousins, had become sufficiently distinct in outlook and manners by the 1770s to create great discord in the empire, and such distinctions are reflected in the appearance of American versions of familiar British dishes. The British who remained at home participated virtually via travel accounts and replicated cooked dishes.

In this context, curry was more than a tasty and exotic meal; it was an artefact of South Asian culture. To eat the dish was to engage the culture in a manner akin to other sensory experiences found in museums, theatres and menageries. Unlike these venues, however, cookery was predominately a domestic affair controlled primarily by women. Both sexes participated in these other spaces just as they did in the world of cookery, but women did not hold sway in them to the degree that they controlled their kitchens and dining tables. Cookery thus has the added benefit of demonstrating that interest in the empire and wider world was neither mainly male nor solely part of the public sphere. In this instance, the empire had infiltrated the home, which, as the next chapter concludes, had severe consequences for imperial rule.

SIX

THE POLITICS OF FOOD

Standing at a mere four and a half inches (11.5 cm), the bowl in the illustration opposite embodies the entangling complexities of Britons' relationships with consumption and the empire. Produced in Britain in the 1820s, the bowl itself is fairly unremarkable in that it is one of the millions of tableware objects born of the hundreds of factories that peppered the English Midlands and used in homes from York in northern England to York in Upper Canada. The social ritual of tea drinking that had spread through the British Empire in the eighteenth century demanded fine accessories, especially cups, saucers, teapots and, as seen here, sugar bowls – the selection and quality of which reflected the status and taste of the owner. The accessories were opportunities to make statements. The statement of this bowl was overtly political. Adopting Josiah Wedgwood's early cameos of an enchained African slave pleading for assistance, the bowl features a kneeling female slave on one side. On the other side is a written message imploring the reader not to buy slave-produced sugar from West Indian plantations, stating that for every six families giving up 'West India Sugar, one Slave less is required'. The bowl, and the many objects like it that first appeared during the popular movements against the African slave trade and slavery, launched in the late 1780s and which continued for the next fifty years, further connected the consumer to the imperial mechanisms of production. In this case, the connection was an ethical one: the civilized practice of taking sugar with one's tea with the repugnant barbarity of slavery. Equally important, the bowl gives a call to action, telling

Sugar dish, England, 1825–30, enamelled and gilded soft-paste porcelain.

its predominately female audience (who were excluded from formal political institutions) that collectively they had the power to alter imperial practices.

Food served as facilitator, metaphor and consumer weapon when it came to public political discourse in Britain during the long eighteenth century. Its production, acquisition and preparation were pillars of the economy, and people typically ate communally. In this context, the ingestibles of imperial rule and trade took on specific, often controversial associations, facilitating important shifts in the meanings of things and popular participation in politics. As discussed in Part One, the widespread consumption of such goods as coffee, tea, sugar and tobacco during the eighteenth century marked important developments in British consumerism. Critically for this chapter, the acquisition of these goods was overwhelmingly public, because they could not be produced in the home. Despite botanists' best efforts, sugar cane simply would not prosper in the British climate. Acquiring these goods fundamentally altered the way ordinary Britons interacted with the empire by making them almost daily consumers of the products of imperial rule and trade. Advertising made them acutely aware of favourite goods' imperial connections. In the cases of coffee and tea, the consumption of the beverages themselves became a social activity in both public and private spaces: coffeehouses became part of the fabric of urban life, just as drinking tea became intrinsic to social visits. The present chapter explores how this socialization fuelled political discourse by providing venues for British men and women from a breadth of social backgrounds to gather and discuss the news of the day. The greatest proof of the important consequences of the mingling of consumption, politics and empire was the advent of the boycott: when British consumers, first in the American colonies and then in the British Isles, rejected specific goods as a form of protest against undesirable elements of the empire.

Facilitating political discussions

Coffeehouses in eighteenth-century Britain consciously acted as spaces in which ordinary Britons engaged with national, international and imperial politics. As discussed earlier, coffeehouses emerged as spaces in which patrons gathered to consume coffee, among other beverages, and socialize. As in the Ottoman Empire, coffeehouses became hubs for personal meetings, business transactions and, notably, political discussions. In fact, in Britain coffeehouses became synonymous with popular politics. There, caffeine-infused Britons not only learned the latest news but found others with whom to debate, discuss and hone their opinions on all manner of political topics.

Coffeehouses' position as centres of popular politics relied heavily upon their symbiotic association with newspapers – a relationship that blossomed during the eighteenth century. Like coffee, newspapers flourished, rising from the few thousand copies of the single legal government-produced newspaper in 1695 to over twelve million copies from over a hundred papers less than a century later.[1] As Samuel Johnson remarked in *The Idler* in 1758, the British had become so obsessed with printed news that imagining life without newspapers was difficult: 'To us, who are regaled every morning and evening with intelligence, and are supplied from day to day with materials for conversation, it is difficult to conceive how man can subsist without a newspaper.'[2]

Newspapers were central to life in coffeehouses, whose proprietors made them freely available to customers, leading contemporaries to estimate that a single printed copy might have as many as eighteen readers.[3] In his *Dictionary of the English Language*, Johnson even defined a 'coffee-house' as 'A house of entertaining where coffee is sold, and the guests are supplied with news-papers', and scarcely an illustration of a coffeehouse interior exists without the inclusion of a newspaper.[4] As the *London Magazine* remarked in August 1780, newspapers were paramount to these businesses' success: 'Without newspapers our Coffee-houses, Ale-houses, and Barber shops, would undergo a change next to depopulation.'[5] Nor was this phenomenon limited to London. By mid-century, coffeehouse culture had established itself outside the metropolis. Bristol had nine coffeehouses, Liverpool had six and almost every market town had at least one.[6] Provincial coffeehouses competed fiercely for the first and greatest number of newspapers, such as one Birmingham coffeehouse, which in 1777 advertised that a special messenger enabled it to offer eleven London newspapers the afternoon following their publication along with an assortment of provincial papers.[7]

Importantly, these were not passive readers. In one of an abundance of examples recorded by visitors, Thomas Campbell, a visiting Irishman, while reading at the Chapter Coffee-House in London in 1773, watched astonished as a 'whitesmith [a worker of tin] in his apron & some of his saws under his arms, came in, sat down and called for his glass of punch and the paper, both of which he used with as much ease as a Lord'.[8] The nature of coffeehouses was such that they encouraged critical discussions of national affairs. As one observer described how the press enabled the flow of information from the august chambers of Parliament to the ordinary Briton in 1775, 'I can easily conceive that the agitation in both Houses of Parliament on the American affairs must be very great. From thence it descends to the coffee-houses and taverns, and then the populace is as violent over a pot of beer.'[9] Contemporaries treated coffeehouse culture as the political pulse of the reading public, with newspapers regularly reporting on discussions transpiring in them and politicians, who could be counted among coffeehouses' regular patrons, referring to them in Parliament. Some coffeehouses even profited directly by enabling patrons to place wagers on projected political outcomes. The *Public Advertiser*, for example, announced in January 1775 that bets could be made at coffeehouses for 6 to 1 against war breaking out with the American colonies by March, or 4 to 1 against war being declared by June.[10] News of the odds went national the following week, with papers across the country printing similar accounts.

James Gillray, 'A Smoking Club' (London, 1793). Featuring the political leaders of the day, the print satirizes the House of Commons, shown in the background, as being little more than a coffeehouse in which men drink, smoke tobacco to excess and rowdily debate the political issues of the day.

Similarly, coffeehouse wagers on treaties and outcomes of battles from across the globe became commonplace during the last decades of the century.

While most conversation was casual, some coffeehouses offered formal debates, often open to men and women, with questions advertised in local papers beforehand. For example, the Queen's Arms, a tavern-turned-coffeehouse and home of the 'Society for Free Debate', held a debate on the evening of 3 January 1776 on the question 'Which are the most loyal subjects, and best friends to liberty, those who in their Addresses to the King approve or those who in the Petitions condemn, the present proceedings against America?' The question referenced the petitions from around Britain that had flooded the government over the issue of whether conciliatory measures or armed coercion was the best way to bring an end to the escalating strife in the American colonies. Often grassroots efforts organized in coffeehouses, the petitions carried tens of thousands of signatures from across the country. Together they represented a scale of popular interest in imperial affairs that was unimaginable a few decades earlier – made possible by the information newspapers provided and the coffeehouse venues in which readers discussed events.[11] As for the organized debate on 3 January 1776, London's *Gazetteer* reported that the question was 'ingeniously handed, and some new matter thrown out on both sides', but that it ended with 'a very small majority' in favour of conciliation.[12]

In this context, the controversial coffeehouse politician was born. Writing in 1726 on the subject of 'Coffee-House Politicians', *The Speculatist* proudly remarked that 'There is no Set of People in the World so curious and inquisitive in the Conduct of their Superiors, as the Natives of this Kingdom.' And, he continued, 'It is truly pleasant to listen sometimes to the odd Notions, and absurd Observations, which one may hear uttered in Coffee-Houses upon this Head, by men of such deep Speculation in the Political way.' However, he warned, listeners should take care not to be one of the 'People of great Curiosity but small Judgment, of strong Appetite for Politicks, but bad Digestion' and fall under a charismatic coffeehouse politician's eloquent influence – something to which even the author admitted to falling prey recently 'at a Coffee-house near Temple-Bar'.[13]

Commentators celebrated the coffeehouse politicians as emblems of the capacity of the ordinary Briton to engage and grapple with the complexities of national politics. Critics regularly used coffeehouses as settings for fictitious political dialogues, readers used them as addresses in their letters to editors, and newspapers reported on their latest debates. Such patrons certainly did not hesitate to correct their social betters. When the language of the press became overly complicated, readers complained, such as when one reader was baffled by the inclusion of the word 'convelescents' in the *London Gazette*'s extract of an official military report from America in 1776. Despite the assistance of his coffeehouse friends, the reader could not determine the word's meaning until his son arrived home and explained it to him. Irritated, he wrote to the *Saint James's Chronicle*: 'I remember, Sir, in the War before last, all our Generals and Admirals wrote in plain English, that every Body could understand them.'[14] When Edmund Burke was overheard making comments sympathetic to the American colonists in a Bristol coffeehouse, one of his constituents immediately complained in a letter to a local newspaper. 'Those who at this critical juncture, feel the unnatural inclination to wish success to the American arms, must not be offended with us if we as Britons disclaim them,' the coffeehouse politician fumed. 'Let them pack up

'The Coffeehous Mob' (London, 1710). Consistent with other visual and written descriptions of coffeehouses, patrons sit around tables reading newspapers, smoking, drinking coffee and debating intensely. A proprietor, in this instance a woman, stands at a bar overseeing operations.

their seditious principles,' he sneered, 'and retire to America; we had rather meet them in the field, as open enemies.'[15]

As much as some admired the pluck of a shopkeeper loudly criticizing the government over a dish of coffee, plenty of others treated him as a subject of amusement, if not derision. Writing as *The Spectator* in 1711, Richard Steele jokingly referred to a haberdasher who presided over the morning news at his local London coffeehouse as 'the oracle'. 'The Haberdasher', Steele cuttingly observed, 'has a Levy of more undissembled Friends and Admirers, than most of the Courtiers or Generals of *Great-Britain*.' 'Every Man about him', he continued, 'has, perhaps, a News-Paper in his Hand; but none can pretend to guess what Step will be taken in any one Court of *Europe*, till Mr. *Beaver* has thrown down his Pipe, and declares what Measures the Allies must enter into upon this new Posture of Affairs.'[16] Other comments were more derisive. A reader's letter printed in *Town and Country Magazine* in 1770 offered a typical complaint about the coffeehouse patrons who had the audacity to comment on public affairs and stir up opinion against the government: 'I frequently met with chattering Quidnuncs who pretend to talk decisively about the English nations, though they are very little acquainted with the English language; and make as many false concords as false conclusions.'[17] During wars, coffeehouse politicians, armed with the tactical maps, military tables and official reports widely printed in magazines and newspapers, hotly debated strategy, sometimes to the fury of more experienced onlookers. As a reader of the *General Evening Post* protested, the 'coffee-house politician ... thinks himself qualified to command the fleet that is to watch the ports of the enemy; and, because he has seen the evolution of a squadron of dragoons, thinks he is entitled to Judge the maneuvers of a squadron of ships.' 'Such are the people who are now busily arraigning the conduct of a General in one quarter of the world, and an Admiral in the other', the reader concluded, 'and do not hesitate to pronounce both the one and the other guilty.'[18]

While coffee consumption played a central role in shaping the predominately male world of public politics, changes in eating and drinking at home helped to instigate a similar transformation in the private and semi-public domestic spaces dominated by women. Elite and middling women, like their male counterparts, were more literate and had greater access to more printed materials than ever before, which, at least when it came to political discussions, rendered the distinction between the public and private spheres fairly permeable.[19] While mostly anecdotal, evidence of female interest in national affairs abounds in the form of subscriptions to newspapers and magazines, remarks in diaries and letters, and visits to public spaces in which affairs of state were presented and discussed, such as coffee-houses, museums and Parliament.[20] Pierre-Jean Grosley, a Frenchman who wrote about his travels in England in the 1770s, remarked extensively about the popular fascination with politics. 'In the present state of that kingdom', he declared, 'public affairs are become the concern of every English-man: each citizen is a politician.' Such sentiments, he noted, were not limited to men: 'Even the fair sex has its share of this pride in England, and it discovers itself with all the violence which melancholy gives to the affections and passions.'[21]

As with men, food brought women together for conversations on a range of topics, including politics, in both mixed and single-sex company. Men and women of all ranks typically ate meals together when in a home. As mentioned earlier, in middling and elite homes this was more formalized, with male-female-male alternating seating patterns to further promote cross-gender conversation.[22] Such conversation included politics. Louis Simond, a French-born American citizen who visited Britain with his wife in 1810, remarked how 'Politics are a subject of such general interest in England, both for

'Le Thé Anglais' (Paris, 1815). The scene depicts the English having tea. Highlighting the relative informality and gender-mixing sociability of such occasions, the conversing group sits in a semi-circle as one of the men serves tea.

Charles Williams, 'A Shrewd Guess, or the Farmers Definition of Parliamentary Debates' (London, *c.* 1813). The scene depicts a farming family, a copy of the *Liverpool Journal* in hand and teapot and cups set on the table, discussing politics.

men and women, that it engrosses the conversations before, as much as after the retreat of the ladies [after dinner].' 'The latter', he continued, 'indeed, are still more violent and extravagant than the men, whenever they meddle at all with politics.'[23]

Within the intimacy of families, political discussions could be equally fierce, with the informality of the breakfast table and the evening fireside serving as favoured backdrops for invented renderings. The *London Chronicle*, for example, carried a two-page fictitious dialogue in early May 1775 entitled 'The City Patriot; a Breakfast Scene' in which a husband and wife debate the American crisis over breakfast and newspapers. Although a witty piece, it is not satirical in that the notion of a husband and wife discussing politics at breakfast is not treated as out of the ordinary. The dialogue's structure merely serves as a vehicle to carry the author's points about the reliability of the press and the need for a more conciliatory tone towards the protesting American colonists. As the scene opens, the husband, sympathetic to the plight of the American colonists, is reading a story extracted from the *New York Gazette*, from which he reads aloud: 'the people in America are so united that they will soon raise a militia to match the very best veterans in Europe.' Attempting to provoke his wife – depicted as the rational supporter of the British government's current coercive policies – he goads her by concluding, 'Do you mark that, my dear?' She responds with a simple 'Yes; but I don't believe it,' which sparks a witty debate in which she attacks the propagandistic nature of the American and British opposition press and pokes fun at those readers, including her husband, who gullibly believe it. The author's point that the British and American colonists could resolve their difference through a mutually respectful dialogue found within the bonds of kinship – familial imagery was commonly used to describe the quarrel between Britain and the colonies – is asserted in the characters' final lines. Despite some heated words, the husband retreats, stating that 'I will not quarrel with a lady.' His wife responds with the equally conciliatory line 'Nor I with a Patriot, whom I have the honour to call my husband.'[24]

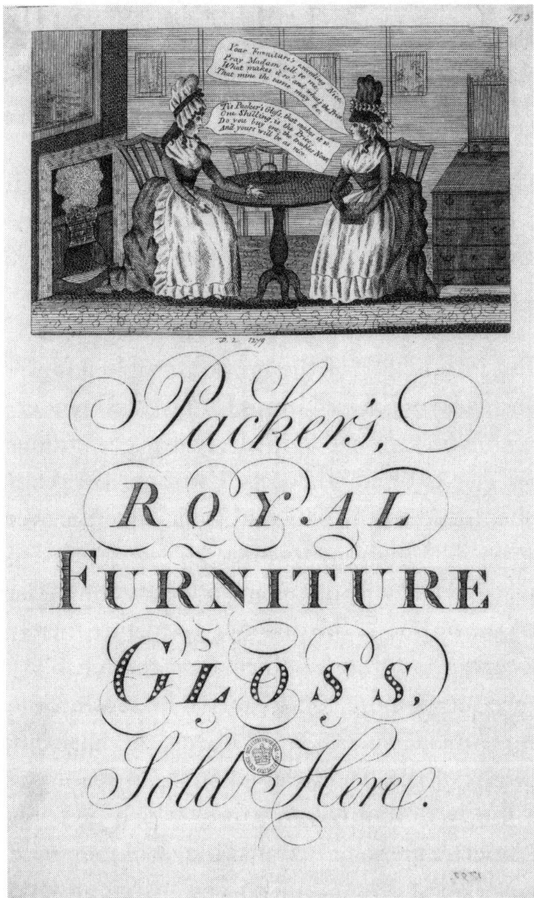

Advertisement for 'Packer's Royal Furniture Gloss', London (1793). In the scene, two women sit at a tea table; the guest praises the hostess on the quality of her furniture, remarking, 'Your furniture's exceeding nice, Pray madam tell me, What makes it so? and what's the price? That mine the same may be.' The hostess responds with the name of the brand of gloss she uses.

Thomas Rowlandson, 'Female Politicians' (London, *c.* 1809). A group of women sit reading newspapers and discussing the latest news of the global war with Napoleonic France.

Visiting, the practice of elite and middling women spending afternoons calling on each other socially, provided ample opportunities for further discussion. Although the practice took root in the seventeenth century, before the popularity of tea, tea became inextricably linked with visiting in the eighteenth century. In fact, by mid-century 'taking tea with . . .' had become synonymous with visiting. As already discussed, the social practice of visiting became a frontstage opportunity for women to demonstrate their social status, economic prosperity and taste through such mediums as the selection of furnishings, dress, chinaware and the quality of the tea itself. Advertisers pressured would-be customers by depicting fictitious conversations in which visiting women admired and commented on the state of an item – the quality of which could be ensured with the marketed product. Many commentators treated the conversation at such occasions as gossipy and frivolous, such as in George Cruikshank's 'A Curious Junto of Slandering Elves', in which three women sit around a tea table discussing the latest gossip while a fourth eavesdrops. Yet national affairs were no less likely to be subjects of conversation than in the coffeehouses, which were also infamous for slanderous gossip and flippant conversation. After

George Cruikshank, 'A Curious Junto of Slandering Elves' (London, 1817).

all, the same newspapers that peppered coffeehouses abounded in middling and elite homes. Cruikshank's 'Curious Junto', like many other depictions of such scenes, even included a copy of a newspaper at the women's feet.

Food as metaphor in politics

The employment of food as metaphor in political discourse is a natural one. After all, eating is a biological necessity that people have in common, irrespective of geography, gender or rank, and, as a result, people spend copious amounts of time procuring, preparing and consuming food. In consequence, food is a common ground that provides a wealth of metaphors in all sorts of genres. In eighteenth-century Britain, where critics typically sought to reach wide audiences, food was a favourite metaphor for commentary on a host of subjects, but during the second half of the eighteenth century, the association of food with politics reached unprecedented heights.

Even abstaining from food carried connotations of one's political convictions. The self-denial of food through fasting has long served as an expression of the devout in both religion and politics across many cultures, and Britain was no exception. The king and Parliament routinely called for days of national fasting and prayer during crises, especially during wartime. Britons were called upon to abstain from or simplify their food and attend church services at which they were to offer dedicated prayers related to the subject of the fast. The growth of interest in national affairs meant that participation in national fast days could be expressions of political beliefs. This was especially evident in Britain during the publicly divisive American Revolution – a time when even the frequency of the fast days attracted derision. A reader of the *Public Advertiser* captured the public sense of futility in the dark humour of a poem:

> First General Gage commenc'd the War in vain;
> Next General Howe continued the Campaign;
> Then General Burgoyne took the Field; and last,
> Our forlorn Hope depends on a General Fast.[25]

Supporters of the government's coercive policies against the American colonies made big shows of observing national fast days, while opponents openly ate and hosted dinner parties. For instance, in response to the 13 December 1776 national day of fasting and prayer for 'the success His Majesty's arms in America', Edmund Burke, an outspoken conciliationist, and his supporters in Bristol held a dinner in protest.[26] In this context, remaining aloof was difficult; participating or not participating could be interpreted as political support for one side or the other. John Marsh, a newlywed young lawyer living in Salisbury, felt conflicted when facing the December 1776 fast day. He had brothers in the Royal Navy, but he was hardly an ardent advocate of coercion, so he dutifully went to the church service with his family and servants. His friend, however, 'who was always averse from, and sometimes very vehement in his disapprobation of the American War, would not go to church, saying it was an unjust war'. Another friend held a musical party that evening in defiance of the day's expected sombre tone. Marsh, who had a passion for music, reluctantly declined an invitation, fearing attendance would send the wrong message about his political convictions.[27]

Visual imagery was especially common and particularly powerful. Artists skilfully employed the imagery of food to complain about everything from the government's use of American Indian allies against the rebelling American colonists to the destructive effect of taxes. James Gillray, arguably the most famous satirist of his age, drew heavily on food and cookery as useful metaphors in his caricatures of politics and society. In his world, Napoleon Bonaparte and his European state-building became the 'Tiddy-Doll' gingerbread baker, in which the French emperor donned an apron to bake a fresh batch of kings and queens for Europe. Gillray's commentary on the state of global affairs in 1805 featured the British prime minister William Pitt and Napoleon sitting at a table carving a globe in the shape of an enormous plum pudding.

The outbreak of the French Revolution in 1789 and its calls for *liberté, égalité, fraternité* posed a metaphysical threat to Britain's identity as a nation that protected and prospered from tolerance and personal freedom. For commentators who took up the pen in defence of Britain, food proved a useful metaphor that at once symbolized French falseness and British prosperity.[28] As *The Times* boasted in its description of a Sunday in the labouring districts of London: 'From twelve to three, in the manufacturing parts of

'The Allies – par nobile Fratrum!' (London, 1780). The print features Lord North and American Indians feasting on the flesh and blood of dismembered American colonists, while supplies of scalping knives and tomahawks are brought over from Britain. The sight causes the watching dog to vomit. William Markham, Archbishop of York, is delivering crates of tomahawks, scalping knives and crucifixes to aid the Indian allies. During the American Revolution, there was public outcry in Britain at the use of Indians as allies against the rebelling colonists. Cannibalism was not widely associated with American Indians and so was metaphoric of their supposed barbarousness and, by association, the British government.

James Gillray, 'John Bull ground down' (London, 1795). In a satirical print designed to protest the effects of increased taxation, John Bull, representing the ordinary Briton, pleads with the Prince of Wales and government ministers as he is ground by a giant coffee grinder into gold coins.

James Gillray, 'Tiddy-Doll the great French Gingerbread-Baker, drawing out a new Batch of Kings' (London, 1806). The print satirizes Napoleon's constant removal and replacement of monarchs by depicting him as a gingerbread maker discarding unwanted old breads in the shape of rulers and baking fresh new ones.

James Gillray, 'The Plumb-Pudding in Danger; or, State Epicures Taking un Petit Souper' (London, 1805). The scene satirizes the British and French division of the world by depicting William Pitt and Napoleon Bonaparte greedily devouring an enormous plum pudding in the shape of a globe.

Thomas Holland, 'Mr and Mrs Bull giving Buonaparte a Christmas Treat!' (London, 1803).

James Gillray, 'French Liberty, British Slavery' (London, 1792).

the metropolis, the streets smoaked with dishes of meat, pies, and puddings, and the bakers seemed to weigh down with their loaded boards.' 'What a view this for a half-starved Frenchman', the paper concluded, 'whose industrious cookery could make a whole week's sustenance for himself and his family out of one British tradesman's Sunday dinner.'[29]

British satirical caricaturists were masters of the use of food as a metaphor during this period. The characterization of John Bull and his wife, invented by artists to represent aspiring Britons of the lower middling and upper manufacturing ranks, often featured food as signals of economic prosperity and pride. For example, Thomas Holland's 1803 Christmas celebration print featured Mr and Mrs Bull, the embodiment of middling and sometimes labouring Britons, enjoying large tankards of beer, a gargantuan joint of roast beef and a truly remarkably-sized Christmas pudding as a tied-up Napoleon longingly watches and endures their jibes. James Gillray's most famous use of food imagery in defence of Britain was his 'French Liberty, British Slavery', in which he censured complaining Britons for their ingratitude and lack of perspective. In the print, he satirically contrasted the 'free' emaciated, onion-eating Frenchman to the 'enslaved' plump John Bull. In it, the ragged Frenchman praises France as the land of 'Milk & Honey' free from slavery and tax as

James Gillray, 'A Voluptuary under the horrors of Digestion' (London, 1792).

he warms his shoeless feet at a pathetic fire of twigs. In the background, live snails, presumably the next course, slither around a cracked pot. In the opposite scene, the rotund John Bull uses his silver cutlery (the Frenchman has none) to slice into the iconic steaming joint of beef with the equally familiar tankard of frothing beer waiting to wash it down, all the while muttering about how the government's taxes were 'making slaves of us all, & starving us to Death'.

Such depictions aligned with the popular new genre of cookery books by the likes of such authors as Hannah Glasse and Elizabeth

Raffald. As discussed in Chapter Four, these books framed the ideal British cuisine as avoiding unnecessary ornamentation, complication or fussiness. Notably, the prints' heroes ate traditional, unadulterated food. Mrs Bull does not cover her family's meat with elaborate French sauces or adorn her table with gaudy decorations. Along these lines is Gillray's memorably unforgiving critique of the Prince of Wales. Widely panned by his critics for his decadence, the prince took the form of 'A Voluptuary under the horrors of Digestion'. In it, the corpulent prince sits spread across his chair picking his teeth with a serving fork and digesting another extravagant meal, the remnants of which are strewn across the room, with his trousers and waistcoat unable to contain his gluttonous girth. In this context of food as metaphor, the popular adoption of tea and sugar as symbols of the empire by critiques of imperialism during the second half of the century was a natural extension, because it required no great stretch of the public imagination.

Tea, imperial tyranny and the first consumer boycotts

While civil disobedience in the forms of refusing to attend a church service or eating in public on a fast day reached new heights during the American Revolution, the most impressive action came in the form of the first consumer boycotts. The term 'boycott' is an anachronism. The term was coined in the late nineteenth century during the events surrounding the controversial eviction practices of Charles C. Boycott, an English land agent in Ireland. Local labourers and shopkeepers, backed by the reformist and overwhelmingly Catholic Irish National Land League, were encouraged to shun Boycott. Following widespread coverage in the press, the British establishment responded by sending troops and constables as labourers and protectors to aid Boycott. While the initial efforts against Boycott failed, the term proved a raging success, quickly spreading across the English-speaking world and into other languages. Yet the modern concept of a consumer boycott – a voluntary, non-governmental, popular action in which a group refuses to purchase specific goods to advance a social, cultural or political agenda – appeared in the eighteenth century.

The first consumer boycotts took place not in the British Isles but in British North America, where the East India Company's tea became a hated symbol of imperial oppression. The case simultaneously highlights the importance of tea to the British imperial economy and imagination. Following the mid-century Seven Years War, Britain was broke.[30] Although the British Empire had been victorious, the global conflict between British and French-led coalitions had sapped the nation's economy, doubling the already exploding national debt to £133 million – roughly twice the national income.[31] A succession of British governments responded to the dilemma with a series of reforms designed to rein in the expanding empire under the central authority of Parliament.[32] For the American colonies, this meant direct taxation by Parliament on a number of consumable goods for the first time.

The war had effectively started when a young and inexperienced George Washington led a group of Virginia militia in 1754 in an unsuccessful bid to push the expanding French Empire out of what is now western Pennsylvania – a move unsanctioned by Parliament. A sizeable chunk of the British wartime expenditure of blood and treasure had gone towards first defeating the French in North America and then their former American Indian allies, who continued to fight for a further two years after French capitulation. The British government primarily blamed the colonists for the poor state of American Indian relations and so proposed leaving an establishment of 10,000 troops and a diplomatic corps to keep the frontier peaceful, the estimated annual cost of which exceeded £350,000. The Sugar Act of 1764 and more infamous Stamp Act the following year were expected to raise £150,000 to offset some of the costs.[33]

On the surface, taxing American internal trade made sense. The British had long done the same, and by the mid-eighteenth century, the mainland American colonies were as awash with overseas goods as Britain itself. One-time luxuries such as Asian spices, tea, coffee, sugar, cotton textiles and British-manufactured goods became commonplace, as the American colonies emerged as the single most important overseas market for British goods.[34] In fact, the American colonists drank as much as twice the amount of tea as their British counterparts.[35] The cumulative result was that the American colonies alone accounted for over a quarter of the export trade in British domestic goods and half of what British merchants re-exported from other parts of the empire by the eve of the American Revolution. This represented a growth of 1,003 per cent and 441 per cent, respectively, during the first three-quarters of the century.[36] Contemporaries were well aware of the colonies' value to the British economy. In Edmund Burke's highly publicized eleventh-hour effort in Parliament to avert war with the colonists in the spring of 1775, he drew on government figures to argue that the value of British trade with the American colonies had become almost 'equal to what this great commercial nation, England, carried on at the beginning of this century with the whole world!'[37]

Critically, however, the colonists had not directly consented to the taxes, and many viewed the taxes as an infringement on their rights. The cumulative response is what historians have long identified as the road to revolution. The flurry of arguments in print and private accounts are too extensive to describe fully here, but the most cited was the argument against Parliament's authority to tax without the consent of the governed, most famously remembered in the cry of 'no taxation without representation'. While the violent protests that erupted in the colonies tend to stand out on the annals of history, far more effective were the threats to British commerce that the disruptive colonists posed. Fearing negative repercussions for Britain's recovering economy, Parliament backed down and repealed the Stamp Act. The British government did not, however, lose its appetite for taxing the American colonists. For the next decade, the British and Americans played a dangerous game of taxation-protest-repeal that galvanized colonial opinion against British imperial authority and, crucial to the subject of this chapter, resulted in increasingly sophisticated methods of protest and resistance, most notably the consumer boycott.

The extent of participation in and the economic impact of the boycotts is difficult to assess.[38] Many colonial newspapers assured readers that the boycotts had dealt a heavy blow, while others openly questioned their effectiveness. However, Parliament, for worry of the potential damage colonial unrest might cause the British economy, repealed most of the taxes before the boycotts could take full effect. The primary exception was the tax on tea, which lingered after the rest had been repealed in 1770. Instead of continuing their protest against British tea, the colonists either paid the duty or, far more commonly, turned to the cheaper Dutch alternative. Although technically smuggled, the importation of Dutch tea was virtually uncontested, rendering the label of 'illegal' a misnomer.

One contemporary assessment estimated that three-quarters of the tea in Boston and nine-tenths of the tea in New York was Dutch.[39]

This state of affairs came to an abrupt halt in 1773, when the British government sought to reform the East India Company, which through corruption, incompetence and an unexpectedly rapid expansion into a territorial power was on the verge of economic ruin. The company, whose taxed trade accounted for roughly 11 per cent of total government revenue from all sources during this period and whose stock had become a bedrock of private investment, was too important for Parliament to let fail.[40] In a corporate bailout that foreshadowed countless others in the centuries to come, the government passed legislation that combined increased government regulation with loans and policy changes designed to increase company revenue. The last part put them inadvertently at odds with the colonists. The Tea Act of 1773 allowed the company to sell tea directly to the colonists, thus eliminating the expensive requirement of selling it first to the London wholesalers, who re-exported the tea. The company's tea, despite carrying a tax, thus became substantially cheaper than the smuggled Dutch tea and ostensibly secured the British monopoly in North America. Nevertheless, the colonies erupted in widespread outrage and popular rejection of the tea, immortalized in the Boston Tea Party in December, when a group of protesters boarded three East India Company ships and dumped an estimated 92,000 pounds of tea into Boston's harbour.

Ultimately, the colonists' boycotts failed in their original mission. The British government continued to administer taxes, colonists did not receive direct representation in Parliament, and eventually the resolution of differences required nearly a decade of war. Moreover, the boycotts failed to develop domestic alternatives or promote lasting self-sufficiency, thereby freeing the colonists from their dependence upon what Samuel Adams, a leader of the Boston resistance, called 'the Baubles of Britain'. In fact, trade with the British Empire actually increased after the American Revolution. Nevertheless, the boycotts proved enormously successful in their ability to muster popular support for the cause of resistance. As the historian T. H. Breen has remarked, 'By all odds the American Revolution should be remembered as a relatively minor event in the long history of the British Empire.' After all, the British Empire was packed full of people unhappy with British rule. What partly enabled the American colonial resistance to succeed was its ability to mobilize popular support by drawing on consumerism and associating everyday things with parliamentary injustice.[41]

Tea was the perfect target. Virtually every household, irrespective of geography, class or gender, drank it, and, as in Britain, it was a social beverage. Even Philadelphia's prisoners had access to it.[42] Moreover, it could not be produced domestically, necessitating the act of public purchase at a shop, coffeehouse or tavern. In consequence, the widespread boycotts meant that buying or not buying tea, serving or not serving it, or drinking or abstaining from it became public, political acts in which most households could participate. Printed calls for boycotts overtly targeted the disenfranchised for participation, particularly women, who, as in Britain, were closely associated with tea drinking. As the closing lines of a poem written by a woman for the *Pennsylvania Gazette* in 1769 and 'Addressed to the Daughters of Liberty in America' declared:

> Stand firmly resolv'd and bid Grenville to see,
> That rather than Freedom we part with our Tea.[43]

Women not only responded, but took leading roles. John Adams, a colonial leader and future president, wrote to his wife about his pleasure at being prompted by the mistress of a house in which he was a guest of the importance of refusing tea:

> I believe I forgot to tell you one Anecdote: When I first came to this House it was late in the Afternoon, and I had ridden 35 miles at least. 'Madam' said I to Mrs. Huston, 'is it lawfull for a weary Traveller to refresh himself with a Dish of Tea provided it has been honestly smuggled, or paid no Duties?' 'No sir, said she, we have renounced all Tea in this Place. I cant make Tea, but I'le make you Coffee.' Accordingly I have drank Coffee every Afternoon since, and have borne it very well. Tea must be universally renounced. I must be weaned, and the sooner, the better.[44]

In this context, tea, once deemed a hallmark of civility and a welcome addition to a home, was denigrated as a prostitute. Reflective of incidents across the American colonies, 'the firm Contenders of the true Interest of America' in Providence, Rhode Island publicly burned 'about Three Hundred Pounds Weight of Tea' along with a copy of the prime minister's speeches, and 'Many worthy Women, from a Conviction of the evil Tendency of continuing the Habit of Tea-drinking, made free-will Offerings of their respective Stocks of the hurtful trash.' A description of the incident was widely reprinted, along with a satirical obituary for 'Madam Souchong', 'a Native of China . . . [who] came into this Colony about forty Years ago'. Although she had been 'greatly caressed by all Ranks' and had initially 'lived in Reputation', she had become 'a common Prostitute', and through 'hard living' she had suffered 'Broken Spirits and Hysterics', leading to her death, given as the day of the burning.[45]

The boycotts made a lasting impression among the British. A begrudgingly impressed Thomas Gage, commander-in-chief of the British forces in the American colonies, representatively remarked in a private letter to Lord Barrington, Secretary at War, 'I never heard of a people, who by general agreement, and without sumptuary laws to force them, that ever denied themselves what their

'A New Method of Macarony Making, as practised at Boston' (London, 1774). Two members of the colonial resistance organization the Sons of Liberty stand on either side of John Malcomb, a Boston customs officer in the Crown's service who was tarred and feathered – a favoured humiliating punishment in the colonies. In the print, the man to the left forces Malcomb to drink the imperially taxed tea.

Philip Dawe, 'A Society of Patriotic Ladies, at Edenton in North Carolina' (London, 1775). The print satirizes American colonial women's effort to boycott tea. In the scene, a group of women draft and sign a petition pledging to abstain from British tea. One of the women holds a gavel to call the meeting to order, another welcomes the amorous advances of a man, and other women empty their tea caddies of the offending article. Meanwhile, a child is neglected on the floor, suggesting that the women are neglecting their domestic duties.

circumstances would afford, and custom and habit prompted them to desire.'[46] In Britain, the American Revolution and the preceding crisis was the dominant news story, ensuring close coverage of the boycotts.[47] Local petitions, troop movements, maps, proceedings and endless commentary packed the pages of newspapers, pamphlets and magazines. As the London *Evening Post* declared after the arrival of news of the Boston Tea Party, 'The Affairs of America at present occupy the whole Attention of the Administration; and it is agreed on all Hands to be now the most important Business that has come under Consideration since the Accession of the present King.'[48] Like many ordinary Britons, Abigail Gathern, the daughter of a Nottingham grocer who sold the very teas Americans boycotted, closely followed the conflict, reading her father's newspapers and pasting clippings in her diary.[49] Tea quickly became inextricably linked in the British coverage of and commentary on American events. Reports of American protesters forcing customs officers and other loyalists to symbolically drink British tea as part of public humiliation rituals riled readers in Britain, and detractors poked fun at the would-be American ladies abstaining from tea.

For critics of the British government on both sides of the Atlantic, tea became a metaphor for loathsome imperial policies, such as in the *London Magazine*'s 1774 'The able Doctor, or American Swallowing the Bitter Draught'. In it, America, depicted as the customary American Indian woman, is held down by leading British ministers while Lord North, the prime minister, forcibly pours tea down her clutched throat. Britannia turns away in shame while two men to the left of the scene, representing France and Spain, watch events unfold with interest. Tea was so omnipresent in discussions surrounding the American crisis that when war seemed likely the *Stamford Mercury* expressed its resolute support for coercion in the language of tea: 'A Correspondent observes, upon the military preparations making against the refractory Bostonians, that they have refused to admit our Hyson and Congo, the Government here have determined to try how they relish our Gunpowder Tea.'[50]

The American Revolutionary experience had a profound effect on Britons' understanding of the empire and their relationships to it. The controversy surrounding the war and preceding crisis fractured British society, resulting in a deluge of public criticism of the government, which in turn prompted equally vigorous defences. One important consequence was that the value of imperial trade and conquest came under serious public scrutiny for the first time. There were, of course, plenty of critics of imperialism in Britain prior to the American conflict, but these were largely disparate voices, rather than anything resembling a sustained, widespread movement. In fact, many later imperial reformers cut their teeth criticizing the British government's handling of the American colonies.[51] In this context, at the conclusion of the war Gilbert Wakefield preached a sermon in Richmond on the national day 'appointed for a General Thanksgiving on Account of the Peace'. 'Our Proficiency in Arts and Sciences had been commensurate to our military Reputation', he proposed, 'But have we been as renowned for our liberal Communication of our Religion and our Laws, as for the Possession of them?' The answer he offered was an unsettling challenge not only because of what Wakefield accused but in that he faulted his countrymen as a whole, repeatedly employing the word 'we':

> Let India and Africa give the Answer to these Questions. The one we have exhausted of her Wealth and her Inhabitants,

'The able Doctor, or America Swallowing the Bitter Draught', from the *London Magazine* (April 1774). A female figure, representing the American colonists, is penned down by leading members of the British government as the Prime Minister, Lord North, forcibly pours tea (representing British imperial policies) down her clutched throat. Britannia turns away in embarrassment as France and Spain watch with interest.

> by Violence, by Famine and every Species of Tyranny and Murder. The children of the other we daily carry off from the Land of their Nativity, like *Sheep for the Slaughter*, to return no more: we tear them from every Object of their Affection; or, sad Alternative! Drag them together to the Horrours of a mutual Servitude.[52]

National guilt, argued Wakefield, required communal repentance.

Rejecting sugar as slavery

Sugar was arguably the most important commodity in the eighteenth-century British Empire. Although available for centuries from Mediterranean and Asian sources, sugar remained expensive in the British Isles until English colonists, like their European rivals, began converting West Indian islands into massive sugar-production centres. By the end of the eighteenth century, virtually everyone in Britain ate it via cooked dishes, confectionery, medicines, rum and, most of all, the hot beverages of empire – coffee and tea. It was the empire's most ubiquitous, and arguably most important, commodity. By mid-century, London boasted eighty sugar refineries, and the thriving port of Bristol was home to another twenty. Per capita consumption by 1800 had increased by 2,500 per cent in the past 150 years, reaching in excess of 20 pounds. To produce the sugar and sustain the infrastructure supporting it, slave ships injected millions of Africans into the Caribbean. Conditions were unforgiving due to the combined effects of the disease-infested environment, the taxing physical conditions of sugar production and the brutality of the planters. Europe's sugar-producing colonies failed to increase their slave populations naturally, instead relying on a steady flow of fresh slaves from Africa.[53]

In consequence of sugar's importance, the British abolitionists faced an overwhelming opponent. The empire relied on slave labour, and those who profited from it infected every imaginable corner of power. By the early 1780s, hardly a Briton of substantial means and authority could separate himself from the profits associated with slavery – direct ownership of slaves, the shipping of slaves, the insuring of those ships, the goods traded in Africa for slaves and the British port cities that served as conduits, to name just a few. As many as one-eighth of all British seamen were engaged in West Indian commerce, leading proponents to describe the West Indies as the navy's nursery.[54] Even the Church of England's primary missionary wing, the Society for the Propagation of the Gospel in Foreign Parts, had been a major slave owner via its Barbados plantations since 1710, unabashedly tallying its profits in the society's published annual budgets.

Opposition to slavery was not entirely new to the late eighteenth century. However, the late 1780s marked an exponential increase in public opposition to slavery, resulting in new tactics that demonstrated both the extent to which Britons associated imperial goods with the empire as well as the perceived collective power of ordinary consumers. The 1788 Manchester petition against the slave trade marked the beginning of a popular movement that would last in various forms for half a century. Signed by 11,000 people, which was roughly 30 per cent of the city's population, the petition sent shockwaves across the country and set important precedents for the anti-slavery movement. First, the petition framed its arguments on moral grounds – humanity and national honour – rather than practical, strategic or economic ones. Second, the petition, like the thousands that would follow, did not restrict itself to enfranchised or elite members of society. In fact, women and men who were ineligible to vote made up the majority of signatories. Whereas other petitioning drives, such as goodwill calls for the king's recovery in 1789 or for the removal of the Fox–North coalition from power in 1783, came predominately from elite groups, abolitionist petitions almost entirely originated with people who could not vote. Third, the organizers invested the money they raised by popular subscriptions in a media campaign, buying advertisements in newspapers across Britain calling for local people to start their own petition drives. Tellingly, pro-slavery pundits initially expected even larger counter-petitions to appear either in Manchester or nearby Liverpool, which was even more closely connected to the trade, but such predictions proved erroneous. They never came.[55]

To rally popular support, the new wave of abolitionists focused on sugar, arguing that, as willing consumers, Britons were accountable for the horrific mechanisms that brought it to their tables. This required two underlying mindsets to be shared by great swathes of the British populace. First, Britons had to identify the products they enjoyed with the peoples and places that produced them. Decades of visual advertising, travel accounts, cookery books and consumer-driven discussions about quality and authenticity positioned British consumers to associate sugar with West Indian slavery. Second, Britons needed to believe they were responsible for their nation's actions. In this regard, working in the reformers' favour was the widespread association of the nation with the individual that developed during the eighteenth century.[56] As Grosley reflected after his visit, 'Each citizen identifying himself with the government, must of necessity extend to himself the high idea which he has of the nation: he triumphs in its victories; he is afflicted by its calamities: he exhausts himself in projects to promote its successes, to second its advantages, and to repair its losses.'[57] While Grosley mockingly compared such people to what he described as self-congratulatory flies in a stable who think their irritating buzzing drives the horse forward, the reformers who sought to end slavery did not. Like tea in the American colonies, the consumption of sugar was a choice made public via the act of purchase at a shop. Moreover, the social nature of the beverages into which most sugar flowed made eating sugar an often-witnessed action. The inclusion generations earlier of sugar bowls in tea services enabled individuals to tailor the sweetness of the tea to their own preference at each setting. Thus, each setting and teaspoon of sugar could now become a watched moment of political, moral action.

In the wake of the American Revolution, which had shattered any semblance of knee-jerk public support for anything a British government did overseas, abolitionists capitalized on people's feelings of personal connection to the nation. First, abolitionists relentlessly publicized the horrors of the slave trade and slavery as antithetical to the principles of Christianity and Britishness. As Samuel Bradburn representatively declared in his widely distributed *Address to the People Called Methodist; Concerning the Evils of Encouraging the Slave Trade*, 'That the unconstitutional principles of slavery, should be fostered in the bosom of the *British Legislature* in this enlightened age, is a dreadful reflection on the boasted love of liberty for which the English have been so famous, and an utter disgrace to any nation of people, *said to be free*.'[58] Second, and most relevant to the subject of this chapter, abolitionists successfully associated those vile practices with the most ubiquitous product slaves produced: sugar. In doing so, they made slavery everyone's responsibility.

Sugar was the obvious target not only because of its ubiquity but in part owing to the people who made up the movement's rank and file membership: women. Women were part of the popular abolitionist cause from the start, as signatories of the 1788 Manchester petition and the others it immediately inspired. The first women-only abolitionist meeting was held in London that same year. Successfully targeting male-dominated worlds of insurance or shipping was out of women's reach but promoting a consumer boycott of sugar was well within their purview, as it combined a moral cause with the household economy. The significance of women in these movements is difficult to overestimate. They were leaders as well as the primary target for membership. Unlike other political causes, framing slavery as a subject that affected the health of the nation enabled women to engage comfortably with it in public. While openly campaigning for candidates during elections proved problematic, especially if the candidate was not a husband or relative, membership in evangelical organizations and moral reform movements was generally acceptable.[59] Women were, after all, lauded as the guardians of the nation's moral well-being. The evils of slavery, reformers carefully argued, threatened that health.

The people who organized the abolitionist movements were not malleable dupes. Rather, they were highly motivated, sophisticated grassroots operators who understood how to rally public support and action. While plenty came from the elite and labouring ranks, pious middling women from across the denominational divide made up the rank and file.[60] They pressured each other and male members of their families, and they produced a wealth of publicity via newspaper articles, letters to editors and cheap pamphlets to persuade everyone else.

The detailed minutes of the 'The London Society for the mitigating and gradually abolishing the state of slavery throughout the British dominion', as they dubbed themselves after some debate at their first meeting at the King's Head Tavern in 1823, offer a window into the hundreds of such societies great and small that emerged throughout the British political and social landscape. After first agreeing that slavery was 'opposed to the spirit and precepts of Christianity as well as repugnant to every dictate of natural humanity and justice', the group of several dozen men and women went to work on an action plan. Within two weeks, they had created a prospectus and detailed business plan for the society. The following week they created five subcommittees, one for finances and the others each assigned with a communicative task – pamphlet publications, the newspaper and periodical press, correspondence with like-minded domestic societies, and correspondence with foreign agents and allies. They immediately set to work identifying abolitionist writers to support, linking with similar societies, monitoring the press for commentary on slavery and inundating editors throughout the country with content favourable to the abolitionist cause. Within three months of forming, they had distributed nearly two thousand pamphlets on a host of anti-slavery topics in 38 counties in the British Isles as well as in North America – all of which were either sold at cost or heavily subsidized. Within six months, they were distributing many thousands of both their own and other societies' pamphlets. As with most abolitionist societies, twopence was the common selling price for the anti-slavery pamphlets, despite a production cost of fourpence and the standard price for similarly sized pamphlets being a shilling or more. Such subsidies enabled greater distribution but required relentless fundraising through lectures, tours and subscriptions.[61]

One such pamphlet was *Reasons for Using East India Sugar* in 1828, produced and initially distributed by the Peckham Ladies' African and Anti-Slavery Association, priced at the usual two-pence.[62] Revealing a sophisticated understanding of both free-market economics and the complexities of imperial trade, the pamphlet sought to explain the value of boycotting West Indian slave sugar and the potential of East Indian sugar as a replacement. Repeating arguments that emerged in the early 1790s, when the target was the slave trade, the pamphlet asserted that the slave sugar of the West Indies was cheaper in consequence of what effectively amounted to a government subsidy. This so-called subsidy had been a bone of contention for decades, as West Indian planters and their supporters in Britain sought to maintain their monopoly on sugar production against the growing threat from South Asia.[63]

Like a host of similar pamphlets and petitions, *Reasons for Using East India Sugar* called for the withdrawal of favourable legislation in favour of a free-market position that would result in East India sugar becoming markedly cheaper – a counterintuitive prospect given India's greater distance. Labour costs, the pamphlet explained in a simple language designed to reach the widest possible audience, were the explanation. Indian labour was so cheap, and the price for maintaining a slavery establishment so great, that costs related to shipping were irrelevant. In support of this argument, the author pointed out how free labour in Ohio produced tobacco more cheaply than slaves in Maryland and Virginia, despite the greater distance from markets. With such arguments, abolitionists found a tenuous ally in the East India Company, which saw an opportunity to profit from Asian sugar production. Yet abolitionists were careful not to overemphasize cost savings for risk of distracting from their main point – an accusation that apologists for slavery launched at abolitionists. As in so many similar pamphlets, the Peckham Ladies' African and Anti-Slavery Association concluded by insisting that the issue was not about how to acquire cheaper sugar. The actual cost of sugar was 'Not eightpence, or tenpence, or twelvepence, or fourteenpence the pound only; but groans, and wounds, and death.' If abstinence was the only possibility, then that was the way forward.

James Gillray, 'Anti-saccharites, or, John Bull and his Family leaving off the use of Sugar' (London, 1792). King George III, Queen Charlotte and their daughters gather around a tea table. As the king encouragingly declares 'O delicious! delicious!' as he drinks the sugarless tea, the queen explains to her frowning daughters, 'O my dear Creatures, do but Taste it! You can't think how nice it is without Sugar: – and then consider how much Work you'll save the poor Blackeemoors by leaving off the use of it!' In an allusion to the king's frugality and accusations that some families embraced the sugar boycott for household economic reasons, the queen adds, 'and above all, remember how much expence it will save your poor Papa!'

Whether targeting the slave trade in the 1790s or slavery itself in the 1820s, abolitionists consistently emphasized Britons' personal responsibility for the actions of the government. The boycotting of sugar fit this message perfectly. William Fox's 1792 seminal *Address to the People of Great Britain*, which went through 26 editions by the end of the next year, struck a popular chord and set the tone. Slavery, the Baptist minister Fox proclaimed, had become too entrenched in the British Empire and enriched too many in power to be toppled through mere words and petitions to Parliament. Only 'the people at large' could effect change. That change was consumer action. While the British laws enabled West Indian planters to produce and sell sugar, the people had no obligation to eat it. 'They may hold it to our lips, steeped in the blood of our fellow-creatures,' he declared, 'but they cannot compel us to accept the potion.' Thus, he continued,

'With us it rests, either to receive it and be partners in the crime, or to exonerate ourselves from guilt, but spurning from us the temptation.'

The link between consumption and culpability was Fox's key point, which he drove relentlessly in the plainest language possible: 'For let us not think, that the crime rests alone with those who conduct the traffic, or the legislature by which it is protected. If we purchase the commodity we participate in the crime.' After all, he stressed, 'The slave-dealer, the slave-holder, and the slave-driver, are virtually the agents of the consumer, and may be considered as employed and hired by him to procure the commodity.' While an individual might absolve himself through abstaining from sugar, only an evangelical approach in the form of a popular boycott would create the necessary economic pressure to ensure change. In a series of calculations that would be repeated and re-tabulated for decades, appearing on everything from pamphlets to china bowls, Fox estimated that a family abstaining from West Indian sugar for a mere 21 months would 'prevent the slavery or murder of one fellow-creature'. With this knowledge, he explained, future enslavements and deaths of slaves were on the consciences of any who henceforth consumed sugar. While the slaveowner was guilty of murder, Fox accused, 'we, who have knowingly done any act which might occasion his being in that situation, are accessories after the fact.'

The tenets of Fox's address resonated throughout the British Isles. The public call to action took a range of forms – letters to newspaper editors, short stories, sermons, poems and dialogues. Each unyieldingly placed responsibility for the horrors of slavery and the slave trade firmly at the feet of sugar consumers, such as in a fictitious dialogue between 'Mr. English (a gentleman) and Cusho, a Jamaican slave'. Published in the immediate wake of Fox's address, the dialogue centres on a well-meaning Englishman asking what he can do after hearing the slave's vivid account of his suffering. Cusho responds plainly, 'Drink Tea as dey do in China, Massa; and Coffee as dey do in Turkey – without Sugar.'[64] Such associations of sugar with physical suffering, what Fox called 'blood-bought luxury', was a common theme designed to replace sugar's clean white sweetness with nauseatingly gory imagery.[65] Faced with such evidence, the abolitionists argued, the only Christian, British and civilized response was to join the boycott. After all, the sacrifice was minimal. As a male reader of the *Newcastle Courant* remarked in a letter to the editor after the 'ladies in my family' had read Fox's address and made the case for abstinence, 'I could not refuse, Mr Printer, to join in the above commendable resolution, and to make the only sacrifice required for the purpose, by giving up a luxury which habit alone has rendered important to us.'[66]

The economic impact of the sugar boycotts is difficult to assess. Petitions and signed pledges to abstain from slave-produced sugar abound, but the sincerity of a signature – perhaps made under intense social pressure – is impossible to measure. In fact, more than one critic of the boycotters claimed that they were actually penny-pinchers who dressed their cheapness in self-righteousness; or, as one sneeringly described, they were 'hiding parsimony under the specious cloak of humanity'.[67] The first boycotts in the 1790s certainly did not succeed in undermining the economic foundations of West Indian slavery.[68] Total participation can only be guessed, but contemporaries' estimate of 300,000 boycotting families is not unreasonable.[69] Although an

James Gillrary, 'Barbarities in the West Indias' (London, 1791). In a graphically violent print highlighting both the cruelty of slavery and its connection with sugar production, the scene depicts a white overseer boiling slaves along with the sugar cane juice, declaring 'B—t your black Eyes! what you can't work because you're not well? – but I'll give you a warm bath, to cure your Ague, & a Curry-combing afterwards to put Spunk into you.' Severed arms and ears of slaves are nailed above the doorway.

Isaac Cruikshank, 'The Gradual Abolition off the Slave Trade, or leaving of Sugar by Degrees' (London, 1792). A family, possibly the royal family, have tea together and discuss abstaining from sugar in their tea. While the central male figure advocates total abstinence, the rest plead for a reduction only. The figure to the right of him, possibly Queen Charlotte, declares, 'Now my Dear's only an ickle Bit, do but tink on de Negro girl dat Captain Kimber treated so cruelly.'

impressive number, it was countered by the slave rebellion in Saint-Domingue in 1791, which began just as the boycotts took root in Britain. The rebellion, which marked the start of the Haitian Revolution, immediately disrupted sugar production in France's most important Caribbean colony. In consequence, any British sugar unwanted by British consumers found a ready market on the European continent, thus ensuring prices remained buoyant. The economic disruptions caused by the Haitian Revolution and the French Revolutionary and Napoleonic wars proceeded to dictate sugar prices for the next two decades.

Nevertheless, by associating one of the most ubiquitous commodities in Britain with African slavery, abolitionists firmly moved the topic of slavery into Britons' daily lives. As the historian Clare Midgley has argued, 'The main importance of the campaign [to boycott sugar] to the abolition movement was probably the role it played in creating in large numbers of men and women a sense of individual responsibility for slavery, and a belief in the possibility of achieving its downfall through extra-Parliamentary action.'[70] With the aid of considerable pressure, the abolitionists ultimately prevailed against the might of the West Indian interest and what many believed to be the economic self-interest of the British state, first with the abolition of the slave trade in 1807 and then with the abolition of slavery in 1833. Moreover, the experience highlighted the widely recognized power that ordinary Britons wielded as consumers. The language of writers on both sides assumed a level of audience sophistication that included a basic understanding of free markets, types of government subsidies, imperial trade routes, taxation and the ancillary benefits of imperial maritime trade. Equally important, this extended to women, the hearts and minds of whom the boycotting abolitionists and their opponents hoped to sway from the start.

BY THE END OF the eighteenth century, the most common ingestibles of empire had clearly moved beyond their initial exoticism. Yet domestication had not rid them of their association with imperial rule and trade. In fact, their consumption facilitated discussions, and acute criticism, of the British Empire. The social nature of drinking coffee and tea created new public and domestic spaces in which ordinary Britons engaged with social and political topics, including those related to the expanding empire. Along with the growth of the newspaper and periodical press, these spaces helped to cultivate a society that was openly critical of the government and ruling elite as a whole. While there had long been interest in the empire and critics of its management, the notion of shopkeepers, tradesmen and women openly following its news and freely commenting on it was unimaginable before the eighteenth century, yet commonplace by its halfway mark.

The sugar boycotts were partly a product of this newfound confidence in the widespread engagement with politics and imperial affairs and Britons' self-awareness as consumers. Advertising the origins of imperial goods extended beyond the purposes of merely providing assurances of authenticity and quality. Knowing a good's origins enabled consumers to make ethics-based choices rooted in their understanding of the circumstances in which the good was produced and transported to shop shelves. When consumers objected to those methods, they believed that they collectively had the power to effect change through the extra-governmental action of the consumer boycott. This marked a watershed in British history – the empowerment of consumers, irrespective of class or gender, to protest in a legal, polite way – and foreshadowed the countless collective consumer boycotts that would transpire in Britain, its empire and around the globe. Such actions irrevocably politicized otherwise disenfranchised individuals by binding the simple process of eating to statements of political support and dissent. As an abolitionist foreshadowed in a public letter to the Duchess of York, pleading with her to abstain from sugar, boycotting sugar was merely the start. 'If there be any other branch of commerce founded in inequity', she challenged, 'let it be brought forward after the slave trade has been abolished.'[71] The genie was out of the bottle.

CONCLUSION

As a thirteen-year-old in 1766, John Marsh fled the doldrums and anxieties of his boarding school in Kent by escaping with some of his classmates to a place they called Yew Tree Bottom. Isolated from the rest of the word, it was a place of respite. Bringing 'tin cups, bread, butter, tea, and sugar', Marsh and his classmates spent Sunday afternoons and holidays making fires and brewing sweet tea, 'and regarded ourselves with great delight'.[1] Reflecting on his childhood decades later, Marsh described these times as some of his happiest.

Although separated by a century and the chasm of social rank from Marsh, Queen Victoria offered similar escapism to Eugénie de Montijo in October 1879. France's last empress, Eugénie, and her husband, Napoleon III, had been deposed following the Franco-Prussian War in 1870 and taken refuge in Britain. He died three years later, and the death of their only son in the summer of 1879 in South Africa fighting as part of the British army in the Anglo-Zulu War – a death that effectively meant the end of the House of Bonaparte – had sent Eugénie reeling into despair. She sought respite with her old friend Victoria, who took Eugénie to her favoured place of solace, the Scottish Highlands. Victoria's son, Prince Arthur, remarked, 'Her Majesty made a long stay in Balmoral that year, for she had a loving and generous desire to help to comfort her suffering friend the Empress Eugenie, whose health had been so much broken by bereavement and sorrow.' In one of their most poignant moments together, the two empresses visited Victoria's much-loved secret escape Ruidh na Bhan Righ, which Victoria described as 'the little Shiel [cottage], which contains only two small rooms and a little kitchen. It stands in a very wild, solitary spot.' There, the two found some peace: 'We walked along the footpath above the Gelder for a mile and a half,' Victoria recorded, 'the dogs, which had come up, following us, and the Empress talked a great deal, and most pleasantly, about former times.' 'When we came back to the little Shiel after walking for an hour,' she continued, 'we had tea.'[2] A century later, once again little had changed, as two of England's greatest recorded electrical power draws followed England's semi-final and quarter-final losses in the 1990 and 2002 World Cups, as viewers switched on their electric kettles to console themselves with cups of tea.[3]

During the eighteenth century, the ingestibles of empire ingrained themselves into British society to the extent that coffeehouses, tea drinking, pipes of tobacco and sugar-filled sweets became quintessentially British. As difficult as imagining Britain without its favoured edible goods may be, comprehending a British Empire without them is near impossible. The domestic desire for the small luxuries found overseas was an engine of the empire. Tea and the porcelain in which the British consumed it fuelled the growth of the East India Company and linked the British and Chinese economies. The desire to control and increase sugar production drew the English, and later British, to the Caribbean, where indigenous peoples and fauna were effectively eradicated in favour of millions of African slaves, sugar cane and coffee plants. And the early Chesapeake bases transformed into settler colonies only after the discovery of a commercially viable strain of tobacco. Foreshadowing later events, among the permanent settlers' first actions was to form an elected assembly, the House of Burgesses, in 1619 (a year before the Pilgrims arrived in New England on the *Mayflower*) to advocate for their rights against the Virginia Company and Crown.

The increasingly business-minded British government in the eighteenth century was acutely aware of the value of such goods to the state. Surpluses in tobacco and, from the second half of the eighteenth century, Caribbean-produced coffee provided Britain lucrative trade balances with other European countries, further adding to its growing wealth and power. In fact, in the decade before the American Revolution, an estimated 85 and 94 per cent, respectively, of Britain's tobacco and coffee imports were re-exported to Europe – an annual trade worth in excess of £1 million, or roughly the equivalent to the 1765 cost of building sixteen HMS *Victorys*, one of the most famous and powerful ships in the Royal Navy.[4] The need to transport these cherished goods drove the formation of the world's largest merchant navy, whose sailors quickly swelled the ranks of the Royal Navy during wartime, providing Britain an unassailable advantage over its rivals. In turn, the Royal Navy protected and forcefully expanded trade and territorial rule, often conflating the two.

None of this was possible without consumer demand. The question of whether demand was driven by the influx of tantalizing new goods or the social changes that enabled consumers to afford them is an age-old conundrum. During the long eighteenth century, the two forces fed off each other. Potential consumers worked longer and harder to acquire the empire's ingestible luxuries, and the market responded by flooding Britain with the goods to such an extent that they became affordable and accessible to even the remotest and poorest of Britons. In so doing, such goods as coffee, tea, tobacco and sugar effectively became staples of the British diet by the latter half of the eighteenth century. When the basic goods themselves became ubiquitous, consumers elevated the stakes by paying more for better quality or selecting more expensive types, such as Hyson tea and Turkish coffee, over more common varieties. Consumers also accessorized their experiences with silver utensils and porcelain cups; even being able to take tea during the working hours of the lower middling and labouring ranks was a sign of leisured status, wealth and refinement.

For Britons, the introduction of these imperial goods fundamentally changed their lives. In addition to introducing large amounts of caffeine and nicotine into Britons' bodies, these goods were central to the creation of the modern retail sector. Shops selling such goods went from relative rarities and the preserve of the elite to numbering in the tens of thousands and attracting rich and poor alike in the space of a couple of generations. In a quest for customers, highly competitive shopkeepers developed window displays, redesigned the interiors of their shops and created marketing schemes, including extensive mail order businesses and liberal personal credit. Equally important, they advertised. While other shopkeepers utilized many of these practices, none did it more prolifically, innovatively or aggressively than those men and women who peddled the empire's ingestible goods.

The story of British consumption of the empire's edible commodities during the long eighteenth century is a blend of adaptation and adoption. For instance, while coffee's flavour was adapted to suit the British palate, the male, politics-infused culture of the typical London coffeehouse directly reflected its Middle Eastern origins. While Asian tea ceremonies were rarely replicated in Britain, tea's highly ritualistic, intimate preparation and drinking practices, along with the connoisseurship surrounding it, continued, at least in middling and elite households. And, as in China, the style of preparation and selection of the tea reflected the quality of the host in Britain.[5] The continued importance of the adopted qualities of these goods is nowhere more evident than in visual advertising, which highly competitive grocers utilized and advanced more than any other retail sector. Taken as a whole, these advertisements heavily emphasized the overseas origins of coffee, tea and tobacco and their association with the empire and imperial trade. Ubiquitous images of Chinese workers and African slaves cultivating the products and loading them onto British ships assured consumers of their authenticity. Promises of unadulterated quality may have been the primary aim of these advertisements, but they also turned the commodities into material objects and endowed them with meaningful associations with the peoples and places that produced the goods – not unlike the guidebooks and labels that explained the significance of objects in the new public museums. In consequence, consumption of these goods was the most common way in which Britons engaged with the peoples connected to Britain through imperial rule and commerce.

Of course, the infusion of British consumer culture with these goods is just one part of how food shaped and reflected Britons' relationships with their empire and the peoples connected to it. Just as goods of imperial trade flooded Britain, so too did information about the peoples that inhabited the world in the form of travel accounts, histories, geographies and newspaper stories. This was a natural by-product of commercial activity and territorial expansion, and Britons, who during the long eighteenth century embraced fact over fantasy, struggled to make sense of it. The Scottish Enlightenment provided the nation's intellectual framework for processing the deluge of information into a system that could explain the incredible socio-economic differences in the world's peoples. To make their concepts relatable, leading philosophers and those who sought to apply their system to people across the globe employed the common ground of food – its production, distribution, preparation and consumption. Thus a society's relationships with food were evaluated in the same manner as its roads and government. Naturally, Britons applied such assessments to their own culture in search of evidence of their progress and rank as a civilization, and of answers to the question of the longevity of their ascendance. The preparation and consumption of food became a national conversation. In this context, remarks on Cherokee utensils and French admiration of Cheshire cheese were not made lightly. Rather, they served as scrutinized evidence for determining the social and economic developmental status of peoples – in this instance the relative primitiveness of American Indians and the emergence of Britain as a highly civilized society worthy of emulation.

What one ate had long been a matter of social status for the elite, but in eighteenth-century Britain, print culture and the public fascination with fashion and status took matters to a whole new level. Some critics chastised the immorality of those who overindulged in the luxuries of eating, while others shamed the baseness of the unfashionable. Food served as a foil to harangue immoral politicians, chastise European rivals and attack consumer culture. By the same token, food was used to describe a domestic ideal and the superiority of the British people. A new genre of female-authored printed cookery books that targeted middling and elite mistresses and their servants emerged as popular guides for navigating the perilous terrain. Together with the men who emulated them, these women and their publishers from the mid-century onwards laid the foundations for a national cuisine that embraced the emerging middle-class values of economy, rejection of ostentatiousness in favour of subtlety, national pride and celebration of regional diversity. The last expressed itself in the assignment of national and regional names to cooked dishes, such as 'Scotch collops', 'Shrewsbury cakes', 'Yorkshire puddings' and 'Welsh Rabbit'. Increasingly mixed in with these recipes were dishes from around the world, particular the British Empire. Emphasizing authenticity, widely available recipes for such dishes as 'Carolina Rice snowballs', 'China-orange juice', West Indian 'Imperial' and 'sangeree' (sangria) drinks, and 'Mullagatawny Soup, as made in India' offered meaningful, multi-sensory opportunities for people in Britain to engage the various peoples connected to the

'A West India Sportsman' (London, 1807). One of a series of satirical prints designed to criticize the slothful lifestyle of West Indian planters, this is a 'sporting' scene in which the planter sportsmen sit and lie comfortably under umbrellas, tended by slaves and surrounded by a feast of treats. Empty bottles of alcohol are strewn across the ground and multi-gallon vats of rum, brandy, Royal Punch and Sangaree (sangria) are at the ready. Ready for action, the planter calls out, 'Make hast with the Sangaree Quashie, and tell Quaco to drive the Birds up to Me – I'm Ready.'

growing British Empire. In this sense, such dishes could serve as material objects in themselves – edible artefacts of distant places and peoples connected to Britain by imperial rule and trade.

Of course, many people ate Carolina rice pudding and drank plantation coffee simply because these items were on offer and pleasant-tasting. However, consumers' awareness of the imperial connections with such foods is increasingly apparent as the century progressed. Although not always linear, the process was accretive, not unlike the increase in imperial consumer goods, advertising, print culture and cookery books during the eighteenth century. In consequence, we should hesitate to aggregate the cosmologies of the women drinking tea in London in 1700 with those doing the same in 1800. Not until nearly the mid-century mark did many of the ingestible commodities of imperial trade begin to become truly ubiquitous – the same time when museums and popular female-authored cookery books first appeared and London newspapers began to reach truly national audiences. Critically, none of these developments happened in isolation; they were all intertwined. A middling family in the 1770s might easily awaken to a breakfast that included coffee, tea and sugar and the reading of the news from around the nation and empire before embarking to see the ethnographic exhibits at the British Museum. They might stop at a coffeehouse on the way home, reading or listening to other patrons debate the latest events in America, and then go home, where they might enjoy a home-cooked 'Curry the Indian way' made from any number of popular cookery books – or even have it delivered. That evening they would sit by the fireside, like most middling families, and take turns reading a popular travel account, perhaps the most widely read of the day – an account of James Cook's voyages to the Pacific.[6] To this can be added any number of trinkets of imperial trade the family might use to adorn their home or persons. Taken in isolation, a curry may just be a curry; eaten in this context, a curry could have meanings for consumers well beyond nutrition.

Because the path to an imperial consciousness was accretive, both for society and for individuals, identifying a watershed is difficult. Spikes in newspaper coverage or the number of published political pamphlets were common during wartime or during the run-up to parliamentary consideration of a particularly divisive issue. As a reader of London's *Morning Post* observed in 1777, at the height of the highly public and contentious American Revolution, 'The desarts [*sic*] of America become a nearer object than the counties of England; and the regions of the Ganges watched with more anxiety than the territory of the Severn.'[7] However, such evidence is not entirely satisfying, not least because of the difficulties in identifying grassroots public opinion in media coverage. Nevertheless, there were clear bellwethers. Among the most important was the popular opposition movement against slavery that began in the late 1780s. Inherently a grassroots movement, the campaigns sought the participation of the unenfranchised, particularly women. Together, they unequivocally demonstrated their conscious connection of eating with empire by boycotting West Indian slave-produced sugar. If sugar was not yet synonymous with the empire and slavery in the minds of all consumers, the campaigners' relentless onslaught with petitions, newspaper articles, pamphlets, sermons and satirical prints would have made the connection inescapable.

Aside from underlining the connections British consumers made between specific commodities and the mechanisms of imperial rule and trade that provided them, the sugar boycotts ultimately highlight how Britons understood their roles in the empire. By focusing on

Britons' specific role as consumers, the campaigners effectively enfranchised everyone. The wealthy London merchant, Devonshire farm labourer and Scottish blacksmith who purchased sugar from various urban and rural shops were all culpable for how it was produced. When ordinary Britons' confronted the dilemma, their responses demonstrate that their imperial consciousness had a conscience. Boycotting sugar was not in their economic interest, or so consumers believed. The West Indian trade was lucrative, it relied on slavery, and sugar was a tasty staple of the British diet. While some public arguments asserted the economic benefits of eliminating African slavery in favour of free labour, popular petitions that emanated from the same ranks of the boycotters did not focus on the economic issues. For them, humanity, justice and national honour trumped economic concerns. Thus, by the end of the eighteenth century, Britons were prepared to critique unsavoury imperial practices with the same vigour they had previously reserved for domestic affairs. They were no longer merely Britons but, in some instances at least, self-aware participants in the British Empire.

Sometimes drinking a warm cup of coffee or eating a spicy bowl of curry is simply about nourishing one's body or tantalizing one's palate. Just as consumers today do not invariably associate the products they buy with the complex mechanisms and ethical implications of how they were sourced, the British in the eighteenth century purchased the edibles of their growing empire for a host of different reasons. However, like consumers today, such considerations of source and production sometimes played a role in the selection and even rejection of products – often contrary to pure economic interest. Brands, connoisseurship, styles of consumption and using goods to self-fashion an image were prevalent in eighteenth-century Britain. These foods, whether tea imported by the East India Company from China or New England pancakes meticulously recreated via a popular cookery book recipe, were the most common ways in which Britons engaged with their rapidly growing empire. Moreover, and again like today's consumers, many Britons came to hold their government, producers and retailers accountable for the conditions of the labourers producing the goods. While certainly not every British consumer consciously participated in this remarkable shift, many did – enough to shape advertising, cookery, popular national politics and the course of the empire.

REFERENCES

INTRODUCTION

1 John Marsh, 'History of my private life', HM 54457, 37 vols, Huntington Library, San Marino, California.
2 B. W. Higman, *How Food Made History* (Oxford, 2012), p. 1.
3 P. J. Marshall, 'Empire and Authority in the Later Eighteenth Century', *Journal of Imperial and Commonwealth History*, 15 (1987), pp. 105–22. See also P. J. Marshall, 'A Nation Defined by Empire, 1755–1776', in *Uniting the Kingdom? The Making of British History*, ed. Alexander Grant and Keith Stringer (London, 1995), pp. 208–22; H. V. Bowen, 'British Conceptions of Global Empire, 1756–83', *Journal of Imperial and Commonwealth History*, 26 (1998), pp. 1–27.
4 Jacob Price, 'The Imperial Economy, 1700–1776', in *The Oxford History of the British Empire*, vol. II: *The Eighteenth Century*, ed. P. J. Marshall (Oxford, 1998), p. 78.
5 Markman Ellis, Richard Coulton and Matthew Mauger, *Empire of Tea: The Asian Leaf that Conquered the World* (London, 2015), chapter 3; Jane T. Merritt, *The Trouble with Tea: The Politics of Consumption in the Eighteenth-century Global Economy* (Baltimore, MD, 2017), chapter 1; John Thornton, *Africa and Africans in the Making of the Atlantic World, 1400–1800*, 2nd edn (Cambridge, 1998); Richard White, *The Middle Ground, Indians, Empires, and Republics in the Great Lakes Region, 1650–1815* (Cambridge, 1991).
6 Frank Trentmann, *Empire of Things: How We Became a World of Consumers, from the Fifteenth Century to the Twenty-first* (London, 2016), pp. 23–4.
7 Arjun Appadurai, ed., *The Social Life of Things: Commodities in Perspective* (Cambridge, 1986); Maxine Berg, *Luxury and Pleasure in Eighteenth-century Britain* (Oxford, 2005); Trentmann, *Empire of Things*, pp. 10–11; Sidney Mintz, *Sweetness and Power: The Place of Sugar in Modern History* (New York, 1985); Lizzie Collingham, *The Taste of Empire: How Britain's Quest for Food Shaped the Modern World* (New York, 2017); Sven Beckert, *Empire of Cotton: A Global History* (London, 2014); Giorgio Riello, *Cotton: The Fabric that Made the Modern World* (Cambridge, 2013).

8 Mark Pendergrast, *Uncommon Grounds: The History of Coffee and How it Transformed the World*, revd edn (New York, 2010); Ellis, Coulton and Mauger, *Empire of Tea*; Erika Rappaport, *A Thirst for Empire: How Tea Shaped the Modern World* (Princeton, NJ, 2017).
9 *Massachusetts Gazette*, 13 December 1773.
10 *The Africa Trade* (London, 1745), cited in Trentmann, *Empire of Things*, p. 91.
11 Malachy Postlethwayt, *The Universal Dictionary of Trade and Commerce, translated from the French of the Celebrated Monsieur Savary* (London, 1757), vol. I, p. xxv.
12 Hannah Barker, *Newspapers, Politics, and Public Opinion in Late Eighteenth-century England* (Oxford, 1998); James Raven, Helen Small and Naomi Tadmor, eds, *The Practice and Representation of Reading in England* (Cambridge, 1996).
13 Benedict Anderson, *Imagined Communities: Reflections on the Origin and Spread of Nationalism*, revd edn (London, 1991).
14 Pendergrast, *Uncommon Grounds*, p. 6.
15 Troy Bickham, *Making Headlines: The American Revolution as Seen through the British Press* (DeKalb, IL, 2009), chapters 1–2; Kathleen Wilson, *The Sense of the People: Politics, Culture and Imperialism in England, 1715–1785* (Cambridge, 1995).
16 John Brewer, *The Sinews of Power: War, Money and the English State, 1688–1783* (Cambridge, MA, 1990).
17 Karen Ordahl Kupperman, *The Jamestown Project* (Cambridge, MA, 2007), chapter 9.
18 For an overview of imperial trade values, see Price, 'Imperial Economy', pp. 81–6.
19 Ann McClintock, *Imperial Leather: Race, Gender and Sexuality in the Colonial Context* (New York, 1995), p. 17. For the eighteenth century, see especially Linda Colley, *Britons: Forging the Nation, 1707–1837* (New Haven, CT, 1992); and Bob Harris, '"American Idols": Empire, War and the Middling Ranks in Mid-eighteenth Century Britain', *Past and Present*, 150 (1996), pp. 111–41.
20 Ronald Hyam, *Understanding the British Empire* (Cambridge, 2010), pp. 11–16.
21 Ibid., p. 16; Bernard Porter, *The Absent-minded Imperialists: Empire, Society, and Culture in Britain* (Oxford, 2006).
22 Troy Bickham, *The Weight of Vengeance: The United States, the British Empire, and the War of 1812* (New York, 2012), pp. 129–32.
23 Stephen Mennell, *All Manners of Food: Eating and Taste in England and France from the Middle Ages to the Present* (Oxford, 1985).
24 *London Magazine* (October 1755), p. 476.
25 Roland Barthes, 'Toward a Psychology of Contemporary Food Consumption', in *European Diet from Pre-industrial to Modern Times*, ed. Elborg Forster and Robert Forster (New York, 1975). See also his 'Ornamental Cookery' in his *Mythologies* (Paris, 1957), trans. Annette Lavers (New York, 1959), and Claude Lévi-Strauss, *The Origin of Table Manners* (New York, 1968), trans. John Weightman and Doreen Weightman.

26 Sara Pennell, '"Great quantities of gooseberry pye and baked clod of beef": Victualling and Eating Out in Early Modern London', in *Londinopolis*, ed. Paul Griffiths and Mark Jenner (Manchester, 2000), pp. 228–9.
27 John Roach, *Roach's London Pocket Pilot, or Stranger's Guide through the Metropolis* (London, 1796), p. 44.
28 Edwina Ehrman, '18th Century', in *London Eats Out: 500 Years of Capital Dining* (London, 1999); and Janet Ing Freeman's introduction to her edition of Ralf Rylance, *The Epicure's Almanack: Eating and Dining in Regency London. The Original 1815 Guidebook* (London, 2013).
29 *The Times*, 16 March 1802.
30 *General Evening Post*, 21 January 1779.
31 Janet Schaw, *Journal of a Lady of Quality, Being the Narrative of a Journey from Scotland to the West Indies, North Carolina, and Portugal, in the years 1774 to 1776*, ed. Evangeline Walker Andrews (New Haven, CT, 1923), p. 139.
32 *The Times*, 25 December 1790.
33 The seminal work on this subject remains Neil McKendrick, John Brewer and J. H. Plumb, *The Birth of a Consumer Society: The Commercialization of Eighteenth-century England* (London, 1982). For just some of the refinements and challenges to their much-debated thesis that have influence the present book, see Maxine Berg, *Luxury and Pleasure in Eighteenth-century Britain* (Oxford, 2005); Ho-cheung Mui and Lorna H. Mui, *Shops and Shopkeeping in Eighteenth-century England* (London, 1989); Carole Shammas, *The Pre-industrial Consumer in England and America* (Oxford, 1990); and Jan de Vries, *The Industrious Revolution: Consumer Behavior and the Household Economy, 1650 to the Present* (Cambridge, 2008).
34 Letter from Anna Letitia Aikin Barbauld, August 1814, in *Memoir, Letters, and a Selection from the Poetry and Prose Writings of Anna Letitia Barbauld*, ed. Grace A. Ellis (Boston, MA, 1874), vol. I, pp. 293–4.
35 *Lady's Monthly Museum* (March 1812).

1 THE EMPIRE'S BOUNTY

1 Adam Smith, *An Inquiry into the Nature and Causes of the Wealth of Nations* (Dublin, 1776), vol. II, p. 132.
2 Frank Trentmann, *Empire of Things: How We Became a World of Consumers, from the Fifteenth Century to the Twenty-first* (London, 2016), p. 81.
3 For an overview of the early reception of these goods and medicines in Europe, see J. Worth Estes, 'The European Reception of the First Drugs from the New World', *Pharmacy and History*, 37 (1995), pp. 3–23; and Rudi Mathee, 'Exotic Substances: The Introduction and Global Spread of Tobacco, Coffee, Cocoa, Tea, and Distilled Liquor, Sixteenth to Eighteenth Centuries', in *Drugs and Narcotics in History*, ed. Roy Porter and Mikuláš Teich (Cambridge, 1995), pp. 24–51.
4 Cited in Erika Rappaport, *A Thirst for Empire: How Tea Shaped the Modern World* (Princeton, NJ, 2017), p. 23.
5 *The Virtues and Excellency of the American Tobacco Plant, for Cure of Diseases and Preservation of Health* (London, 1712).

6 Steven Blankaart, *The Physical Dictionary. Wherein the Terms of Anatomy, the Names and Causes of Diseases, Surgical Instruments, and Their Use are Accurately Explained* (London, 1702), p. 304.
7 *Materia Medica; or, a Description of Simple Medicines Generally Us'd in Physick* (London, 1708), p. 323.
8 On the medical benefits and potential injuries of drinking tea espoused at the time, see especially Markman Ellis, Richard Coulton and Matthew Mauger, *Empire of Tea: The Asian Leaf that Conquered the World* (London, 2015), pp. 103–8.
9 For just a handful of examples of the recommended medical uses of tobacco, see *The Country Physician; Containing Several Easie and Useful Remedies* (Edinburgh, 1701), p. 37; *Dr. Willis's Receipts for the Cure of all Distempers* (London, 1701), pp. 76 and 139; *Dr. Lower's, and several other Eminent Physicians Receipts: Containing the Best and Safest Method for Curing most Diseases in Humane Bodies* (London, 1704), pp. 18, 24, 86, 96–7; *New Curiosities in Art and Nature; or, a Collection of the Most Valuable Secrets in all Arts and Sciences* (London, 1711), p. 21; John Marten, *A Treatise of the Venereal Disease* (London, 1711), p. 231; and *Practical Scheme for Explaining the Symptoms and Nature of the Venereal or Secret Disease* (London, 1725).
10 *Pharmacopoeia Londinensis; or, the new London Dispensatory* (London, 1702), pp. 81–2; John Locke, *Some Thoughts Concerning Education* (London, 1710), p. 28.
11 Thomas Boydell, *Medicaster Exenteratus, or the Quack's Pourtrait* (London, 1714), p. 11.
12 On tobacco as an insect pesticide and repellent, see Richard Weston, *The Gardeners Pocket-Calendar*, 3rd edn (London, 1783), pp. 39 and 44; and John Abercrombie, *Every Man His Own Gardener* (London, 1788), p. 189. *Joe Miller's Jests: or, the Wits Vade-Mecum* (London, 1745), p. 61.
13 *London Tradesman* (London, 1757), pp. 273–4.
14 *Minutes of several conversations, between the Rev. John Wesley, A.M. and the preachers in connection with him* (London, 1779), p. 57; Jeremy Bentham, *Management of the Poor* (Dublin, 1796), p. 490.
15 Emanuel Mendes da Costa, *A Natural History of Fossils* (London 1757).
16 James Walvin, *Fruits of Empire: Exotic Produce and British Taste, 1660–1800* (London, 1997), pp. 118–21.
17 Trentmann, *Empire of Things*, p. 81; National Archives, Kew, Treasury T 64/276B/316.
18 Karen Ordahl Kupperman, *The Jamestown Project* (Cambridge, MA, 2007), chapter 9; David Price, *Love and Hate in Jamestown: John Smith, Pocahontas, and the Heart of a New Nation* (New York, 2003).
19 Walvin, *Fruits of Empire*, pp. 73–4.
20 National Archives, T 64/276B/330.
21 On England's early tea trade, see especially Ellis, Coulton and Mauger, *Empire of Tea*, pp. 23–4 and 56; Jane T. Merritt, *The Trouble with Tea: The Politics of Consumption in the Eighteenth-century Global Economy* (Baltimore, MD, 2017), pp. 17–22; and Rappaport, *Thirst for Empire*, pp. 40–42.
22 On the importance of silver, see Merritt, *Trouble with Tea*, p. 29, and Trentmann, *Empire of Things*, p. 25.
23 Ellis, Coulton, and Mauger, *Empire of Tea*, p. 56.

24 Merritt, *Trouble with Tea*, p. 19; Ho-cheung Mui and Lorna H. Mui, *Shops and Shopkeeping in Eighteenth-century England* (London, 1989), pp. 200 and 179; Andrew Melrose & Co., *Brief Notices of the Tea Plant, Together with some Account of Coffee, Sugar, Rice, Tapioca, Sago, and Several of the Spices collected from the ship bills of Andrew Melrose & Co.* (Edinburgh, 1835), p. 5.

25 Jacob M. Price, 'The Rise of Glasgow in the Chesapeake Tobacco Trade, 1707–1775', *William and Mary Quarterly*, 11 (1954), pp. 179–99; Robert C. Nash, 'The English and Scottish Tobacco Trades in the Seventeenth and Eighteenth Centuries: Legal and Illegal Trade', *Economic History Review*, 35 (1982), pp. 354–72.

26 The average annual duty on sugar between 1767 and 1771 was about £500,000: National Archives, T 64/276B/388. The duty on coffee in 1774 was £115,126 8*s* 8*d*, T 64/276B/316. For the costs of naval ships and their maintenance, see John Brewer, *The Sinews of Power: War, Money and the English State, 1688–1783* (Cambridge, MA, 1990), pp. 34–5.

27 The duty on coffee in 1774 was £115,126 8*s* 8*d*: T 64/276B/316. For taxes on printed goods, see Victoria E. M. Gardner, *The Business of News in England, 1760–1820* (London, 2016), pp. 40–41.

28 Melrose, *Brief Notices on the Tea Plant*, p. 3.

29 Ellis, Coulton and Mauger, *Empire of Tea*, p. 37; S. D. Smith, 'Accounting for Taste: British Coffee Consumption in Historical Perspective', *Journal of Interdisciplinary History*, 27 (1996), p. 184; Anthony Wild, *Coffee: A Dark History* (New York, 2004).

30 Jonathan Eacott, *Selling Empire: India in the Making of Britain and America, 1600–1830* (Chapel Hill, NC, 2016), p. 181; *H. V. Bowen, The Business of Empire: The East India Company and Imperial Britain, 1756–1833* (Cambridge, 2006), chapter 4; and Merritt, *Trouble with Tea*, pp. 17–19, 30 and 89.

31 Mark Pendergrast, *Uncommon Grounds: The History of Coffee and How it Transformed the World*. revd edn (New York, 2010), p. 17.

32 Londa Schiebinger, *Plants and Empire: Colonial Bioprospecting in the Atlantic World* (Cambridge, MA, 2004), p. 7; Kate Loveman, 'The Introduction of Chocolate into England: Retailers, Researchers, and Consumers, 1640–1730', *Journal of Social History*, 47 (2013), pp. 27–46.

33 Jacob Price, 'The Imperial Economy, 1700–1776', in *The Oxford History of the British Empire*, vol. II: *The Eighteenth Century*, ed. P. J. Marshall (Oxford, 1998), p. 86; S. D. Smith, 'Sugar's Poor Relation: Coffee Planting in the British West Indies, 1720–1833', *Slavery and Abolition*, 19 (1998), pp. 68–9; James Walvin, *Fruits of Empire: Exotic Produce and British Taste, 1660–1800* (London, 1997), pp. 32–47.

34 Merritt, *Trouble with Tea*, pp. 25–8.

35 Ibid., p. 23, table 1.2.

36 T. H. Breen, *The Marketplace of Revolution: How Consumer Politics Shaped American Independence* (Oxford, 2004); Kariann Akemi Yokota, *Unbecoming British: How Revolutionary America Became a Postcolonial Nation* (New York, 2011).

37 Maxine Berg, *Luxury and Pleasure in Eighteenth-century Britain* (Oxford, 2005), pp. 302–4; T. H. Breen, 'An Empire of Goods: The Anglicization of Colonial America, 1690–1776', *Journal of British Studies*, 25 (1996), pp. 333–57; James Raven, *The Business of Books: Booksellers and the English Book Trade*

(London, 2011), pp. 144–53; Carole Shammas, *The Pre-industrial Consumer in England and America* (Oxford, 1990); S. D. Smith, 'The Market for Manufactures in the Thirteen Continental Colonies, 1698–1776', *Economic History Review*, 51 (1998), pp. 676–708.

38 Merritt, *Trouble with Tea*, pp. 34 (table 2.1), 39 (table 2.2), and 43.

39 Berg, *Luxury and Pleasure*, pp. 308–10; Gloria L. Main and Jackson T. Main, 'Economic Growth and the Standard of Living in Southern New England, 1640–1774', *Journal of Economic History*, 48 (1988), pp. 27–46.

40 British Library, Add. MS 36666, fols 41–5.

41 Mui and Mui, *Shops and Shopkeeping*, p. 161.

42 Papers of Ann Gomm, Oxfordshire Record Office, OA/B/118.

43 T.A.B. Corley, 'Fortnum, Charles', *Oxford Dictionary of National Biography* (Oxford, 2004).

44 From 'Our History', www.fortnumandmason.com, accessed 15 August 2018.

45 For an example, see Sun Fire Office policy registers, Guildhall Library, London, MS 11936/481/968004, MS 11936/510/1051128, MS 11936/499/1023330.

46 Daniel Defoe, *The Compleat English Tradesman* (London, 1726), pp. 4–5.

47 Ibid., p. 10.

48 For a description of the grading systems employed, see Ellis, Coulton and Mauger, *Empire of Tea*, pp. 123–7.

49 T.A.B. Corley, 'Twining, Richard', *Oxford Dictionary of National Biography* (Oxford, 2004); Tom Standage, *A History of the World in 6 Glasses* (London, 2005), p. 193; 'History of Twinings', www.twinings.co.uk/about-twinings, accessed 15 August 2018, which largely draws from Stephen Herbert Twining, *The House of Twining, 1706–1956* (London, 1956).

50 Mui and Mui, *Shops and Shopkeeping*, pp. 173 and 179; Andrew Hann and Jon Stobart, 'Sites of Consumption: The Display of Goods in Provincial Shops in Eighteenth-century England', *Cultural and Social History*, 2 (2005), pp. 165–87.

51 National Records of Scotland, Court of Session Records CS96/3341.

52 Ibid., CS96/3374. The 'modest' label is based on the assessed value of the shop inventory and the extent of customers' debts, both of which were in the low hundreds of pounds rather than the thousands of pounds of large provincial groceries.

53 T. S. Willan, *An Eighteenth-century Shopkeeper: Abraham Dent of Kirkby Stephen* (Manchester, 1970). See also Jon Stobart, *Sugar and Spice: Grocers and Groceries in Provincial England, 1650–1830* (Oxford, 2013), p. 82.

54 Account and papers of Alexander Hog, MSS 8601 and 8623, Guildhall Library, London.

55 'Proceedings of the Old Bailey: London's Central Criminal Court, 1674 to 1913', www.oldbaileyonline.org, case t16770425-1.

56 William J. Ashworth, *Customs and Excise: Trade, Production, and Consumption in England, 1640–1845* (Oxford, 2003).

57 'Proceedings of the Old Bailey', cases t16791210-1 and t16800421-7.

58 *A Scheme Humbly Offer'd to Prevent the Clandestine Importation of Tea* (London, 1736).

59 Ellis, Coulton and Mauger, *Empire of Tea*, pp. 168–70.

60 Hoh-cheung Mui and Lorna H. Mui, 'Smuggling and the British Tea Trade Before 1784', *American Historical Review*, 74 (1968), pp. 65–6.

61 Ibid., pp. 44–73.

62 Richard Twining, *Observations on the Tea and Window Act, and on the Tea Trade* (London, 1784), p. 22.
63 Cited in Rappaport, *Thirst for Empire*, p. 45.
64 Nancy F. Koehn, *The Power of Commerce: Economy and Governance in the First British Empire* (Ithaca, NY, 1994), p. 211.
65 Price, 'The Imperial Economy, 1700–1776', p. 83.
66 Eacott, *Selling Empire*, pp. 194–213; Paul Langford, *A Polite and Commercial People: England, 1727–1783* (Oxford, 1989), pp. 532–4; Merritt, *Trouble with Tea*, chapter 4.
67 Eacott, *Selling Empire*; James R. Fichter, *So Great a Proffit: How the East Indies Trade Transformed Anglo-American Capitalism* (Cambridge, MA, 2010).
68 Ellis, Coulton and Mauger, *Empire of Tea*, pp. 175–6; Mui and Mui, *Shops and Shopkeeping*, pp. 61–4.
69 *A Scheme to Secure and Extend the Credit and Strength of the British Nation* (London, 1747), p. 15.
70 Jack Lynch, *Deception and Detection in Eighteenth-century Britain* (Aldershot, 2008).

2 THE NEW BRITISH CONSUMER

1 John Marsh, 'History of my private life', HM 54457, Huntington Library, San Marino, California, box 1, vol. 1.
2 Lorna Weatherill, *Consumer Behaviour and Material Culture in Britain, 1660–1760*, 2nd edn (London, 1996), pp. 153–5; Carole Shammas, *The Pre-industrial Consumer in England and America* (Oxford, 1990), pp. 76–86.
3 James Walvin, *Fruits of Empire: Exotic Produce and British Taste, 1660–1800* (London, 1997), p. 120; A.J.S. Gibson and T. C. Smout, *Prices, Food, and Wages in Scotland, 1550–1780* (Cambridge, 1995), pp. 233–4.
4 On the contentiousness of the dates and early impact of the Industrial Revolution, see especially Robert Allen, 'Technology', in *The Cambridge Economic History of Modern Britain*, vol. I: *1700–1870*, ed. Roderick Floud, Jane Humphries and Paul Johnson (Cambridge, 2014), pp. 292–4; N.F.R. Crafts, *British Economic Growth during the Industrial Revolution* (Oxford, 1985); J. Mokyr, ed., *The British Industrial Revolution: An Economic Perspective* (Boulder, CO, 1993); and Jeff Horn, Leonard Rosenband and Merritt Smith, eds, *Reconceptualizing the Industrial Revolution* (Cambridge, MA, 2010).
5 Jan de Vries, *The Industrious Revolution: Consumer Behavior and the Household Economy, 1650 to the Present* (Cambridge, 2008). On the widespread acceptance of the industrious revolution, see Hugh Cunningham, *Time, Work and Leisure: Life Changes in England since 1700* (Manchester, 2016), pp. 45–7; Carole Shammas, 'Food Expenditures and Economic Well-being in Early Modern England', *Journal of Economic History*, 43 (1983), pp. 89–100; Frank Trentmann, *Empire of Things: How We Became a World of Consumers, from the Fifteenth Century to the Twenty-first* (London, 2016), pp. 23–4; and Hans-Joachim Voth, *Time and Work in England, 1750–1830* (Oxford, 2000).
6 Paul Slack, *The Invention of Improvement: Information and Material Progress in Seventeenth-century England* (Oxford, 2015); David Spadafora, *The Idea of Progress in Eighteenth-century Britain* (New Haven, CT, 1990).

7 For some of the challenges to de Vries's narrative of the industrious revolution, see Sara Horrell, 'Consumption, 1700–1870', in *The Cambridge Economic History of Modern Britain*, vol. I, ed. Roderick Floud, Jane Humphries and Paul Johnson (Cambridge, 2014), pp. 237–63; Craig Muldrew, *Food, Energy and the Creation of Industriousness* (Cambridge, 2011); Gregory Clark and Ysbrand Van Der Werf, 'Work in Progress? The Industrious Revolution', *Journal of Economic History* (1998), pp. 830–43.
8 Jane T. Merritt, *The Trouble with Tea: The Politics of Consumption in the Eighteenth-century Global Economy* (Baltimore, MD, 2017), pp. 6–7 and 23–8.
9 Neil McKendrick, 'The Consumer Revolution of Eighteenth-century England', in *The Birth of a Consumer Society: The Commercialization of Eighteenth-century England*, ed. Neil McKendrick, John Brewer and J. H. Plumb (London, 1982). For two recent critiques of McKendrick's thesis that have challenged both Britain's uniqueness and the rapidity of his account of consumer revolution, see especially Horrell, 'Consumption, 1700–1870', pp. 247–8; Trentmann, *Empire of Things*, pp. 10–11 and 20.
10 Shammas, *Pre-industrial Consumer*, pp. 148 and 299.
11 Jonas Hanway, *Advice from a Farmer to His Daughter, in a Series of Discourses, Calculated to Promote the Welfare and True Interest of Servants* (London, 1770), vol. III, p. 344.
12 William Cobbett, *Cottage Economy* [London, 1821] (New York, 1833), pp. 23–7.
13 See especially Amanda Vickery, *Behind Closed Doors: At Home in Georgian England* (New Haven, CT, 2009), p. 9; Karen Harvey, *The Little Republic: Masculinity and Domestic Authority in Eighteenth-century Britain* (Oxford, 2012); Philip Carter, *Men and the Emergence of Polite Society, Britain, 1660–1800* (London, 2000); Margot Finn, 'Men's Things: Masculine Possession in the Consumer Revolution', *Social History*, 25 (2000), pp. 133–55; Lorna Weatherill, 'A Possession of One's Own: Women and Consumer Behavior in England, 1660–1740', *Journal of British Studies*, 25 (1986), pp. 131–56.
14 'Proceedings of the Old Bailey: London's Central Criminal Court, 1674 to 1913', www.oldbaileyonline.org, originally published as *Proceedings of the Old Bailey*, 11 December 1678, p. 35.
15 *The Fugitive. Containing, Several Very Pleasant Passages, and Surprizing Adventures, Observ'd by a Lady in her Country Ramble* (London, 1705), pp. 184–5.
16 Maxine Berg, *Luxury and Pleasure in Eighteenth-century Britain* (Oxford, 2005), chapter 7; Nancy Cox, *The Complete Tradesman: A Study of Retailing, 1550–1820* (Aldershot, 2000); McKendrick, Brewer and Plumb, eds, *The Birth of a Consumer Society*; Ho-cheung Mui and Lorna H. Mui, *Shops and Shopkeeping in Eighteenth-century Englands* (London, 1989).
17 Jon Stobart, Andrew Hann and Victoria Morgan, *Spaces of Consumption: Leisure and Shopping in the English Town, c. 1680–1830* (London, 2007).
18 William Burnaby, *The Ladies Visiting-Day. A Comedy. As it was Acted at the Theatre in Lincolns-Inn-Fields, by His Majesties Servants* (London, 1701), p. 27.
19 Cesar de Saussure, *A Foreign View of England*, trans. Mme Van Muden (London, 1902), pp. 80–81.
20 On shops' designs, see especially Claire Walsh, 'Shop Design and the Display of Goods in Eighteenth-century London', *Journal of Design History*, 8 (1995), pp. 157–76.

21 *The Diary of Thomas Turner, 1754–1765*, ed. David Vaisey (Oxford, 1984).

22 Sarah Harrison, *Housekeeper's Pocket-Book, and Compleat Family Cook* (London, 1733); Helen Berry, 'Prudent Luxury: The Metropolitan Tastes of Judith Baker, Durham Gentlewoman', in *Women and Urban Life in Eighteenth-century England*, ed. Rosemary Sweet and Penelope Lane (London, 2003), pp. 148–50. See also Lucy A. Bailey, 'Squire, Shopkeeper and Staple Food: The Reciprocal Relationship between the Country House and the Village Shop in the Late Georgian Period', *History of Retailing and Consumption*, 1 (2015), pp. 8–27.

23 T. S. Willan, ed., *An Eighteenth-century Shopkeeper: Abraham Dent of Kirkby Stephen* (Manchester, 1970).

24 Accounts of Alexander Hog, MSS 8601, Guildhall Library, London.

25 This was overwhelmingly the case in Scotland versus surviving records from England or Wales.

26 National Archives of Scotland, Court of Sessions Papers, 96/158.

27 Ibid., 96/898.

28 Accounts of Ann Gomm, Oxfordshire Record Office, OA/B/118.

29 Ann Bermingham and John Brewer, eds, *The Consumption of Culture, 1600–1800: Image, Object, Text* (London, 1995).

30 For the classic theory of fashion, see Georg Simmel, 'Fashion', *International Quarterly*, 10 (1904), pp. 130–55. For broader discussions of food and fashion during this period, see especially Woodruff D. Smith, 'Complications of the Commonplace: Tea, Sugar, and Imperialism', *Journal of Interdisciplinary History*, 23 (1992), pp. 259–78; Stephen Mennell, *All Manners of Food: Eating and Taste in England and France from the Middle Ages to the Present* (Oxford, 1985), pp. 20–39 and 54–61.

31 For a summary of the emergence of the different types of retailed tea, see Markman Ellis, Richard Coulton and Matthew Mauger, *Empire of Tea: The Asian Leaf that Conquered the World* (London, 2015), pp. 36–40 and 74–8.

32 Sara Horrell, Jane Humphries and Ken Sneath, 'Cupidity and Crime: Consumption as Revealed by Insights from the Old Bailey Records of Thefts in the Eighteenth and Nineteenth Centuries', in *Large Databases in Economic History*, ed. Mark Casson and Nigar Hashimzade (London, 2013), pp. 246–67, as well as their 'Consumption Conundrums Unravelled', *Economic History Review*, 68 (2015), pp. 830–57.

33 'Proceedings of the Old Bailey', www.oldbaileyonline.org, case t17210301-1.

34 Ibid., cases t17480224-17 and t17590117-34.

35 Accounts of Ann Gomm, Oxfordshire Record Office; Cobbett, *Cottage Economy*, p. 24.

36 Berg, *Luxury and Pleasure*, p. 117.

37 Vickery, *Behind Closed Doors*, pp. 15–16 and 272; Weatherill, *Consumer Behaviour and Material Culture*, pp. 153–5; Berg, *Luxury and Pleasure*, chapter 4.

38 *Records of Social and Economic History, new series 26: The Diary of Robert Sharp of South Cave: Life in a Yorkshire Village, 1812–1837*, ed. Janice E. Crowther and Peter A. Crowther (Oxford, 1997), p. 43.

39 Caroline Lybbe Powys Diaries, British Library, Add MS, 42160, fol. 31.

40 Marsh, HM 54457, Box 1, vol. IV.

41 Paul Langford, *A Polite and Commercial People: England, 1727–1783* (Oxford, 1989), chapter 3.
42 *The Elements of a Polite Education; Carefully Selected from the Letters of the Late Right Honorable Philip Dormer Stanhope, Earl of Chesterfield* (London, 1800), p. 34.
43 John Trusler, *The Honours of the Table, or, Rules for Behaviour During Meals . . . For the Use of Young People* (London, 1788). A recent use is the Michelin-starred Martin Wishart's The Honours Brasserie in Glasgow.
44 Ibid., p. 24.
45 Trentmann, *Empire of Things*, p. 118. See also Cunningham, *Time, Work and Leisure*, chapter 3.
46 Bernard Mandeville, *The Fable of the Bees; or, Private Vices, Public Benefits* (London, 1705).
47 *London Chronicle*, 2 February 1773.
48 Philip Carter, *Men and the Emergence of Polite Society, Britain, 1660–1800* (London, 2000).
49 William Burnaby, *The Ladies Visiting Day* (London, 1701), p. 25.
50 Allan Ramsay, *Poems* (Edinburgh, 1720), p. 156.
51 John Wesley, *A Letter to a Friend Concerning Tea* (Bristol, 1749).
52 Jonas Haywood, *Letter on the Importance of the Rising Generation of the Labouring Part our Fellow-Subjects* (London, 1768), vol. II, pp. 178–85.
53 *The Spectator*, 10, 12 March 1711.
54 Eliza Fowler Haywood, *The Tea-Table* (London, 1725).
55 James Bland, *The Charms of Women; or, a Mirrour for Ladies. Wherein the Accomplishments of the Fair Sex are Impartially Delineated* (London, 1736), p. 193.
56 James Bland, *An Essay in Praise of Women* (Edinburgh, 1767), p. 61.
57 *Tea-Table Dialogues* (London, 1772).
58 Mark Pendergrast, *Uncommon Grounds: The History of Coffee and How it Transformed the World*, revd edn (New York, 2010), p. 6.
59 Ralph S. Hattox, *Coffee and Coffeehouses: The Origins of a Social Beverage in the Medieval Near East* (Seattle, WA, 1985), pp. 74–81; Antony Wild, *Coffee: A Dark History* (New York, 2004), p. 53.
60 Wild, *Coffee: A Dark History*, p. ix.
61 Trentmann, *Empire of Things*, p. 86; Wild, *Coffee: A Dark History*, p. 88. Andrew Clark, ed., *The Life and Times of Anthony Wood, antiquary, of Oxford, 1632–1695, described by Himself. Collected from His Diaries and Other Papers* (Oxford, 1891), p. 168.
62 The story of Rosée can be found in most of histories of coffee, but for one of the most detailed accounts, see Markman Ellis, *The Coffee House: A Cultural History* (London, 2004), chapter 3.
63 Ellis, *The Coffee House*, p. 87; S. D. Smith, 'Accounting for Taste: British Coffee Consumption in Historical Perspective', *Journal of Interdisciplinary History*, 27 (1996), pp. 183–214.
64 Brian Cowan, *The Social Life of Coffee: The Emergence of the British Coffeehouse* (New Haven, CT, 2005).
65 Ellis, *The Coffee House*, p. 75.
66 The king made the proclamation on 29 December 1675, and the *London Gazette* published it the following day.

67 Andrew Chambers, *Godly Reading: Print, Manuscript, and Puritanism in England, 1580–1720* (Cambridge, 2011), pp. 183–5.

68 Walvin, *Fruits of Empire*, p. 39.

69 John Roach, *Roach's London Pocket Pilot, or Stranger's Guide through the Metropolis* (London, 1796), p. 50.

70 Ibid., p. 44.

71 John Trusler, *The London Adviser* (London, 1786), pp. 163–5.

72 William Hicks, *Coffee-House Jests: Being a Merry Companion* (London, 1677). The description is taken from the advertisement for the 1730 edition.

73 *The Spectator*, 49 (1711).

74 'Proceedings of the Old Bailey', www.oldbaileyonline.org, case t16800707-4.

75 On women in business, see especially Hannah Barker, *The Business of Women: Female Enterprise and Urban Development in Northern England, 1760–1830* (Oxford, 2006) and her *Family and Business During the Industrial Revolution* (Oxford, 2016).

76 *The Life and Character of Moll King, Late Mistress of King's Coffee-House in Covent-Garden* (London, 1747). Most of the details of her life come from this colourful, if not inflammatory, account.

77 Nicola Jane Phillips, *Women in Business, 1700–1850* (London, 2006), p. 192; Paula R. Backscheider, 'King, Mary', *Oxford Dictionary of National Biography*, www.oxforddnb.com, accessed 25 August 2018.

78 *The Spectator*, 49.

79 *Roach's London Pocket Pilot*, pp. 51–2.

80 Bryant Lillywhite, *London Coffee Houses: A Reference Book of Coffee Houses of the Seventeenth, Eighteenth and Nineteenth Centuries* (London, 1963). On the New England and American coffeehouses, see *The Journal of Samuel Curwen, Loyalist*, ed. Andrew Oliver (Cambridge, MA, 1972), vol. II, pp. 26 and 565.

81 For more on the history of Edward Lloyd and the coffeehouse he founded, see Sarah Palmer, 'Lloyd, Edward (*c.* 1648–1713)', *Oxford Dictionary of National Biography*, www.oxforddnb.com, accessed 25 August 2018. Charles Wright and Charles Ernest Fayle, *A History of Lloyd's: From the Founding of Lloyd's Coffee House to the Present Day* (London, 1928).

82 Troy Bickham, *The Weight of Vengeance: The United States, the British Empire and the War of 1812* (Oxford, 2012), pp. 129–30.

83 *Roach's London Pocket Pilot*, pp. 52–3.

84 Herbert S. Klein, *The Atlantic Slave Trade*, 2nd edn (Cambridge, 1999), chapter 4.

85 Lists of modern corporations and banks whose early success is attributed to involvement in the slave trade almost invariably include Lloyd's namesakes. Most recently Lloyd's of London was sued in 2004 by a group of U.S. citizens who traced their ancestry to African slaves transported on ships insured by Lloyd's and demanded compensation. For details, see *Evening Standard*, 29 March 2004.

3 ADVERTISING AND IMPERIALISM

1 Igor Kopytoff, 'The Cultural Biography of Things: Commodification as Process', in *The Social Life of Things: Commodities in Cultural Perspective*, ed. Arjun Appadurai (Cambridge, 1986), pp. 64–91; Daniel Miller, *Material*

Culture and Mass Consumption (Oxford, 1987); Alan Warde, *Consumption, Food and Taste: Culinary Antinomies and Commodity Culture* (London, 1997), p. 194.

2 Alison Games, *The Web of Empire: English Cosmopolitanism in an Age of Expansion, 1560–1660* (Oxford, 2008), pp. 124–37; Peter C. Mancall, *Hakluyt's Promise: An Elizabethan's Obsession for an English America* (New Haven, CT, 2007), pp. 189–207; Stuart Piggott, *Ancient Britons and the Antiquarian Imagination: Ideas from the Renaissance to the Regency* (London, 1989), p. 73.

3 Andrew A. Mitchell and Jerry C. Olson, 'Are Product Attribute Beliefs the Only Mediator of Advertising Effects on Brand Attitude?', *Journal of Marketing Research*, 19 (1981), pp. 318–32; Lars Hermerén, *English for Sale: A Study of the Language of Advertising* (Lund, Sweden, 1999); James Shanteau, 'Consumer Impression Formation: The Integration of Visual and Verbal Information', in *Nonverbal Communication in Advertising*, ed. Sidney Hecker and David W. Stewart (Lexington, MA, 1988); Thomas J. Madden, William R. Dillon and Jacquelyn L. Twible, 'Construct Validity of Attitude Toward the Ad: An Assessment of Convergent/Discriminant Dimension', in *Advertising and Consumer Psychology*, ed. Jerry Olson and Keith Sentis (New York, 1986), vol. III, pp. 74–92; Karen A. Machleit and R. Dale Wilson, 'Emotional Feeling and Attitude toward the Advertisement: The Roles of Brand Familiarity and Repetition', *Journal of Advertising*, 17 (1988), pp. 27–35; and Meryl Lichtenstein and Thomas K. Srull, 'Conceptual and Methodological Issues in Examining the Relationship Between Consumer Memory and Judgment', in *Psychological Processes and Advertising Effects: Theory, Research, and Applications*, ed. Linda F. Alwitt and Andrew A. Mitchell (London, 1985).

4 John Brewer, *Party Ideology and Popular Politics at the Accession of George III* (Cambridge, 1976), p. 142. See also Hannah Barker, *Newspapers, Politics and English Society, 1695–1855* (London, 2000); Jeremy Black, *The English Press in the Eighteenth Century* (Philadelphia, PA, 1987).

5 Troy Bickham, *Making Headlines: The American Revolution as Seen through the British Press* (DeKalb, IL, 2009), tables 1.2 and 1.3.

6 Maurizio Gotti, 'The English of 18th Century Advertisements', *Merope*, 13 (1994), pp. 97–118.

7 Ambrose Heal, *The Signboards of Old London Shops* (New York, 1972), p. 3.

8 For a collector's account of trade cards, see Ambrose Heal, *London Tradesmen's Cards of the XVIII Century: An Account of their Origin and Use* (New York, 1968). For a more recent examination, see Maxine Berg and Helen Clifford, 'Selling Consumption in the Eighteenth Century: Advertising and the Trade Card in Britain and France', *Cultural and Social History*, 4 (2007), pp. 145–70.

9 For an overview, see especially Julie A. Edell, 'Nonverbal Effects in Ads: A Review and Synthesis', in *Nonverbal Communication in Advertising*, ed. Hecker and Stewart. See also R. N. Shepard, 'Recognition Memory for Words, Sentences, and Pictures', *Journal of Verbal Learning and Verbal Behavior*, 6 (1967), pp. 156–63; Gordon H. Bower, *Cognition in Learning Memory* (New York, 1972); Jolita Kisielius and Brian Sternthal, 'Examining the Vividness Controversy: An Availability-Valence Interpretation', *Journal of Consumer Research*, 12 (1986), pp. 418–31; K. A. and R. J. Lutz, 'Effects of Interactive Imagery on Learning: Applications to Advertising', *Journal of Applied Psychology*, 62 (1977), pp. 493–8.

10 These are all examples from the Bodleian Library, John Johnson Collection, Oxford Trade, box 4 and Trade Cards, box 11.
11 Johnson Collection, Trade Cards, box 11 (100).
12 Sun Fire Office policy registers, Guildhall Library, London, MS 11936/492/995380.
13 Ibid., MS 11936/481/968004, MS 11936/510/1051128, MS 11936/499/1023330.
14 Theodore R. Crom, *Trade Catalogues, 1542–1842* (Gainesville, FL, 1989), p. 309; Johnson Collection, Trade Cards, box 4.
15 Markman Ellis, Richard Coulton and Matthew Mauger, *Empire of Tea: The Asian Leaf that Conquered the World* (London, 2015), pp. 197–8.
16 See especially Jack Lynch, *Deception and Detection in Eighteenth-century Britain* (Aldershot, 2008); Bee Wilson, *Swindled: The Dark History of Food Fraud, From Poisoned Candy to Counterfeit Coffee* (Princeton, NJ, 2008), chapter 1.
17 Bodleian Library, Oxford, John Johnson Collection, Trades and Professions 6 (54a), cited in Jon Stobart, *Sugar and Spice: Grocers and Groceries in Provincial England, 1650–1830* (Oxford, 2013), p. 149.
18 Wilson, *Swindled*, pp. 31–3.
19 Barbara Shapiro, *A Culture of Fact: England, 1550–1720* (Ithaca, NY, 2000).
20 *Geography and History. Selected by a Lady, for the Use of Her Own Children* (London, 1790).
21 On the growth of useful knowledge, see John Brewer, *Sinews of Power: War, Money and the English State, 1688–1783* (Cambridge, MA, 1990), especially chapter 8; on antiquarianism, see Rosemary Sweet, *Antiquaries: The Discovery of the Past in Eighteenth-century Britain* (London, 2004); on the shift of objects from fantastical curiosities to artefacts representing specific cultures, see Troy Bickham, '"A conviction of the reality of things": Material Culture, North American Indians and Empire in Eighteenth-century Britain', *Eighteenth-century Studies*, 39 (2005), pp. 29–47.
22 *A Frenchman in England 1784, being the Melanges sur l'Angleterre of Francois de la Rochefoucauld*, ed. Jean Marchand and trans. S. C. Roberts (London, 1995), pp. 16–17.
23 See for example *A Companion to Every Place of Curiosity and Entertainment in and about London and Westminster* (London, 1767), pp. 62–109; *The Ambulator; or, the Stranger's Companion in a Tour Round London* (London, 1774), pp. xix–xxii; *Britannica Curiosa*, 2nd edn (London, 1777), pp. 111–37; *A Companion to all the Principal Places of Curiosity and Entertainment in and about London and Westminster*, 8th edn (London, 1796), pp. 164–85.
24 *The Ambulator*, p. xix.
25 Carl Philip Moritz, *Journeys of a German in England in 1782,* trans. and ed. Reginald Nettell (London, 1965), p. 59.
26 *Morning Post*, 19 July 1777.
27 Caroline Lybbe Powys Diaries, British Library, Add. MS 42160, fols 8–9.
28 Bickham, '"A conviction of the reality of things"', pp. 34–6.
29 The most popular seems to have been *The General Contents of the British Museum: With Remarks. Serving as a Directory in Viewing that Noble Cabinet* (London, 1762), which sold cheaply and enjoyed multiple editions. The second edition of the guide was, according to the editor, 'printed in a Duodecimo, to make it more conveniently portable in the Pocket'.

30 *European Magazine and London Review* (January 1782), pp. 17–21. For a more detailed examination of Lever's showmanship see also Clare Haynes, 'A "Natural" Exhibitioner: Sir Ashton Lever and his Holosphusikon', *British Journal for Eighteenth-century Studies*, 24 (2001), pp. 1–14.
31 *Morning Post*, 19 July 1777.
32 On the representation of American Indians in Britain during this period, see especially Troy Bickham, *Savages within the Empire: Representations of American Indians in Eighteenth-century Britain* (Oxford, 2005) and the essays in Tim Fulford and Kevin Hutchings, eds, *Native Americans and Anglo-American Culture, 1750–1850: The Indian Atlantic* (Cambridge, 2009).
33 *London Chronicle*, 9 October 1759.
34 S. D. Smith, 'Accounting for Taste: British Coffee Consumption in Historical Perspective', *Journal of Interdisciplinary History*, 27 (1996), p. 184.
35 National Archives, Kew: Treasury, T64/276B/316.
36 Francis Grose, *A Classical Dictionary of the Vulgar Tongue* (London, 1796).
37 *The New London Cookery and Complete Domestic Guide* (London, 1827), p. 631.
38 Cited in Sidney Mintz, *Sweetness and Power: The Place of Sugar in Modern History* (New York, 1985), p. 157.
39 For a summary of the movement of British sugar sources, see Philip Curtain, *The Rise and Fall of the Plantation Complex*, 2nd edn (Cambridge, 1998), pp. 3–28; and Nuala Zahedieh, 'Economy', in *The British Atlantic World*, ed. David Armitage and Michael J. Braddick (New York, 2002), pp. 56–9.
40 Walvin, *Fruits of Empire*, pp. 117–18.
41 Heal, *Signboards of Old London Shops*, p. 3.
42 On adoption versus adaptation, see especially Marcy Norton, *Sacred Gifts, Profane Pleasures: A History of Tobacco and Chocolate in the Atlantic World* (Ithaca, NY, 2008).
43 Margarette Lincoln, *Representing the Royal Navy: British Seapower, 1750–1815* (London, 2002), p. 6; Brewer, *Sinews of Power*, p. 59.

4 DEFINING A BRITISH CUISINE

1 *Chester Chronicle*, 30 September 1814.
2 Quoted in John Brooke, *King George III* (London, 1972), p. 612.
3 On the emergence of a British national identity in this period, see especially Linda Colley, *Britons: Forging the Nation, 1707–1837* (New Haven, CT, 1992).
4 On food as a language and expression of culture, see especially the seminal works of Roland Barthes, 'Toward a Psychology of Contemporary Food Consumption', in *European Diet from Pre-industrial to Modern Times*, ed. Elborg Forster and Robert Forster (New York, 1975), trans. Annette Lavers (New York, 1959), and 'Ornamental Cookery' in his *Mythologies* (Paris, 1957); and Claude Lévi-Strauss, *The Origin of Table Manners* (New York, 1968), trans. John Weightman and Doreen Weightman (New York, 1978).
5 For an excellent examination of postcolonial cookery and the emergence of a national cuisine, see Arjun Appadurai, 'How to Make a National Cuisine: Cookbooks in Contemporary India', *Comparative Studies in Society and History*, 30 (1988), pp. 3–24.
6 Alan Warde, *Consumption, Food and Taste: Culinary Antinomies and Commodity Culture* (London, 1997), especially pp. 183–4.

7 Ann Shackleford, *The Modern Art of Cookery Improved* (London, 1767), p. 172.
8 See especially the highly influential Benedict Anderson, *Imagined Communities: Reflections on the Origin and Spread of Nationalism*, revd edn (London, 1991). For selected use of Anderson's thesis to Britain during this period, see Colley, *Britons*, and Kathleen Wilson, *The Sense of the People: Politics, Culture and Imperialism in England, 1715–1785* (Cambridge, 1995).
9 David Spadafora, *The Idea of Progress in Eighteenth-century Britain* (New Haven, CT, 1990).
10 Troy Bickham, *Savages within the Empire: Representations of American Indians in Eighteenth-century Britain* (Oxford, 2005), chapter 5; and Ronald Meek, *Social Science and the Ignoble Savage* (Cambridge, 1979).
11 On eighteenth-century antiquarianism, see Rosemary Sweet, *Antiquaries: The Discovery of the Past in Eighteenth-century Britain* (London, 2004).
12 James Macpherson, *An Introduction to the History of Great Britain and Ireland* (London, 1771), pp. 193–4.
13 Hugo Arnot, *The History of Edinburgh* (Edinburgh, 1779), pp. 84–5. For other examples of descriptions, and dismissals, of medieval Scottish cookery, see Abbé Milot, *Elements of the History of England, from the Invasion of the Romans to the Reign of George the Second. Translated from the French of Abbé Milot* (London, 1777), vol. II, pp. 15–17; and Robert Heron, *History of Scotland, from the Earliest Times, to the Era of the Abolition of the Hereditary Jurisdictions of Subjects, in the Year 1748* (Edinburgh, 1798), vol. I, p. 145.
14 Alexander Gerard, *An Essay on Taste* (London, 1759), p. 206.
15 John Adams, *Curious Thoughts on the History of Man*, pp. 136–7.
16 *The French Family Cook: Being a Complete System of French Cookery* (London, 1748).
17 John Thacker, *The Art of Cookery*, revd edn (Newcastle upon Tyne, 1758). For an excellent analysis of this subject, see Elizabeth M. Schmidt, 'Elegant Dishes and Unrefined Truths: A Culinary Search for Identity in Eighteenth-century Britain', *Eighteenth-century Thought*, 6 (2016), pp. 61–81.
18 *Gazetteer*, 10 May 1779.
19 Pierre Jean Grosley, *A Tour to London: or, New Observations on England, and Its Inhabitants* (London, 1772), vol. I, p. 75.
20 *Salisbury and Winchester Journal*, 10 November 1823.
21 *Derby Mercury*, 5 November 1762.
22 *Chester Chronicle*, 25 September 1818.
23 *Yorkshire Gazette*, 25 December 1818.
24 Adams, *Curious Thoughts*, p. 318.
25 First published in 1774, the quotation is taken from Kames, *Sketches of the History of Man* (Philadelphia, PA, 1776), book I, sketch ii, pp. 66–9.
26 *Caledonian Mercury*, 25 February 1731.
27 Edward Gibbon, *The History of the Decline and Fall of the Roman Empire* (London, 1776–88).
28 Gibbon, *Decline and Fall*, vol. VI (1776), p. 74. Modern historians have attributed Attila's willingness to accept a negotiated withdrawal to a lack of local supplies for his army, owing partly to crop failures and famine in Italy in AD 451 and 452.
29 Edward Wortley Montagu, *Reflections on the Rise and Fall of the Ancient Republicks, Adapted to the Present State of Great Britain* (London, 1760), pp. 264–5.

30 Thomas Leland, *The History of the Life and Reign of Philip King of Macedon* (London, 1784), p. 78.
31 [George Lyttelton], *Letters from a Persian in England to His Friend in Ispahan* (London, 1761), p. 208.
32 R. Campbell, *The London Tradesman* (London 1747), pp. 276–8.
33 *London Magazine* (January 1773).
34 *Oxford Journal*, 28 June 1817.
35 *Hereford Journal*, 27 February 1793.
36 *The Times*, 10 December 1803, reporting the previous day's debates.
37 'Proceedings of the Old Bailey: London's Central Criminal Court, 1674 to 1913', www.oldbaileyonline.org, case t17990911-31.
38 For details of Glasse's life, see Gilly Lehmann, *The British Housewife: Cookery Books, Cooking and Society in Eighteenth-century Britain* (Blackawton, Devon, 2003), pp. 108–17, and A.H.T. Robb-Smith, 'Glasse, Hannah', *Oxford Dictionary of National Biography* (Oxford, 2004). On Raffald, see Nancy Cox, 'Raffald, Elizabeth', *Oxford Dictionary of National Biography*, and Lehmann, *British Housewife*, pp. 129–32.
39 Hannah Barker, *The Business of Women: Female Enterprise and Urban Development in Northern England, 1760–1830* (Oxford, 2006), especially pp. 47–9, 76–7 and 132–3.
40 For the most detailed history of British cookery books, see Lehmann, *British Housewife*. For a bibliographic compilation of the books and their various editions, see Arnold Whitaker, *English Cookery Books to the Year 1850* (Oxford, 1913).
41 John Farley, *The London Art of Cookery* (London, 1783); and Francis Collingwood and John Woollams, *The Universal Cook, and City and Country Housekeeper* (London, 1792).
42 Edwina Ehrman, '18th Century', in *London Eats Out: 500 Years of Capital Dining* (London, 1999), p. 53.
43 Collingwood and Woollams, *The Universal Cook*.
44 There has been some debate over how much Farley wrote himself, as much of it appears to have been compiled by Richard Johnson (apparently without complaint from Farley) from other cookery books. See Fiona Lucraft, 'The London Art of Plagiarism: Part 1', *Petits Propos Culinaires*, 42 (1992), and Peter Targett, 'Johnson or Farley', *Petits Propos Culinaires*, 58 (1998).
45 Lehmann, *British Housewife*, p. 120; Raffaella Sarti, *Europe at Home: Family and Material Culture, 1500–1800*, trans. Allan Cameron (New Haven, CT, 2002), pp. 159–62.
46 On skilled labourer's wages, see Maxine Berg, *Luxury and Pleasure in Eighteenth-century Britain* (Oxford, 2005), pp. 122, 134 and 174.
47 William Augustus Henderson, *The Housekeeper's Instructor; or, Universal Family Cook* (London, 1793).
48 On servants' reading, see Jan Fergus, 'Provincial Servants' Reading in the Late Eighteenth Century', in *The Practice and Representation of Reading in England*, ed. James Raven, Helen Small and Naomi Tadmor (Cambridge, 1996), pp. 202–25.
49 *The Times*, 7 January 1811.
50 For further discussions of prescription versus practice regarding cookery books, see especially Ken Albala, 'Cookbooks as Historical Documents',

in *The Oxford Handbook of Food History*, ed. Jeffrey M. Pilcher (Oxford, 2012), pp. 227–40; Sara Pennell, 'Making Livings, Lives and Archives: Tales of Four Eighteenth-century Recipe Books', in *Reading and Writing Recipe Books, 1550–1800*, ed. Michelle DiMeo and Sara Pennell (Manchester, 2013), p. 225; and Simon Varey, 'Pleasures of the Table', in *Pleasure in the Eighteenth Century*, ed. Roy Porter and Marie Mulvey Roberts (London, 1996), p. 45. For a comprehensive look at English kitchens during this period, see especially Sarah Pennell, *The Birth of the English Kitchen, 1600–1850* (London, 2016).

51 Julie Powell, *Julie and Julia: 365 Days, 524 Recipes, 1 Tiny Apartment Kitchen* (New York, 2005). The ensuing film released in 2009 was *Julie and Julia*.

52 Entry for 19 August 1773, *The Early Diary of Frances Burney, 1768–1778*, ed. Annie Raine Ellis (London, 1889), vol. I, p. 244.

53 James Boswell, *The Life of Samuel Johnson* (London, 1791), vol. II, pp. 22–3.

54 For example, British Library, Add. MS 33,343 (Table-plans for dinner parties of Thomas, Lord Pelham, afterwards 1st Earl of Chichester, 1774–1802); British Library, Add. MSS 33,325–33,336 (Registers of the bills of fare in the household of the Duke of Newcastle, and, after his death, the Duchess of Newcastle, 1761–1774); and National Archives, Kew, LS 9/50–226 (Royal Bills of Fare for 1660–1812).

55 Hannah Glasse, *The Art of Cookery made Plain and Easy*, 5th edn (London, 1755).

56 Richard Briggs, *The English Art of Cookery, According to the Present Practice; Being a Complete Guide to all Housekeepers, on a Plan Entirely New* (London, 1788).

57 Martha Bradley, *The British Housewife: or, the Cook, Housekeeper's, and Gardiner's Companion* (London, *c.* 1770).

58 Jeremy Black, *A Subject for Taste: Culture in Eighteenth-century England* (London, 2005), p. xvi.

59 *The Times*, 1 October 1802.

60 Anderson, *Imagined Communities*.

61 For a broader examination of the role of cookbooks in the creation of communities, see especially Janet Theophano, *Eat My Words: Reading Women's Lives through the Cookbooks They Wrote* (New York, 2002).

62 Mrs Frazer, *The Practice of Cookery, Pastry, Pickling, Preserving, &c.* (Edinburgh and London, 1791).

63 [Maria Rundell], *A New System of Domestic Cookery; Formed upon Principles of Economy: And Adapted to the Use of Private Families* (London, 1807). The book had at least 63 editions by 1840.

64 Schmidt, 'Elegant Dishes and Unrefined Truths', pp. 76–7.

65 John Brewer, *The Sinews of Power: War, Money and the English State, 1688–1783* (Cambridge, MA, 1990), chapter 8.

66 *The Prudent Housewife; Or, Complete English Cook for Town and Country* (London, *c.* 1750); and Susannah Carter, *The Frugal Housewife, or, Complete Woman Cook* (London, 1790).

67 Sarah Harrison, *The House-keeper's Pocket-Book* (London, 1733).

68 Preface to Charlotte Mason, *The Lady's Assistant for Regulating and Supping her Table, being a Complete System of Cookery*, 5th edn (London, 1786).

69 James Jenks, *The Complete Cook: Teaching the Art of Cookery in All its Branches* (London, 1768).
70 Frazer, *Practice of Cookery*.
71 Maximilian Hazlemore, *Domestic Economy; or, a Complete System of English Housekeeping* (London, 1794).
72 Rundell, *New System of Domestic Cookery*, preface.
73 On the decline of manuscript collections, see Lehmann, *British Housewife*, p. 72; and Varey, 'Pleasures of the Table', p. 42. For two useful studies of the emergence of national cuisines, see Arjun Appadurai, 'How to Make a National Cuisine: Cookbooks in Contemporary India', *Comparative Studies in Society and History*, 30 (1988), pp. 3–24; and Alison K. Smith's consideration primarily of Russia in her 'Natural Cuisines', in *The Oxford Handbook of Food History*, ed. Jeffrey M. Pilcher (Oxford, 2012), pp. 444–60.
74 Mary Cole, *The Lady's Complete Guide; or Cookery in all its Branches* (London, 1788).
75 Elizabeth Cleland, *A New and Easy Method of Cookery*, 2nd edn (Edinburgh, 1759).
76 Daniel Defoe, *A Tour Thro' the Whole Island of Great Britain,* 6th edn (1761–2), vol. IV, p. 61. When Defoe encountered good cookery in Scotland, he credited it to the area being anglicized.
77 Linda Colley, *Britons: Forging the Nation, 1707–1837* (New Haven, CT, 1992).
78 Samuel Johnson, *A Journey to the Western Islands of Scotland* (Dublin, 1775), vol. I, pp. 125–7.
79 William Guthrie, *New Geographical, Historical, and Commercial Grammar* (London, 1771), vol. I, p. 179.
80 *Morning Post*, 2 December 1815.
81 *Carlisle Patriot*, 1 February 1817.
82 The painting is David Wilkie's *George IV in Kilt* (1829).
83 *The Examiner*, 1 September 1822.
84 Reprinted in the *Dublin Evening Mail*, 31 May 1826.

5 AN EDIBLE MAP OF MANKIND

1 *London Magazine* (January 1779), p. 53.
2 Edmund Burke to William Robertson, 9 June 1777, in *The Correspondence of Edmund Burke*, ed. Thomas W. Copeland (Chicago, IL, 1958–78), vol. III, pp. 350–51.
3 Christopher J. Berry, *The Idea of Commercial Society in the Scottish Enlightenment* (Edinburgh, 2015); Alexander Broadie, ed., *The Cambridge Companion to the Scottish Enlightenment* (Cambridge, 2003).
4 James Horn, 'British Diaspora: Emigration from Britain, 1680–1815', in *The Oxford History of the British Empire*, vol. II: *The Eighteenth Century*, ed. P. J. Marshall (Oxford, 1998), table 2.1.
5 On Scottish participation in the eighteenth-century empire, see especially Ned Landsman, *Scotland and its First American Colony, 1683–1765* (Princeton, NJ, 1985); G. J. Bryant, 'Scots in India in the Eighteenth Century', *Scottish Historical Review*, 64 (1985), pp. 22–41; and Eric Richards, 'Scotland and the Uses of the Atlantic Empire', in *Strangers within the Realm: Cultural Margins of the First British Empire*,

ed. Bernard Bailyn and Philip Morgan (Chapel Hill, NC, 1991), pp. 67–114. On the imperial experience and national identity, see Linda Colley, *Britons: Forging of the Nation, 1707–1837* (New Haven, CT, 1992). For a contrasting view, see especially John M. MacKenzie, 'Empire and National Identities: The Case of Scotland', *Transactions of the Royal Historical Society*, 8 (1998), pp. 215–32.

6 Jacob M. Price, 'Who Cared about the Colonies? The Impact of the Thirteen Colonies on British Society and Politics, circa 1714–1775', in *Strangers within the Realm*, ed. Bailyn and Morgan, p. 427.

7 Roger L. Emerson, 'American Indians, Frenchmen, and Scots Philosophers', *Studies in Eighteenth-century Culture*, 19 (1979), p. 217.

8 An exception to this was Lord Kames, who proposed a second creation for American Indians, although he did not suggest they were any less human than Europeans.

9 Richard B. Sher, *The Enlightenment and the Book: Scottish Authors and Their Publishers in Eighteenth-century Britain* (Chicago, IL, 2007).

10 *Scots Magazine* (April 1772), p. 196.

11 Maxine Berg, *Luxury and Pleasure in Eighteenth-century Britain* (Oxford, 2005), pp. 207–8.

12 *Monthly Review* (July 1759), p. 1.

13 Mark Duckworth, 'An Eighteenth-century Questionnaire: William Robertson on the Indians', *Eighteenth-century Life*, 21 (1987), pp. 36–49.

14 Troy Bickham, *Savages with the Empire: Representations of American Indians in Eighteenth-century Britain* (Oxford, 2005), pp. 200–209. On literacy, see Lawrence Stone, 'Literacy and Education in England, 1640–1900', *Past and Present*, 42 (1969), pp. 69–139; and Peter Earle, *The Making of the English Middle Class: Business, Society and Family Life in London, 1660–1730* (Berkeley, CA, 1989), p. 10.

15 *Edinburgh Magazine* (March 1759), pp. 130–32. On female reading, see especially Naomi Tadmor, '"In the even my wife read to me": Women, Reading and Household Life in the Eighteenth Century', in *The Practice and Representation of Reading in England*, ed. James Raven, Helen Small and Naomi Tadmor (Cambridge, 1996), pp. 162–74; and Jan Fergus, 'Women, Class, and Growth of Magazine Readership in the Provinces, 1746–1780', *Studies in Eighteenth-century Culture*, 16 (1986), pp. 41–53.

16 *London Chronicle*, 29 June 1762.

17 Silvia Sebastiani, *The Scottish Enlightenment: Race, Gender, and the Limits of Progress* (London, 2013).

18 William Robertson, *The History of America* (London, 1777), vol. I, p. 314.

19 *Leeds Intelligencer*, 6 September 1768.

20 Stewart J. Brown, ed., *William Robertson and the Expansion of Empire* (Cambridge, 1997).

21 For the best synopsis of conjectural, stadial history, see H. M. Hopfl, 'From Savage to Scotsman: Conjectural History in the Scottish Enlightenment', *Journal of British Studies*, 17 (1978), pp. 19–40.

22 Michael Eamon, *Imprinting Britain: Newspapers, Sociability, and the Shaping of British North America* (Montreal, 2015), pp. 61–2.

23 See Paul Kaufman's examination of the borrowing records of Bristol Library in his *Borrowings from the Bristol Library, 1733–1784: A Unique Record of*

Reading Vogues (Charlottesville, VA, 1960), which shows that history and travel works were borrowed 6,121 times versus theology's 607 and jurisprudence's 447.

24 Paul Kaufman, 'English Book Clubs and their Role in Social History', *Libri*, 14 (1964), p. 23; James Raven, 'From Promotion to Proscription: Arrangements for Reading in Eighteenth-century Libraries', in *The Practice and Representation of Reading in England*, ed. Raven, Small and Tadmor (Cambridge, 1996), pp. 175–201.

25 Joshua Toulmin, *The History of Taunton in the Country of Somerset* (Taunton, 1791), p. 187.

26 John Marsh, 'History of my private life', HM 54457, Huntington Library, San Marino, California, Box 1, vol. XII.

27 C.-F. (Constantin-François) Volney, *Travels through Syria and Egypt, in the years 1783, 1784, and 1785. Containing the present natural and political state of those countries . . .* (Dublin, 1788), vol. 1, p. 236.

28 Cowper to John Newton, 6 October 1783, in *The Letters and Prose Writings of William Cowper*, ed. James King and Charles Ryskamp (Oxford, 1981), vol. 1, p. 168.

29 James Murray, *The Travels of the Imagination; a true journey from Newcastle to London, in a Stage-Coach. With observations on the metropolis* (London, 1773).

30 Jeremy Black, *Italy and the Grand Tour* (New Haven, CT, 2003), especially chapter 7.

31 For more on this subject, see Troy Bickham, 'American Indians in the British Imperial Imagination', in *The American Colonies in the British Empire*, ed. Stephen Foster (Oxford, 2014).

32 *Annual Register* for 1777, p. 214.

33 *Jackson's Oxford Journal*, 7 March 1772.

34 For more on the connections between the Scottish Enlightenment and American Indians, see Bickham, *Savages within the Empire*, chapter 5.

35 William Russell, *The History of America, from its Discovery by Columbus to the Conclusion of the Late War* (London, 1778), vol. II, p. 130.

36 Robert Beverly, *The History and Present State of Virginia* (London, 1705), pp. 14–18.

37 Cadwallader Colden, *The History of the Five Indian Nations of Canada* (London, 1755), vol. 1, pp. 12–13.

38 Henry Timberlake, *The Memoirs of Lieut. Henry Timberlake (who accompanied the three Cherokee Indians to England in the year 1762) Containing Whatever He Observed* (London, 1765), pp. vii and 34–5.

39 *The Juvenile Library, Including a Complete Course of Instruction on Every Useful Subject* (London, 1800), vol. 1, pp. 169–77.

40 Cornelis de Bruyn, *A New and More Correct Translation than has hitherto Appeared in Public of Mr. Cornelius Le Brun's Travels into Moscovy, Persia, and Divers Parts of the East-Indies . . . by a Gentleman in Oxford* (London, 1759), p. 10.

41 *A Compendium of the travels of Mr. Hanway, Sir John Mandeville and Mr. Lionel Wafer, and a Description of Greenland* (London, 1765), p. 94.

42 Johann Gottlieb Georgi, *Russia; or, a Compleat Historical Account of all the Nations which Compose that Empire* (London, 1783), vol. III, p. 229.

43 Daniel Fenning, *A New System of Geography: or, a General Description of the World* (London, 1765), vol. I, p. 99.

44 In William Mayor, *Historical Account of the Most Celebrated Voyages, Travels, and Discoveries, from the Time of Columbus to the Present Period* (London, 1796), vol. IX, p. 95.

45 Priscilla Wakefield, *Human Manners: Delineated in Stories Intended to Illustrate the Characters, Religion, and Singular Customs of the Inhabitants of Different Parts of the World* (London, 1814), pp. 2–5.

46 For examples of Tahitians being utilized as noble savages in Britain, see the series of articles that first appeared in the *London Chronicle*, 24 July 1774, 21 July, 1, 15 and 20 August and 26 December 1778; *A Letter from Oberea, Queen of Otaheite* (London, 1774). Bernard Smith deals with British depictions and perceptions in much more substantial detail than is possible here in *European Vision and the South Pacific*, 2nd edn (New Haven, CT, 1985) and *Imagining the Pacific: In the Wake of the Cook Voyages* (New Haven, CT, 1992). See also Kathleen Wilson, *This Island Race: Empire and Gender in the Eighteenth Century* (London, 2002), pp. 54–91 and 169–200; and Richard Grove, *Green Imperialism: Colonial Expansion, Tropical Edens and the Origins of Environmentalism, 1600–1800* (Cambridge, 1995).

47 John Walker, *Elements of Geography, and of Natural and Civil History* (London, 1800), p. 160.

48 David Henry, *An Historical Account of all the Voyages Round the World, Performed by English Navigators* (London, 1774), p. 103.

49 John Hawkesworth, *Account of the Voyages . . . for Making Discoveries in the Southern Hemisphere* (London, 1773). See also Alan Frost, 'New Geographical Perspectives and the Emergence of the Romantic Imagination', in *Captain James Cook and his Times*, ed. Robin Fisher and Hugh Johnston (London, 1979), pp. 5–19.

50 Thomas Blake Clark, *Omai: First Polynesian Ambassador to England* (Honolulu, HI, 1969), p. 58.

51 According to the *Oxford English Dictionary*, its first known use in relation to cooking meats is in late seventeenth-century Jamaica.

52 John Hawkesworth, *A New Voyage, Round the World . . . Performed by Captain James Cook* (London, 1774), p. 125.

53 *By the King's Royal License and Authority. A New Royal Authentic and Complete System of Universal Geography Antient and Modern* (London, 1790), p. 49.

54 Ibid., p. 50.

55 William Chambers, *Designs of Chinese Buildings, Furniture, Dresses, Machines and Utensils* (London, 1757).

56 Louis-Pierre Anquetil, *A Summary of Universal History . . . Exhibiting the Rise, Decline, and Revolutions of the Different Nations of the World* (London, 1800), vol. V, pp. 550–51.

57 Edward Terry, *A Voyage to East-India*, revd edn (London, 1777).

58 Anquetil, *A Summary of Universal History*, vol. V, pp. 592–3.

59 John Henry Grose, *A Voyage to the East-Indies, with Observations on Various Parts There* (London, 1757), p. 241.

60 Mark H. Smith, *Sensory History* (Oxford, 2007), pp. 3–10.

61 Mary Wortley Montagu, *Letters of the Right Honourable Lady M—y W—y M—e: written, during her travels in Europe, Asia and Africa* (London, 1764),

p. 125; this particular passage was selected for reprinting in the *London Magazine* (May 1763), p. 202.

62 Samuel Derrick, *A Collection of Travels, Thro' Various Parts of the World; but More Particularly, Thro' Tartary, China, Turkey, Persia, and the East-Indies* (London, 1762), vol. II, p. 257.

63 John Trusler, *Honours of the table, or rules for behaving during meals* (London, 1791), p. 6.

64 Amanda Vickery, *The Gentleman's Daughter: Women's Lives in Georgian England* (New Haven, CT, 1998), pp. 147–53.

65 Martha Bradley, *The British Housewife: or, the Cook, Housekeeper's, and Gardiner's Companion* (London, *c.* 1770); Robert Abbot, *The Housekeeper's Valuable Present: or, Lady's Closet Companion* (London, 1790).

66 Hannah Glasse, *The Art of Cookery Made Plain and Easy* (London, 1777); William Augustus Henderson, *The Housekeeper's Instructor; or, Universal Family Cook* (London, 1793).

67 University College, Oxford: UC: 01/A1/1, 2 July 1804.

68 Amanda Vickery, '"Neat and Not Too Showey": Words and Wallpaper in Regency England', in *Gender, Taste and Material Culture in Britain and North America, 1700–1830*, ed. John Styles and Amanda Vickery (New Haven, CT, 2006), pp. 201–24.

69 Rosamond Bayne-Powell, *Housekeeping in the Eighteenth Century* (London, 1956), especially chapter 2.

70 Jon Stobart and Mark Rothery, *Consumption and the Country House* (Oxford, 2016), pp. 75 and 269.

71 Berg, *Luxury and Pleasure*, p. 130.

72 For a comprehensive discussion of the importance of replication, innovation and design to the economic history of Britain during this period, see Berg, *Luxury and Pleasure*, chapter 1.

73 For more on the abundance and appeal of ethnographic objects, see Troy Bickham, '"A conviction of the reality of things": Material Culture, North American Indians and Empire in Eighteenth-century Britain', *Eighteenth-century Studies*, 39 (2005), pp. 29–47.

74 Ibid.

75 Lot 1444 in the annotated catalogue with prices of the *A Catalogue of the Portland Museum* (London, 1786), Bodleian Library, Oxford University, 2591 d.8.

76 Sarah Harrison, *The House-keeper's Pocket-Book, and Compleat Family Cook*, 6th edn (London, 1757).

77 Henderson, *The Housekeeper's Instructor*, p. 3.

78 From the preface of Francis Collingwood and John Woollams, *The Universal Cook, and City and Country Housekeeper* (London, 1792).

79 Hannah Glasse, *The Art of Cookery, Made Plain and Easy*, 13th edn (London, 1778), pp. 102, 334, 331–2, 101, 385, 372, 377 and 373.

80 John Farley, *London Art of Cookery*, 7th edn (London, 1792), pp. 267, 271–2, 202 and 294.

81 For examples, see Ann Peckham, *The Compleat English cook; or, the Prudent Housewife* (Leeds, 1767); *The New London cookery and Complete Domestic Guide* (London, 1827), pp. 570–71; *Mrs. Cole's cookery: the Lady's Complete Guide; or, Cookery in all its Branches*, 3rd edn (London, 1791), p. 183;

Charlotte Mason, *The Lady's Assistant for Regulating and Supping her Table, being a Complete System of Cookery*, 5th edn (London, 1786), p. 388; Harrison, *House-keeper's Pocket-Book*, 8th edn (London, 1764), p. 179; Richard Briggs, *The English Art of Cookery, According to the Present Practice* (London, 1788), p. 42, and 2nd edn (London, 1793), p. 207; Margaret Dods, *The Cook and Housewife's Manual* (Edinburgh, 1826), pp. 59 and 61.

82 See for example J. Skeat, *The Art of Cookery and Pastry Made Easy and Familiar* (London, 1769), p. 41; *Mrs. Cole's Cookery*, p. 191; Dods, *Cook and Housewife's Manual*, pp. 242–3 and 181–2; Mrs Frazer, *The Practice of Cookery, Pastry, Pickling, Preserving, &c.* (Edinburgh, 1791), pp. 69–70.

83 Martha Bradley, *The British Housewife: or, the Cook, Housekeeper's, and Gardiner's Companion* (London, 1758), pp. 13 and 118.

84 *The Young Lady's Geography; Containing, an Accurate Description of the Several Parts of the Known World* (London, 1765).

85 See for example Glasse, *Art of Cookery*, 5th edn (1755), p. 101, and editions thereafter; Shackleford, *Modern Art of Cookery Improved*, p. 28; Duncan Macdonald, *The London Family Cook; or, Town and Country Housekeeper's Guide* (London, 1812), p. 217; Maria Rundell, *A New System of Domestic Cookery; Formed upon Principles of Economy: And Adapted to the Use of Private Families*, new edition (London, 1812), p. 86; Briggs, *English Art of Cookery*, p. 297; and Mason, *Lady's Assistant*, p. 265.

86 *New London cookery and Complete Domestic Guide*, p. 627.

87 Elizabeth Raffald, *The Experienced English Housekeeper* (Manchester, 1769), p. 175. The recipe grew in grandness and design over the course of the books' editions.

88 Farley, *The London Art of Cookery*, pp. 373–4, which is a modified version of the recipe from Raffald's *Experienced English Housekeeper*, 7th edn (1786), pp. 189–90.

89 Henderson, *Housekeeper's Instructor*, p. 256.

90 Eliga Gould, *The Persistence of Empire: British Political Culture in the Age of the American Revolution* (Chapel Hill, NC, 2000); Bob Harris, '"American Idols": Empire, War and the Middling Ranks in Mid-eighteenth Century Britain', *Past and Present*, 150 (1996), pp. 111–41; Kathleen Wilson, *The Sense of the People: Politics, Culture and Imperialism in England, 1715–1785* (Cambridge, 1995).

91 *The Diary of Thomas Turner, 1754–1765*, ed. David Vaisey (Oxford, 1984), p. 191.

92 See for example, Mason, *The Lady's Assistant*, pp. 175–6; Farley, *London Art of Cookery*, 7th edn (London, 1792), pp. 127–8; and Briggs, *English Art of Cookery* (1788), p. 264, who placed the recipe in between ones for curry, pilau and West Indian turtle.

93 The first American-related designation appears to have been 'Carolina rice pudding' and 'Carolina Snow-Balls' in Glasse, *Art of Cookery*, 13th edn (1778), p. 385. The designation 'New England' appeared shortly after the war, when it was applied to a number of foods, including hams, oatmeal and pancakes. On the shift of the colonists from fellow Britons to foreigners, see Stephen Conway, 'From Fellow-nationals to Foreigners: British Perceptions of the Americans, circa 1739–1783', *William and Mary Quarterly*, 49 (2002), pp. 65–100.

94 Rebecca L. Spang, *The Invention of the Restaurant: Paris and Modern Gastronomic Culture* (Cambridge, MA, 2000), pp. 76–8.
95 For national coverage of the feasts, see *Ruddiman's Weekly Mercury* [Edinburgh], 13 November 1782, and *Derby Mercury*, 28 November 1782.
96 For a lively and comprehensive history of 'Indian' food and its mutations and migrations to Europe, see Lizzie Collingham, *Curry: A Biography* (London, 2005); and Cecilia Leong-Salobir, *Food Culture in Colonial Asia: A Taste of Empire* (London, 2014), pp. 39–59.
97 See for example Collingham, *Curry*, pp. 129–56; Susan Zlotnick, 'Domesticating Imperialism: Curry and Cookbooks in Victorian England', *Frontiers*, 16 (1996), pp. 51–68; and Nupur Chaudhuri, 'Shawls, Jewelry, Curry, and Rice in Victorian Britain', in *Western Women and Imperialism*, ed. Nupur Chaudhuri and Margaret Strobel (Bloomington, IN, 1992), pp. 238–44. Chaudhuri notes that curry was first offered publicly in 1733 at the Norris Street Coffeehouse in London, but this appears to be an editing error, because the source Chaudhuri cites gives the year as 1773.
98 Glasse, *Art of Cookery* (1747), p. 101.
99 David Burton, *The Raj at the Table: A Culinary History of the British in India* (London, 1993), p. 3; Chaudhuri, 'Shawls, Jewelry, Curry, and Rice', pp. 231–2.
100 Harrison, *House-keeper's Pocket-Book*, 8th edn (1764), preface and p. 30.
101 *Mrs. Cole's cookery*, 3rd edn (London, 1791), pp. vi and 148–9.
102 *Public Advertiser*, 6 December 1773.
103 Skeat, *Art of Cookery and Pastry Made Easy and Familiar*, p. 41.
104 See for example Glasse, *Art of Cookery*, 16th edn (London, 1796), p. 129; and Rundell, *A New System of Domestic Cookery* (1807), p. 86. In such instances, the 'easier' recipe appeared underneath lengthier ones.
105 Robert H. Goodsall, *A Kentish Patchwork* (London, 1966), p. 20; The first to use 'curree-powder' was likely Mason, *Lady's Assistant*, p. 265, and it appeared regularly after that.
106 Sarah Martin, *The New Experienced English-Housekeeper, for the Use and Ease of Ladies, Housekeepers, Cooks &c.* (Doncaster, 1795), p. 35.
107 'Proceedings of the Old Bailey: London's Central Criminal Court, 1674 to 1913', www.oldbaileyonline.org, case t18030112-2.
108 Margaret Dods, *Cook and Housewife's Manual* (Edinburgh, 1826), pp. 242–3.
109 Michael H. Fisher, *The First Indian Author in English: Dean Mahomed (1759–1851) in India, Ireland, and England* (Oxford, 1996), pp. 257–63; *The Times*, 27 March 1811; *The Epicure's Almanack* (London, 1815), pp. 123–4.

6 THE POLITICS OF FOOD

1 Hannah Barker, *Newspapers, Politics and English Society, 1695–1855* (London, 2000), chapter 2.
2 *The Idler*, 27 May 1758.
3 The estimate is from Edmund Burke, and it is on a par with historians' estimates. On newspaper readership, see especially Hannah Barker, *Newspapers, Politics and English Society, 1695–1855* (London, 2000), p. 47; Troy Bickham, *Making Headlines: The American Revolution as Seen through*

the British Press (DeKalb, IL, 2009), chapter 1; Jeremy Black, *The English Press in the Eighteenth Century* (London, 1987), pp. 104–5.

4 Samuel Johnson, *A Dictionary of the English Language* (London, 1785).

5 *London Magazine* (August 1780), p. 355.

6 John Brewer, *Party Ideology and Popular Politics at the Accession of George III* (Cambridge, 1976), p. 7.

7 Don Herzog, *Poisoning the Minds of the Lower Orders* (Princeton, NJ, 1998), p. 58.

8 Cited in John Brewer, *Pleasures of the Imagination: English Culture in the Eighteenth Century* (London, 1997), pp. 183–4.

9 Letter from Horace Mann to Horace Walpole, 8 April 1775, *The Yale Edition of Horace Walpole's Correspondence*, ed. W. S. Lewis et al. (London, 1937–83), vol. XXIV, p. 87.

10 *Public Advertiser*, 2 January 1775.

11 For an analysis of the petitions, see James E. Bradley, 'The British Public and the American Revolution: Ideology, Interest and Opinion', in *Britain and the American Revolution*, ed. H. T. Dickinson (London, 1998), pp. 124–54.

12 *The Gazetteer*, 4 January 1776.

13 *The Speculatist: A Collection of Letters and Essays, Moral and Political, Serious and Humourous: Upon Various Subjects* (London, 1732), p. 126.

14 *Saint James's Chronicle*, 12 October 1776.

15 *Bristol Journal*, 2 March 1776.

16 *The Spectator*, 49 (1711).

17 *Town and Country Magazine* (August 1770), p. 267.

18 *General Evening Post*, 25 April 1781.

19 On how print culture eroded some of the distinctiveness of public and private spheres during this period, see especially the Harriet Guest, *Small Change: Women, Learning, Patriotism, 1750–1810* (Chicago, IL, 2000); Kathleen Wilson, *The Sense of the People: Politics, Culture and Imperialism in England, 1715–1785* (Cambridge, 1995); Lawrence Klein, 'Gender and the Public/Private Distinction in the Eighteenth Century: Some Questions about Evidence and Analytical Procedure', *Eighteenth-century Studies*, 29 (1995); Karen O'Brien, *Women and Enlightenment in Eighteenth-century Britain* (Cambridge, 2009).

20 Jan Fergus, 'Women, Class, and Growth of Magazine Readership in the Provinces, 1746–1780', *Studies in Eighteenth-century Culture*, 16 (1986), pp. 41–53; and Kathryn Shevelow, *Women and Print Culture: The Construction of Femininity in the Early Periodical* (New York, 1989).

21 Pierre Jean Grosley, *A Tour to London: or, New Observations on England, and Its Inhabitants* (London, 1772), vol. I, pp. 208 and 211.

22 John Trusler, *The Honours of the Table, Or, Rules for Behaviour During Meals . . . For the Use of Young People* (London, 1788).

23 Louis Simond, *An American in Regency England: The Journal of a Tour in 1810–1811*, ed. Christopher Hibbert (London, 1968), p. 35.

24 *London Chronicle*, 13 May 1775.

25 *Public Advertiser*, 4 March 1777.

26 Peter Marshall, *Bristol and the American War of Independence* (Bristol, 1977), p. 6.

27 John Marsh, 'History of my private life', HM 54457, Huntington Library, San Marino, California, Box 1, vol. V.

28 See Tamara L. Hunt, *Defining John Bull* (London, 2003), pp. 91 and 160; and Ben Rodgers, *Beef and Liberty: Roast Beef, John Bull and the English Nation* (London, 2003).

29 *The Times*, 13 April 1789.

30 The Seven Years War was the British name for a conflict that played out globally, with various regions assigning different names and fighting the war for different periods. For example, the British colonists in North America typically referred to the conflict as the French and Indian Wars, which effectively lasted from 1754 to 1765, while in the Indian subcontinent it is described as the Third Carnatic War.

31 John Brewer, *The Sinews of Power: War, Money and the English State, 1688–1783* (Cambridge, MA, 1990), pp. 40–41 and 114; and Nancy F. Koehn, *The Power of Commerce: Economy and Governance in the First British Empire* (Ithaca, NY, 1994), pp. 3–18.

32 For the most influential and succinct description of this shift, see P. J. Marshall, 'Empire and Authority in the Later Eighteenth Century', *Journal of Imperial and Commonwealth History*, 15 (1987), pp. 105–22.

33 P.D.G. *Thomas, British Politics and the Stamp Act Crisis* (Oxford, 1975), pp. 86–7.

34 Jacob Price, 'The Imperial Economy, 1700–1776', in *The Oxford History of the British Empire*, vol. II: *The Eighteenth Century*, ed. P. J. Marshall (Oxford, 1998), pp. 78–104.

35 Jane T. Merritt, *The Trouble with Tea: The Politics of Consumption in the Eighteenth-century Global Economy* (Baltimore, MD, 2017), pp. 34 (table 2.1), 39 (table 2.2) and 43.

36 Price, 'The Imperial Economy, 1700–1776', table 4.4.

37 *Edmund Burke's Speech on Conciliation with the American Colonies, Delivered in the House of Commons March 22, 1775*, ed. William I. Crane (New York, 1900), p. 66.

38 T. H. Breen, *The Marketplace of Revolution: How Consumer Politics Shaped American Independence* (Oxford, 2004); Merritt, *The Trouble with Tea*, chapter 3.

39 The estimates came from Thomas Hutchinson, Governor of Massachusetts, cited in James R. Fichter, *So Great a Proffit: How the East Indies Trade Transformed Anglo-American Capitalism* (Cambridge, MA, 2010), p. 18.

40 Jonathan Eacott, *Selling Empire: India in the Making of Britain and America, 1600–1830* (Chapel Hill, NC, 2016), p. 181; for East India Company shareholding, see *H. V. Bowen, The Business of Empire: The East India Company and Imperial Britain, 1756–1833* (Cambridge, 2006), chapter 4.

41 T. H. Breen, *The Marketplace of Revolution: How Consumer Politics Shaped American Independence* (Oxford, 2004), p. xii.

42 Fichter, *So Great a Profit*, pp. 16–18.

43 Cited in Breen, *Marketplace of Revolution*, p. 285. George Grenville's ministry was responsible for creating the Sugar and Stamp acts.

44 John Adams to Abigail Adams, 6 July 1774, *Adams Family Correspondence*, ed. L. H. Butterfield, Wendell D. Garrett and Marjorie Sprague (Cambridge, MA, 1963), vol. I, pp. 130–31.

45 *Providence Gazette*, 4 March 1775. I am grateful to James R. Fichter for calling my attention to this source.

46 Cited in Breen, *Marketplace of Revolution*, p. xvi.
47 Bickham, *Making Headlines*.
48 *Evening Post*, 4 February 1774.
49 *The Diary of Abigail Gathern of Nottingham, 1751–1810*, ed. Adrian Henstock (Nottingham, 1980), p. 33.
50 *Stamford Mercury*, 24 March 1774.
51 Christopher Leslie Brown, *Moral Capital: Foundations of British Abolitionism* (Chapel Hill, NC, 2006); and Jack P. Greene, *Evaluating Empire and Confronting Colonialism in Eighteenth-century Britain* (Cambridge, 2013), especially chapter 8.
52 Gilbert Wakefield, *A Sermon Preached at Richmond in Surry on July 29th, 1784, The Day Appointed for a General Thanksgiving on Account of the Peace* (London, 1784), pp. 16–17.
53 On the importance of sugar to the English, and later British, Empire, its centrality to the Atlantic world and its destructive consequences, see especially Lizzie Collingham, *The Taste of Empire: How Britain's Quest for Food Shaped the Modern World* (New York, 2017), chapter 4; Sidney Mintz, *Sweetness and Power: The Place of Sugar in Modern History* (New York, 1985); Walvin, *Fruits of Empire*, chapter 8, and his *Sugar: The World Corrupted* (London, 2018).
54 On the value of the West Indian trade to British naval power, see James Epstein, *The Scandal of Colonial Rule: Power and Subversion in the British Atlantic during the Age of Revolution* (Cambridge, 2012), p. 5. For examples of contemporary awareness of its value, see *The Present Ruinous Situation of the West India Islands, Submitted to the People of the British Empire* (London, 1811), p. 11; and 'General Meeting Minutes, 15 May 1811', Glasgow West Indian Association: Minutes, Mitchell Library, Glasgow.
55 On the Manchester Petition, see Seymour Drescher, *Capitalism and Antislavery: British Mobilization in Comparative Perspective* (Oxford, 1997), pp. 70–74 and table 4.1.
56 See especially Linda Colley, *Britons: Forging the Nation, 1707–1837* (New Haven, CT, 1992); Wilson, *Sense of the People*; and Bob Harris, '"American Idols": Empire, War and the Middling Ranks in Mid-eighteenth-century Britain', *Past and Present*, 150 (1996), pp. 111–41.
57 Grosley, *Tour to London*, pp. 210–11.
58 Samuel Bradburn, *An Address to the People Called Methodist; Concerning the Evils of Encouraging the Slave Trade* (Manchester, 1792), p. 6.
59 Colley, *Britons*, chapter 6; Amanda Foreman, *Georgiana, Duchess of Devonshire* (London, 1999); Kathryn Jane Gleadle, *Borderline Citizens: Women, Gender and Political Culture in Britain, 1815–1867* (London, 2009); Guest, *Small Change*; Brien, *Women and Enlightenment*; Clare Midgley, *Feminism and Empire: Women Activists in Imperial Britain, 1790–1865* (New York, 2007); Srividhya Swaminathan, *Debating the Slave Trade: Rhetoric of British National Identity, 1759–1815* (Farnham, Surrey, 2009), pp. 189–90.
60 Elizabeth J. Clapp and Julie Roy Jeffrey, *Women, Dissent, and Anti-slavery in Britain and America, 1790–1865* (Oxford, 2011).
61 Minute books, Rhodes House, Oxford University, MSS Brit Emp s 20, E2/1–20.

62 William Nash, *Reasons for Using East India Sugar. Printed for The Peckham Ladies' African and Anti-Slavery Association* (London, 1828).
63 The East India Company noted the potential for its sugar early on in *A Report from the Committee of Warehouses of the United East-India Company, Relative to the Culture of Sugar* (London, 1792), but its public calls for the end of the West Indian subsidy and marketing of its sugar as 'free' did not gain momentum until the 1820s. Conditions of sugar production were, like most commercial agriculture under British rule in South Asia, poor and hardly free. See Andrea Major, *Slavery, Abolitionism and Empire in India, 1772–1843* (Liverpool, 2012), especially chapter 8.
64 *No Rum! No Sugar! Or, the Voice of Blood, Being Half an Hour's Conversation, between a Negro and an English Gentleman, Shewing the Horrible Nature of the Slave-Trade, and Pointing out an Easy and Effectual Method of Terminating It, by an Act of the People* (London, 1792), p. 21.
65 Timothy Morton, *The Poetics of Spice: Romantic Consumerism and the Exotic* (Cambridge, 2000), chapter 4.
66 *Newcastle Courant*, 5 January 1792.
67 *A Plain Man's Thoughts on the Present Price of Sugar, &c.* (London, 1792), p. 11.
68 Clare Midgley, *Women Against Slavery: The British Campaigns, 1780–1870* (London, 1992), pp. 39–40; Drescher, *Capitalism and Antislavery*, p. 79.
69 Drescher, *Capitalism and Antislavery*, pp. 78–9.
70 Midgley, *Women Against Slavery*, p. 40.
71 *An Address to Her Royal Highness the Duchess of York, Against the Use of Sugar* (London, 1792), p. 21.

CONCLUSION

1 John Marsh, 'History of my private life', HM 54457, Huntington Library, San Marino, California, Box 1, vol. 11.
2 The event is described in Alexander Inkson McConnochie, *Lochnagar* (Aberdeen, 1891), pp. 79–80; and Thomas Archer, *Our Sovereign Lady Queen Victoria: Her Life and Jubilee* (London, 1888), vol. IV, pp. 93–4.
3 'Can You Have a Big "Switch Off"?', BBC News, 6 September 2007, www.news.bbc.co.uk; *Daily Telegraph*, 11 June 2010.
4 Jacob Price, 'The Imperial Economy, 1700–1776', in *The Oxford History of the British Empire*, vol. II: *The Eighteenth Century*, ed. P. J. Marshall (Oxford, 1998), pp. 85–6; Elizabeth B. Schumpeter, *English Overseas Trade Statistics, 1697–1808* (Oxford, 1960), p. 60; Michael Duffy, *The Military Revolution and the State, 1500–1800* (Exeter, 1980), pp. 61–2; John Brewer, *The Sinews of Power: War, Money and the English State, 1688–1783* (Cambridge, MA, 1990), pp. 34–5.
5 Bret Hinsch, *The Rise of Tea Culture in China: The Invention of the Individual* (London, 2018).
6 John Hawkesworth, *Account of the Voyages . . . for Making Discoveries in the Southern Hemisphere* (London, 1773).
7 *Morning Post*, 5 July 1777.

SELECTED SOURCES

PRIMARY SOURCES

The National Archives at Kew (formerly the Public Record Office) is home to the Board of Customs and Excise's Ledgers of Imports and Exports and Board of Trade records, as well as other Treasury papers, which form the basis of most of the statistics on imperial and foreign trade listed here – noted either directly or, more often, indirectly via secondary sources.

Shop records provide important details on commodities' journeys from ships to tables. Although shops numbered in the tens of thousands during the eighteenth century, relatively few ledgers detailing their operations survive. The papers of Ann Gomm in the Oxfordshire Record Office offer a rare glimpse into the business dealings of a village shop. Shopkeepers' ledgers are most prolific and detailed in the proceedings of bankruptcy cases, because lawyers and creditors typically produced detailed lists of a shop's contents, money owed to suppliers and customers with outstanding debts. Many of these can be found in London's Guildhall Library, English county records offices and the Court of Chancery records in the National Archives. By far the most consistently detailed are the bankruptcy records in the Court of Session Records at the National Records of Scotland. Somewhat uniquely, these papers provide detailed information on customers in arrears, including names, addresses, job titles and amounts owed. The largest collections of British trade cards, all consulted here, are found in the Banks and Heal collections held by the British Museum (many of which have been digitized and are free to view via the museum's online catalogue), the John Johnson Collection held by the Bodleian Library, Oxford University, and London's Guildhall Library.

The Sun Fire Office policy registers, held by London's Guildhall Library, are an excellent resource for gauging the size and wealth of a particular shop. The 'Proceedings of the Old Bailey: London's Central Criminal Court, 1674 to 1913', which are freely available and searchable online (www.oldbaileyonline.org), are an invaluable source for estimating the appearance, circulation and value of specific goods. For a detailed explanation and application of this methodology, see Sara Horrell, Jane Humphries and Ken Sneath, 'Cupidity and Crime: Consumption as Revealed by Insights from the Old Bailey Records of Thefts in the Eighteenth and Nineteenth Centuries', in *Large Databases in Economic History*, ed. Mark Casson and Nigar Hashimzade (London, 2013), pp. 246–67, as well as their 'Consumption Conundrums Unravelled', *Economic History Review*, 68 (2015), pp. 830–57.

Unfortunately, relatively few people from the eighteenth century kept detailed accounts of their lives, and, worse still, few of those accounts have survived. Even so, there is still an abundance of material to consider. By no means is what follows exhaustive, but the accounts that have been the most informative to the present study are Daniel Defoe, *A Tour Thro' the Whole Island of Great Britain*, 6th edn (1761–2); *The Diary of Abigail Gathern of Nottingham, 1751–1810*, ed. Adrian Henstock (Nottingham, 1980); Pierre Jean Grosley, *A Tour to London: or, New Observations on England, and Its Inhabitants* (London, 1772); James Boswell, *The Life of Samuel Johnson* (London, 1791); John Marsh, 'History of my private life', HM 54457, Huntington Library, San Marino, California; the Caroline Lybbe Powys Diaries, British Library, Add. MS 42160; Cesar de Saussure, *A Foreign View of England*, trans. Mme Van Muden (London, 1902); *Records of Social and Economic History*, new series 26: *The Diary of Robert Sharp of South Cave: Life in a Yorkshire Village, 1812–1837*, ed. Janice E. Crowther and Peter A. Crowther (Oxford, 1997); and *The Diary of Thomas Turner, 1754–1765*, ed. David Vaisey (Oxford, 1984).

Printed books, newspapers, pamphlets, essays and medical and political treatises account for a large swathe of the material considered in the present study. They are far too numerous to be listed here in full, but the wealth of material considered is evident in the notes. These sources abound in physical and digital form in libraries throughout the world, just as they once adorned eighteenth-century coffeehouse and domestic tables. Printed travel guides exploded as a genre in the latter half of the eighteenth century, as tourism and leisure grew. Although almost exclusively focused on London, the cheaply printed guides offer details about the eateries and entertainments on offer. Some of the most notable are *The Ambulator; or, the Stranger's Companion in a Tour Round London* (London, 1774) *Britannica Curiosa*, 2nd edn (London, 1777); *A Companion to Every Place of Curiosity and Entertainment in and about London and Westminster* (London, 1767); *The Epicure's Almanack* (London, 1815); John Roach, *Roach's London Pocket Pilot, or Stranger's Guide through the Metropolis* (London, 1796); and John Trusler, *The London Adviser* (London, 1786). Copies of cookery books abound, and some, such as Hannah Glasse, *The Art of Cookery made Plain and Easy*, remain in print. The most detailed guide to the titles, editions and publishers of each book is Arnold Whitaker, *English Cookery Books to the Year 1850* (Oxford, 1913). Gilly Lehmann, *The British Housewife: Cookery Books, Cooking and Society in Eighteenth-century Britain* (Blackawton, Devon, 2003) includes a similarly useful appendix.

The satirical prints that offered such lively social and political commentary are increasingly available in digital form online from a number of institutions. Similarly, museums have digitized images of artefacts such as teapots and sugar bowls. Some of the largest collections consulted for the present study are held by the British Library, British Museum, Colonial Williamsburg Foundation, Library of Congress, Metropolitan Museum of Art of New York City and Lewis Walpole Library at Yale University.

SECONDARY SOURCES

The general subject of this book – how certain foods affected Britain and shaped its inhabitants' views of the empire in the long eighteenth century – engages with a wide range of historical subjects with deep historiographies. The lists of works below are by no standard comprehensive, either of my reading or of the subjects engaged in this book. What follows is a summary of the sources that were most influential in the present study. In consequence, the reader should imagine a 'see especially' prefacing almost every sentence. Of course, influence should not be equated with agreement; therefore, none of the authors should be held responsible for my arguments or conclusions.

Broader histories of eighteenth-century Britain and its relationships with its empire are not in short supply. John Brewer, *The Sinews of Power: War, Money and the English State, 1688–1783* (Cambridge, MA, 1990); Linda Colley, *Britons: Forging the Nation, 1707–1837* (New Haven, CT, 1992); Julian Hoppit, *A Land of Liberty? England, 1689–1727* (Oxford, 2000); and Paul Langford, *A Polite and Commercial People: England, 1727–1783* (Oxford, 1989), though decades old, remain the most influential. Equally important is the work of P. J. Marshall, whose prolific contributions are to some extent encapsulated in his reflective *Making and Unmaking of Empires: Britain, India, and America, c. 1750–1783* (Oxford, 2005). Other works that have significantly shaped the present book include Jeremy Black, *A Subject for Taste: Culture in Eighteenth-century England* (London, 2005), among his many other works; John Brewer, *Pleasures of the Imagination: English Culture in the Eighteenth Century* (London, 1997); Hugh Cunningham, *Time, Work and Leisure: Life Changes in England since 1700* (Manchester, 2016); Nicholas B. Dirks, *The Scandal of Empire: India and the Creation of Imperial Britain* (Cambridge, MA, 2006); Bob Harris, '"American Idols": Empire, War and the Middling Ranks in Mid-eighteenth-century Britain', *Past and Present*, 150 (1996), pp. 111–41; Robert Markley, *The Far East and the English Imagination, 1600–1730* (Cambridge, 2006); James Raven, Helen Small and Naomi Tadmor, eds, *The Practice and Representation of Reading in England* (Cambridge, 1996); Amanda Vickery's *The Gentleman's Daughter: Women's Lives in Georgian England* (London, 1998) and *Behind Closed Doors: At Home in Georgian England* (New Haven, CT, 2009); and Kathleen Wilson, *The Sense of the People: Politics, Culture and Imperialism in England, 1715–1785* (Cambridge, 1995). Although to some extent at odds with the conclusions reached in this book, Ronald Hyam, *Understanding the British Empire* (Cambridge, 2010), offers a grounding challenge to cultural historians of Britain and its empire.

While commerce, the economy and trade are recurring themes in many works already listed, important to include here are Robert C. Allen, *The Industrial Revolution in Global Perspective* (Cambridge, 2009); William J. Ashworth, *Customs and Excise: Trade, Production, and Consumption in England, 1640–1845* (Oxford, 2003); H. V. Bowen, *The Business of Empire: The East India Company and Imperial Britain, 1756–1833* (Cambridge, 2006); K. N. Chaudhuri, *The Trading World of Asia and the English East India Company, 1660–1760* (Cambridge, 1978); Jonathan Eacott, *Selling Empire: India in the Making of Britain and America, 1600–1830* (Chapel Hill, NC, 2016); James R. Fichter, *So Great a Proffit: How the East Indies Trade Transformed Anglo-American Capitalism* (Cambridge, MA, 2010); Nancy F. Koehn, *The Power of Commerce: Economy and Governance in the First British Empire* (Ithaca, NY, 1994); Jacob M. Price, 'The Rise of Glasgow in the Chesapeake Tobacco Trade, 1707–1775', *William and Mary Quarterly*, 11 (1954), pp. 179–99; and Nuala Zahedieh, 'Economy', in *The British Atlantic World*, ed. David Armitage and Michael J. Braddick (New York, 2002).

The intellectual currents of Enlightenment and progress have substantial historiographies of their own. The most influential works on the present study's interest in how they shaped Britons' views of foreign peoples, particularly non-Europeans, include Thomas Ahnert, *The Moral Culture of the Scottish Enlightenment, 1690–1805* (New Haven, CT, 2015); Christopher J. Berry, *The Idea of Commercial Society in the Scottish Enlightenment* (Edinburgh, 2015); Troy Bickham, *Savages within the Empire: Representations of American Indians in Eighteenth-century Britain* (Oxford, 2005), chapter 5; Alexander Broadie, ed., *The Cambridge Companion to the Scottish Enlightenment* (Cambridge, 2003); Stewart J. Brown, ed., *William Robertson and the Expansion of Empire* (Cambridge, 1997); Arthur Herman, *How the Scots Invented the Modern World: The True Story of How Western Europe's Poorest Nation Created Our World and Everything in It* (London, 2001); H. M. Hopfl, 'From Savage to Scotsman: Conjectural History in the Scottish Enlightenment', *Journal of British Studies*, 17 (1978), pp. 19–40; Karen O'Brien, *Women and Enlightenment in Eighteenth-century Britain* (Cambridge, 2009); Stuart Piggott, *Ancient Britons and the Antiquarian Imagination: Ideas from the Renaissance to the Regency* (London, 1989); Silvia Sebastiani, *The Scottish Enlightenment: Race, Gender, and the Limits of Progress* (London, 2013); Barbara Shapiro, *A Culture of Fact: England, 1550–1720* (Ithaca, NY, 2000); Richard B. Sher, *The Enlightenment and the Book: Scottish Authors and Their Publishers in Eighteenth-century Britain* (Chicago, IL, 2007); Paul Slack, *The Invention of Improvement: Information and Material Progress in Seventeenth-century England* (Oxford, 2015); David Spadafora, *The Idea of Progress in Eighteenth-century Britain* (New Haven, CT, 1990); and E. C. Spary, *Eating the Enlightenment: Food and the Sciences in Paris* (Chicago, IL, 2012).

B. W. Higman, *How Food Made History* (Oxford, 2012), has argued that histories of food generally fall into two general categories: either histories of the foods themselves or histories that use food to explore a broader historical problem. While the present book fits firmly into the latter category, it draws heavily on the scholarship of both. The classic studies are Stephen Mennell, *All Manners of Food: Eating and Taste in England and France from the Middle Ages to the Present* (Oxford, 1985); and James Walvin, *Fruits of Empire: Exotic Produce and British Taste, 1660–1800* (London, 1997). Paul S. Lloyd, *Food Identity in England, 1540–1650* (London, 2015) is a careful examination of the period immediately prior to the deluge of imperial goods. In addition to many of the other books noted here, informative specific studies of eighteenth-century eating habits also include James McWilliams, *A Revolution in Eating: How the Quest for Food Shaped America* (New York, 2007); Sarah Pennell, *The Birth of the English Kitchen, 1600–1850* (London, 2016); Joan Thirsk, *Food in Early Modern England: Phases, Fads, Fashions, 1500–1760* (London, 2007); and Simon Varey, 'Pleasures of the Table', in *Pleasure in the Eighteenth Century*, ed. Roy Porter and Marie Mulvey Roberts (London, 1996). David Burton, *The Raj at the Table: A Culinary History of the British in India* (London, 1993), and Lizzie Collingham, *The Taste of Empire: How Britain's Quest for Food Shaped the Modern World* (New York, 2017) both offer broad studies of how British tastes shaped the overseas empire.

To these can be added what Frank Trentmann, *Empire of Things: How We Became a World of Consumers, from the Fifteenth Century to the Twenty-first* (London, 2016),

p. 79, calls 'commodity biographies'. Shaped by Sidney Mintz, *Sweetness and Power: The Place of Sugar in Modern History* (New York, 1985), the genre has exploded in recent decades. Just some of the highlights include Lizzie Collingham, *Curry: A Biography* (London, 2005); Mark Kurlansky, *Salt: A World History* (London, 2003); Marcy Norton, *Sacred Gifts, Profane Pleasures: A History of Tobacco and Chocolate in the Atlantic World* (Ithaca, NY, 2008); Marjorie Shaffer, *Pepper: A History of the World's Most Influential Spice* (New York, 2013); Julia Skinner, *Afternoon Tea: A History* (New York, 2019); Tom Standage, *A History of the World in Six Glasses* (New York, 2006); and Reaktion Books' substantial Edible series. Although not dealing with edible commodities, Jennifer L. Anderson, *Mahogany: The Costs of Luxury in Early America* (Cambridge, MA, 2012); Sven Beckert, *Empire of Cotton: A Global History* (London, 2014); and Giorgio Riello, *Cotton: The Fabric that Made the Modern World* (Cambridge, 2013) have been influential forces in the genre. For an overview of early receptions of some of these goods as medicines in Europe, see J. Worth Estes, 'The European Reception of the First Drugs from the New World', *Pharmacy and History*, 37 (1995), pp. 3–23; and Rudi Mathee, 'Exotic Substances: The Introduction and Global Spread of Tobacco, Coffee, Cocoa, Tea, and Distilled Liquor, Sixteenth to Eighteenth Centuries', in *Drugs and Narcotics in History*, ed. Roy Porter and Mikuláš Teich (Cambridge, 1995), pp. 24–51. Markman Ellis, Richard Coulton and Matthew Mauger, *Empire of Tea: The Asian Leaf that Conquered the World* (London, 2015); Jane T. Merritt, *The Trouble with Tea: The Politics of Consumption in the Eighteenth-century Global Economy* (Baltimore, MD, 2017); and Erika Rappaport, *A Thirst for Empire: How Tea Shaped the Modern World* (Princeton, NJ, 2017) are three recent studies that place British tea consumption in a wider global context. Coffee arguably has the most robust scholarship of any single commodity, which includes Ralph S. Hattox, *Coffee and Coffeehouses: The Origins of a Social Beverage in the Medieval Near East* (Seattle, WA, 1985); Mark Pendergrast, *Uncommon Grounds: The History of Coffee and How it Transformed the World*, revd edn (New York, 2010); S. D. Smith, 'Accounting for Taste: British Coffee Consumption in Historical Perspective', *Journal of Interdisciplinary History*, 27 (1996); and Antony Wild, *Coffee: A Dark History* (New York, 2004). On the history of the coffeehouse, see Brian Cowan, *The Social Life of Coffee: The Emergence of the British Coffeehouse* (New Haven, CT, 2005), which is as much an influential book about the development of a middling public culture of critical conversation as it is about coffeehouses; Markman Ellis, *The Coffee House: A Cultural History* (London, 2004); and Bryant Lillywhite, *London Coffee Houses: A Reference Book of Coffee Houses of the Seventeenth, Eighteenth and Nineteenth Centuries* (London, 1963).

While the consideration of food in cultural and social history has increased remarkably in the past few decades, the approach has deep roots in the 'foodways' studies of anthropology and sociology, which have long examined food as a form of individual and communal expression and communication. To a great extent, the discussion of food as communication has been shaped by the works of Roland Barthes, 'Toward a Psychology of Contemporary Food Consumption', in *European Diet from Pre-industrial to Modern Times*, ed. Elborg Forster and Robert Forster (New York, 1975). See also his 'Ornamental Cookery' in his *Mythologies* (Paris, 1957) and Claude Lévi-Strauss, *The Origin of Table Manners* (New York, 1968). A more recent, largely complementary, applied study is Arjun Appadurai, 'How to Make a National Cuisine: Cookbooks in Contemporary India', *Comparative Studies in Society and History*, 30 (1988), pp. 3–24. To this should be added Linda Civitello, *Cuisine and Culture: A History of Food and People*, 3rd edn (Oxford, 2011); the essays in Ishita Banerjee-Dube, ed., *Cooking Cultures: Convergent Histories of Food and Feeling* (Cambridge, 2016); Dan Jurafsky, *The Language of Food: A Linguist Reads the Menu* (New York, 2014); Rachel Laudan, *Cuisine and Empire: Cooking in World History* (Berkeley, CA, 2013); and Maguelonne Toussaint-Samat, *A History of Food*, 2nd edn (Oxford, 2008). Particularly thought-provoking in terms of thinking about the meanings of things, including food, are the essays in Anne Gerritsen and Giorgio Riello, eds, *The Global Lives of Things: The Material Culture of Connections in the Early Modern World* (London, 2016); and Arjun Appadurai, ed., *The Social Life of Things: Commodities in Cultural Perspective* (Cambridge, 1986), pp. 64–91.

The pioneering work on consumption and material culture in Britain and its empire during the long eighteenth century is Neil McKendrick, John Brewer and J. H. Plumb, *The Birth of a Consumer Society: The Commercialization of Eighteenth-century England* (London, 1982). Although challenged by a number of studies, it remains an important work not least because it has provoked over a generation's worth of scholarship. For just some of the studies on these subjects, see Maxine Berg, *Luxury and Pleasure in Eighteenth-century Britain* (Oxford, 2005); Ann Bermingham and John Brewer, eds, *The Consumption of Culture, 1600–1800: Image, Object, Text* (London, 1995); T. H. Breen, *The Marketplace of Revolution: How Consumer Politics Shaped American Independence* (Oxford, 2004); Troy Bickham, '"A conviction of the reality of things": Material Culture, North American Indians and Empire in Eighteenth-century Britain', *Eighteenth-century Studies*, 39 (2005), pp. 29–47; John Brewer and Roy Porter, eds, *Consumption and the World of Goods* (London, 1993); Margot Finn, 'Men's Things: Masculine Possession in the Consumer Revolution', *Social History*, 25 (2000), pp. 133–55; Ann McClintock, *Imperial Leather: Race, Gender and Sexuality in the Colonial Context* (New York, 1995); David Porter, *The Chinese Taste in Eighteenth-century England* (Cambridge, 2010); Carole Shammas, *The Pre-industrial Consumer in England and America* (Oxford, 1990); Woodruff D. Smith, 'Complications of the Commonplace: Tea, Sugar, and Imperialism', *Journal of Interdisciplinary History*, 22 (1992), pp. 259–78; John Styles and Amanda Vickery, eds, *Gender, Taste and Material Culture in Britain and North America, 1700–1830* (New Haven, CT, 2006); Frank Trentmann, *Empire of Things: How We Became a World of Consumers, from the Fifteenth Century to the Twenty-first* (London, 2016); Alan Warde, *Consumption, Food and Taste: Culinary Antinomies and Commodity Culture* (London, 1997); and Lorna Weatherill, *Consumer Behaviour and Material Culture in Britain, 1660–1760*, 2nd edn (London, 1996).

Related studies of the development of retail and marketing include Lucy A. Bailey, 'Squire, Shopkeeper and Staple Food: The Reciprocal Relationship between the Country House and the Village Shop in the Late Georgian Period', *History of Retailing and Consumption*, 1 (2015), pp. 8–27; Hannah Barker, *The Business of Women: Female Enterprise and Urban Development in Northern England, 1760–1830* (Oxford, 2006) and her *Family and Business During the Industrial Revolution* (Oxford, 2016); Maxine Berg and Helen Clifford, 'Selling Consumption in the Eighteenth Century: Advertising and the Trade Card in Britain and France', *Cultural and Social History*, 4 (2007), pp. 145–70; Helen Berry, 'Prudent Luxury: The Metropolitan Tastes of Judith Baker, Durham Gentlewoman', in *Women and Urban Life in Eighteenth-century England*, ed. Rosemary Sweet and Penelope Lane (London, 2003); Nancy Cox, *The Complete Tradesman: A Study of Retailing,*

1550–1820 (Farnham, Surrey, 2000); Ian Mitchell, *Tradition and Innovation in English Retailing, 1700–1850* (Farnham, Surrey, 2014); Ho-cheung Mui and Lorna H. Mui, *Shops and Shopkeeping in Eighteenth Century* (London, 1989); Nicola Jane Phillips, *Women in Business, 1700–1850* (London, 2006); Jon Stobart, *Sugar and Spice: Grocers and Groceries in Provincial England, 1650–1830* (Oxford, 2013); Jon Stobart, Andrew Hann and Victoria Morgan, *Spaces of Consumption: Leisure and Shopping in the English Town, c. 1680–1830* (London, 2007); Claire Walsh, 'Shop Design and Display of Goods in Eighteenth-century London', *Journal of Design History*, 8 (1995), pp. 157–76; T. S. Willan, *An Eighteenth-century Shopkeeper: Abraham Dent of Kirkby Stephen* (Manchester, 1970); and Bee Wilson, *Swindled: The Dark History of Food Fraud, from Poisoned Candy to Counterfeit Coffee* (Princeton, NJ, 2008).

Arguably the most important recent theses advanced on consumption is Jan de Vries, *The Industrious Revolution: Consumer Behavior and the Household Economy, 1650 to the Present* (Cambridge, 2008). Although widely embraced, it has not gone unchallenged. Some of these can be found in Sara Horrell, 'Consumption, 1700–1870', in *The Cambridge Economic History of Modern Britain*, vol. I, ed. Roderick Floud, Jane Humphries and Paul Johnson (Cambridge, 2014), pp. 237–63; Craig Muldrew, *Food, Energy and the Creation of Industriousness* (Cambridge, 2011); and Gregory Clark and Ysbrand Van Der Werf, 'Work in Progress? The Industrious Revolution', *Journal of Economic History*, 58 (1998), pp. 830–43.

The most comprehensive study of British cookery books in this period is Gilly Lehmann, *The British Housewife: Cookery Books, Cooking and Society in Eighteenth-century Britain* (Blackawton, Devon, 2003). Janet Theophano, *Eat My Words: Reading Women's Lives through the Cookbooks they Wrote* (New York, 2002) provides a broader perspective. Other illuminating studies include Ken Albala, 'Cookbooks as Historical Documents', in *The Oxford Handbook of Food History*, ed. Jeffrey M. Pilcher (Oxford, 2012), pp. 227–40; Sara Pennell, 'Making Livings, Lives and Archives: Tales of Four Eighteenth-century Recipe Books', in *Reading and Writing Recipe Books, 1550–1800*, ed. Michelle DiMeo and Sara Pennell (Manchester, 2013); Elizabeth M. Schmidt, 'Elegant Dishes and Unrefined Truths: A Culinary Search for Identity in Eighteenth-century Britain', *Eighteenth-century Thought*, 6 (2016), pp. 61–81; and Susan Zlotnick, 'Domesticating Imperialism: Curry and Cookbooks in Victorian England', *Frontiers*, 16 (1996).

Opposition to the slave trade and slavery during the eighteenth and early nineteenth centuries is explored in Christopher Leslie Brown, *Moral Capital: Foundations of British Abolitionism* (Chapel Hill, NC, 2006); Elizabeth J. Clapp and Julie Roy Jeffrey, *Women, Dissent, and Anti-slavery in Britain and America, 1790–1865* (Oxford, 2011); Seymour Drescher, *Capitalism and Antislavery: British Mobilization in Comparative Perspective* (Oxford, 1987); Kathryn Jane Gleadle, *Borderline Citizens: Women, Gender and Political Culture in Britain, 1815–1867* (London, 2009); Harriet Guest, *Small Change: Women, Learning, Patriotism, 1750–1810* (Chicago, IL, 2000); Clare Midgely, *Feminism and Empire: Women Activists in Imperial Britain, 1790–1865* (New York, 2007) and *Women Against Slavery: The British Campaigns, 1780–1870* (London, 1992); Timothy Morton, *The Poetics of Spice: Romantic Consumerism and the Exotic* (Cambridge, 2000); and Srividhya Swaminathan, *Debating the Slave Trade: Rhetoric of British National Identity, 1759–1815* (Farnham, Surrey, 2009).

ACKNOWLEDGEMENTS

This book's origins, like so many scholars' ideas, began during my graduate studies nearly two decades ago. Since then, I pursued it in fits and starts, as I set it aside to start and finish other books, lines of historical enquiry and administrative roles. In consequence of this lengthy and often circuitous route, I have incurred too many debts – intellectual, professional and personal – to recount fully here. Nevertheless, I will make the attempt to note a few, with profuse apologies to those that go unmentioned.

The main ideas and versions of chapters benefited greatly through exposure at a number of conference and workshops, including those hosted by the American Society for Eighteenth Century Studies, British Society for Eighteenth Century Studies, North American Conference on British Studies and Western Conference on British Studies, as well as the 'Economies of Empire' workshop at the University of Chicago's Nicholson Center for British Studies, Education City Faculty Forum in Doha, 'Strangers, Aliens and Foreigners' project conference in Prague, the 'War, Empire and Slavery' conference at York University, the 'Food and History' conference at the University of Central Lancashire, and the Anglo-American Conference's 'Food in History'. Some of the central themes of the book received their first published airing in 2008 as an article with a similar title in *Past and Present*, which later won the Belasco Prize from the Association for the Study of Food and Society. I am grateful both for the journal's permission to use some of the article's material in the book, especially in chapters Three and Four, as well as the generous and constructive comments of the journal's editors and readers, which aided me in conceptualizing the project as a book. An early fellowship at the Huntington Library enabled me to share and shape my ideas and engage with the diaries of John Marsh, whose recorded experiences pepper the pages of this book and likely many others to come. My research also benefited from the advice and assistance of the staff at numerous other institutions where I researched this book, including the Bodleian Library, British Library, British Museum, City of London's Guildhall, Lewis Walpole Library at Yale University, National Archives at Kew, National Library of Scotland, National Records of Scotland, Oxfordshire Record Office, Qatar National Library, libraries of Texas A&M University, libraries of the University of Maine, Scottish National Archives, and the Wellcome Library.

This project at various stages has benefited throughout its long history from the conversations, answered questions, read drafts and support of a host of colleagues and scholars – far too many to remember, let alone include, here: Quince Adams, Jeremy Black, Brian Cowan, Yannis Economou, Zohreh Eslami, James Fichter, Joanna Innes, Mark van de Logt, César Malavé, Eyad Masad, Jeremy Osborn, Antonio La Pastina, Sara Pennell, James Rosenheim, Mysti Rudd, Elizabeth Schmidt, Rebecca Schloss, Karine Walther, Dror Wahrman and Kathleen Wilson. Of course, none should be held accountable for the book's final outcome, but they are more than welcome to take some credit if they like the result. I have also benefited, undeservedly, from the patience of Reaktion's editors, first Ben Hayes and then Michael Leaman, because I embarked on a six-year intensive administrative assignment at my university's campus in Qatar shortly after signing a contract with Reaktion that kept me from completing the book. Their comments along with those of the diverse group of readers they identified both at the starting and finishing stages were greatly appreciated and extremely influential in the final result. My family has been unfailingly supportive (if not always equally interested in the subject!) throughout.

My home institution, Texas A&M, has been reliably supportive. The Glasscock Center for the Humanities granted a semester-long fellowship during the early stages of the project, and the College of Liberal Arts and the Office of the Vice-President for Research provided a steady flow of financial support for me to attend conferences and pursue archival research. Texas A&M's campus in Qatar was my home for a decade, and as I now return to Texas to rejoin my department in College Station, I realize that I am only just beginning to understand how formative the experience has been for me and my family. Although the Qatar campus offers exclusively engineering degrees, students must still meet the core curriculum requirements of any Texas A&M student, and that includes history. Despite being something of an intellectual oddity among a faculty comprised mainly of engineers and scientists, I never once felt marginalized, and this book benefited from the generous support from the campus, the Qatar Foundation of which the campus was a part, and colleagues in the humanities and social sciences at the other five American branch campuses. When I finished my administrative service in Qatar, I benefited from a semester free of teaching, which enabled me to transition mentally back to a historian and finish a draft of the book manuscript. The College of Liberal Arts at Texas A&M University provided a year of development leave, during which I have completed the book.

As I progress in my own career, I have had ample opportunity to reflect upon and appreciate those who taught and mentored me. Even now, two decades later, I cannot write academically without hearing the voice of Joanna Innes asking the overarching 'So what?' question about my subject or highlighting the poor structure of an individual sentence. Although these were humbling experiences for me, and no doubt sometimes exasperating ones for her, she always managed to keep me from feeling belittled. Today I regularly find myself using her adages and examples with my own students and, hopefully, also tempering criticism with kindness. It is to her that I dedicate this book.

PHOTO ACKNOWLEDGEMENTS

The author and publishers wish to express their thanks to the below sources of illustrative material and/or permission to reproduce it.

From Rudolph Ackermann, *Microcosm of London*, vol. II (London, 1809): pp. 60, 86; Archenback Foundation for Graphic Arts, Fine Arts Museums of San Francisco, California: p. 76; from John Ashton, *Chap-books of the Eighteenth Century with Facsimiles, Notes, and Introduction* (London, 1882): p. 83; Bodleian Library, University of Oxford University (John Johnson Collection – photographs reproduced by permission of the Bodleian Library): pp. 94 (Trade Cards box 11 (100)), 97 (Trade Cards box 11 (80b)), 111 foot (Trade Cards box 11 (96a)), 112 (Trade Cards box 11 (18)), 114 (Bill Headings, box 12 (28c)), 116 (Bill Headings, box 11 (13)); photos Boston Public Library, Digital Commonwealth: pp. 206, 219; The British Library, London (photo © The British Library Board): p. 119; British Museum, London (Prints & Drawings Department – photos © copyright the Trustees of the British Museum): pp. 62–3, 68, 69, 81, 96 (top), 100, 105, 176, 180, 200, 208 (foot); British Museum, London (Prints & Drawings Department [Banks Collection] – photos © copyright the Trustees of the British Museum): pp. 42, 58, 59, 96 (middle and foot), 110, 111 (top), 117, 202; British Museum, London (Prints & Drawings Department [Heal Collection] – photos © copyright the Trustees of the British Museum): pp. 40, 98, 107, 108, 115, 118; from [Francis Collingwood and John Woollams], *The Universal Cook, and City and Country Housekeeper* . . . (London, 1792): p. 143; Colonial Williamsburg, Virginia (museum purchase: Mr and Mrs John C. Austin, Phyllis M. Carstens, Mrs Joyce Longworth Ann Winter Odette, John F. Orman Jr, M. Robert Prioleau, Joan N. Woodhouse, the Dwight P. and Ann-Elisa W. Black Fund and the John R. and Carolyn J. Maness Family Foundation – reproduced courtesy of The Colonial Williamsburg Foundation): p. 193; from *A Companion to the Museum, late Sir Ashton Lever's, removed to Albion Street, the Surry end of Black Friars Bridge* (London, 1790): p. 103; from the *Derby Mercury*, 31 January 1782: p. 45; from [John Farley], *The London Art of Cookery* . . . (London, 1783): p. 142; from *The Fortunes and Misfortunes of Moll Flanders, who was Born in Newgate* . . . (London, n.d. [1760?]): p. 83; from [Hannah Glasse], *The Art of Cookery, Made Plain and Easy* . . . (London, 1747): p. 139; from [Hannah Glasse], *The Art of Cookery, made plain and easy*... (London, n.d. [1777?]): p. 178; collection of Guildhall Library, London: p. 44; photo Guildhall Library, London: p. 106; from Thomas Hariot, *A Briefe and True Report of the New Found Land of Virginia*... (London, 1588): p. 88; from Sarah Harrison, *The House-keeper's Pocket-Book, and Compleat Family Cook*... (London, 1757): p. 149; from Eliza Fowler Haywood, *A New Present for a Servant Maid: Containing Rules for her Moral Conduct both with Respect to Herself and her Superiors*... (London, 1771): p. 145; from [William Augustus Henderson], *The Housekeeper's Instructor; or, Universal Family Cook*... (London, 1793): p. 179; photos courtesy of The Lewis Walpole Library, Yale University, Farmington, Connecticut: pp. 13, 19, 47, 49, 164, 196, 203, 207 (top), 225, 227; photos Library of Congress, Washington, DC (Prints and Photographs Division): pp. 21, 35, 51, 74, 77, 136, 177, 201, 204, 216, 217, 228, 236; from the *London Magazine*, vol. XLIII (May 1774): p. 219; from [Charlotte Mason], *The Lady's Assistant*... (London, 1787): p. 148; photos The Metropolitan Museum of Art (Open Access): pp. 109, 135, 207 (foot), 208 (top), 209, 210; from [Elizabeth Raffald], *The Experienced English Housekeeper, For the Use and Ease of Ladies, Housekeepers, Cooks, &c.* (London, 1782): p. 140; from [Elizabeth Raffald], *The Experienced English Housekeeper, For the Use and Ease of Ladies, Housekeepers, Cooks, &c.... A New Edition: In which are inserted some celebrated Receipts by other modern Authors* (London, 1803): p. 141; from [Walter Raleigh], *A New History of England, Ecclesiastical and Civil... by Walter Raleigh* (London, 1746): p. 6; from John Trusler, *The Honours of the Table; or, Rules for Behaviour During Meals; with the whole Art of Carving, illustrated by a variety of cuts. Together with Directions for going to Market, and the Method of distinguishing good Provisions from bad; to which is added A Number of Hints or concise Lessons for the Improvement of Youth, on all occasions in Life... for the use of young People* (London, 1788): p. 71; photo U.S. National Archives and Records Administration: p. 88; photos Wellcome Collection: pp. 142, 179; from *Westminster Magazine*, 3 February 1781: p. 206.

INDEX

Page numbers in *italics* indicate illustrations.